‘This is an essential book for anyone seeking to understand the Sex Offender Register in the UK. The book provides a comprehensive overview of the development of the “register” by examining the socio-historical context within which it emerged and developed. The impact of the register, how it is implemented and monitored are also examined in-depth, providing readers with a thorough understanding of the operationalisation of the register nationally. This unique book is ideal for students, practitioners, policy makers and academics in search of a one-stop source on sex offender management in the UK.’

***Sarah Kingston**, Professor of Criminal Justice and Policing, Co-Director of the Criminal Justice Partnership, University of Central Lancashire*

‘This book is the most comprehensive of its kind. Whether you’re an academic or practitioner, if you want to know anything about the Sex Offender Register and if it succeeds in its aim to protect the public then this is the book for you.’

***Caro Gorden**, Senior Lecturer, Criminology and Criminal Justice Programme Leader for MA Criminology and Criminal Justice, Wrexham Glyndwr University*

The Sex Offender Register

The Sex Offender Register examines the origins, history, structure and legalities of the UK sex offender register, and explores how political and public opinion has influenced the direction the policy of registration has taken.

Delving into the origins of the UK sex offender register and how the registration policy has evolved, this book provides an understanding of the register and its contribution to public protection while attempting to see the register as a policy that has grown and developed and as having an organic life of its own. The sex offender register is designed as a form of public protection rather than a punishment, requiring offenders to notify the police of their circumstances and to accept a degree of offender management from the police.

The book:

- puts the development of the register in its political, social and ethical context
- considers the position of children and young people as offenders
- outlines the movement of registered offenders across international borders
- analyses how offenders can be removed from the register
- explores how other countries in the UK manage sex offenders through registers
- asks questions about the efficacy of the register and what contribution it makes to public protection
- looks at specific aspects of registration including the management of information
- delves into the experience of life on the register
- examines the influence of public opinion
- discusses the role of the police as custodians of the register and as offender managers.

Exploring the different pressures brought to bear on the register, this book provides an authoritative starting point for police officers, social workers, probation officers, magistrates, students of Criminology, Criminal Justice and Policing, and the general reader wanting to understand where the UK sex offender register originated from and how it operates today.

Terry Thomas is Emeritus Professor of Criminal Justice Studies at Leeds Beckett University. He is the author of *Sex Crime: Sex Offending and Society* (2016 3rd edn), *Policing Sexual Offences and Sex Offenders* (2016) and *Privacy and Criminal Justice* (co-author with Daniel Marshall 2017).

Daniel J. Marshall is a Senior Lecturer in Criminal Justice at Liverpool John Moores University. His research interests are in the fields of youth justice, criminal justice, privacy and enterprise education.

The Sex Offender Register

Politics, Policy and Public Opinion

Terry Thomas and Daniel J. Marshall

Routledge
Taylor & Francis Group
LONDON AND NEW YORK

First published 2021
by Routledge
2 Park Square, Milton Park, Abingdon, Oxon OX14 4RN

and by Routledge
52 Vanderbilt Avenue, New York, NY 10017

Routledge is an imprint of the Taylor & Francis Group, an informa business

British Library Cataloguing-in-Publication Data
A catalogue record for this book is available from the British Library

Library of Congress Cataloging-in-Publication Data
A catalog record has been requested for this book

ISBN: 978-0-367-54285-6 (hbk)
ISBN: 978-0-367-54284-9 (pbk)
ISBN: 978-1-003-08850-9 (ebk)

Typeset in Times New Roman
by Taylor & Francis Books

Contents

Illustrations

Figures

Tables

Acknowledgements

Thanks to Laura Bui, Bill Hebenton, Steve Lister, Richard Ward and Eva Kemecsei. Thanks also to Grace for showing no interest at all.

List of abbreviations

ACHE	Action on Child Exploitation
ACOP	Association of Chief Officers of Probation
ACPO	Association of Chief Police Officers
ACRO	ACPO Criminal Record Office
APCC	Association of Police and Crime Commissioners
ARMS	Active Risk Management System
ASORMC	Area Sex Offender Risk Management Committee
BASW	British Association of Social Workers
BOT	British Overseas Territories
CCCJS	Coordination of Computerisation of the Criminal Justice System
CEOP	Child Exploitation and Online Protection
CJJIT	Criminal Justice Joint Inspection Teams
CPPC	Critical Public Protection Case
CPS	Crown Prosecution Service
CSOD	Child Sex Offender Disclosure scheme
DRM	Designated Risk Manager
ECHR	European Convention on Human Rights
ECPAT	Every Child Protected Against Trafficking
ECRIS	European Criminal Records Information System
EWS	Early Warning System
FLO	Family Liaison Officers
FTO	Foreign Travel Order
GPMS	Government Protective Marking Scheme
GSCS	Government Secure Classifications Scheme
IICSA	Independent Inquiry into Child Sexual Abuse
IPP	Imprisonment for Public Protection
ISSG	Information Sharing Steering Group
JBOC	Joint Border Operations Centre
JMAPPA	Jersey Multi-Agency Public Protection Arrangements
LSCB	Local Safeguarding Children Board
MAPPA	Multi-Agency Public Protection Arrangements
MASH	Multi-Agency Safeguarding Hub

MASRAM	Multi-Agency Sex Offender Risk Assessment and Management
MoJ	Ministry of Justice
MOSOVO	Management of Sexual Offenders and Violent Offenders
NBTC	National Border Targeting Centre
NCB	National Central Bureau
NOTA	National Organisation for the Treatment of Abusers
NOMS	National Offender Management Service
NPCC	National Police Chiefs Council
NPS	National Probation Service
NSPIS	National Strategy for Police Information Systems
OASYS	Offender Assessment System
OM	Offender Manager(s)
PBNI	Probation Board Northern Ireland
PIMR	Police Internal Management Review
PPANI	Public Protection Arrangements Northern Ireland
PSA	Police Superintendents Association
PSNI	Police Service of Northern Ireland
RM2000	Risk Matrix 2000
RSO	Registered Sex Offender
RSOMU	Registered Sex Offender Management Units
SCR	Serious Case Review
SHPO	Sexual Harm Prevention Order
SMB	Strategic Management Boards
SONR	Sex Offender Notification Requirements
SOPO	Sexual Offences Prevention Order
SOTP	Sex Offender Treatment Programme
SOU	Sex Offender Unit
SRO	Sexual Risk Order

1 Introduction

On 1 September 1997 the UK introduced its new legal arrangements that required all people convicted or cautioned for a designated sexual offence to notify the police each time their personal circumstances changed. In this way the police database of 'known' sex offenders would be more accurate and up to date and the police better able to track sex offenders and know where they were in case of future reoffending. This tracking would continue for given periods of time depending on the seriousness of the offence and the severity of the sentence handed down; some people would be required to notify the police for a lifetime. Although the law never used the terminology, these arrangements became known as the sex offender register.

Since September 1997 the list of designated sexual offences has lengthened, and various changes have been made to the registration requirements. Risk assessment and risk management has become an additional feature for all those on the register. Risk assessment is the initial assessment made to try to determine the future behaviour of a convicted sex offender. In the past practitioners such as probation officers or police officers tried to determine future levels of dangerousness, and now we are more specific in trying to assess the likelihood of someone causing future sexual harm or future sexual offending. To assist these risk assessments various instruments have been introduced to assist the practitioner. At present the people on the sex offender register are assessed as:

- very high risk
- high risk
- medium risk
- low risk.

As we shall see, most of the offenders fall into the low risk group.

Risk management is the devising of a plan of intervention to prevent or reduce the possibility of the subject causing future sexual harm or further sexual offending. Such plans are devised by probation or police officers acting as offender managers. Sometime the intervention is accompanied by civil orders from the courts prohibiting the subject of the order from engaging in certain activities that have been identified in his or her assessment as being precursors to inappropriate sexual behaviour. The subject of risk assessment and risk management will be returned to.

The numbers that are required to notify the police have inevitably increased over the years. By 28 February 1999 some 8,161 individuals had notified the police of their details (*Hansard House of Commons 12 May 1999 col.159*) and by 31 March 2019 this figure had risen to 60,294 registered sex offenders living in the community in England and Wales (MoJ 2019a: 5). The vast majority of these people complied fully with their requirements to notify the police; one study at the time put it at 94% (Plotnikoff and Woolfson 2000: 6). Failure to comply was an offence in itself. This book looks at the background to the sex offender registration requirements and the history of this policy as a part of the public protection agenda.

The purpose of any sentence has been outlined in law as being an amalgam of retributive and utilitarian justifications of punishment. The appropriate sentence in the UK is decided upon in terms of a custodial sentence, a community sentence or a financial penalty. The Criminal Justice Act 2003 states that a court in making a sentence 'must have regard to the following purposes of sentencing':

a the punishment of offenders
b the reduction of crime (including its reduction by deterrence)
c the reform and rehabilitation of offenders
d the protection of the public
e the making of reparation by offenders to persons affected by their offences.

(CJA 2003 s142(1))

The protection of the public at section 142(1) (d) usually invokes the aim of custodial sentences when someone may pose a risk of further harm or offending if they are not imprisoned. The sex offender register is an administrative form of public protection, and not a part of the punishment. The punishment is decided upon at the point of sentencing; the public protection element is then automatically added on in the form of registration. The seriousness of the punishment dictates the length of registration required.

Public protection is a form of intervention to prevent recidivism that used to be solely provided by probation officers who originally held social work qualifications and were sometimes referred to as 'social workers to the court'. More recently probation officers have moved towards their own forms of qualification and a more managerial approach. The police have brought in their own form of offender management in the interests of public protection for those on the register. The new National Offenders Management Service was introduced in 2004 using more targeted and rigorous sentences driven by information on what works to reduce reoffending; today it has been renamed as HM Prison and Probation Services. Private and voluntary providers have also been turned to in the interests of effectiveness and value for money crime prevention and public protection (Carter Report 2003).

From the outset it has always been government policy that the details of sex offenders on the register are kept locally and, in that sense, there is no actual national register:

> There is no central register as such; individual sex offenders currently notify their details to the local police and are identified on the Police National Computer. This enables police across the country to know who is a 'registered' sex offender and to check their details with the local police force if required.
>
> (Home Office 2002a: para.18)

To that extent the 'register' is a misnomer and references to offenders being asked to 'sign the sex offenders' register' are slightly wide of the mark. There is no large book on to which is inscribed the names of sex offenders. A computer database called ViSOR has been developed to hold personal information on a national scale of those required to notify the police.

For ease of expression the use of the word 'register' will be adopted in this book. Offenders are required to notify changes in their circumstances (to register) to designated or 'prescribed' police stations. Offender managers will assess the risk posed by those on the register and devise ways to manage that risk. The register was not retrospective and only applied to new cases, or to those offenders already in the criminal justice system for sexual offences on 1 September 1997.

Criminal justice is delivered under the umbrella 'criminal justice system', which indicates a system of closely linked parts working together efficiently with a clear input at one end and output at the other. Those linked parts include the police, probation service, Crown Prosecution Service (CPS), magistrates, judiciary, lawyers, prison service, Children's Departments, mental health agencies and voluntary agencies. The perceived linear and unified nature of this system masks the complex nature of sexual offending and responses to this offending.

Registered sex offenders are a disparate group of all sorts of people. Too often they are lumped together as one monolithic group bound only by the registered sex offender label that has been applied to them. In terms of possible reoffending, some are assessed as 'high risk' while far more are assessed as 'low risk'. Some are referred to as 'paedophiles' where their victim has been a child. In journalistic and parliamentary discussions, the word paedophile has been used freely in talk about the register which in the early days, was often referred to as a 'paedophile register'.

The word 'paedophile' has a medical background and is not a term recognised in UK law where the term 'child sex offender' is preferred. The term 'paedophile' was first used by medical professionals in the late nineteenth century and has become a widely used term in contemporary life beyond that of the medical world. Today it is indiscriminately applied to any person who has committed a sexual offence against a child (Thomas 2016); in common currency 'paedophile' refers to adults who are sexually attracted to children of any age. The term has no status as a specific offence in UK law, where, as noted above, the term 'child sexual offender' is used.

The American Psychiatric Association (APA) *Diagnostic and Statistical Manual of Mental Disorders* (DSM-5) terms paedophilia as a 'Paedophilic Disorder' which is 'recurrent, intense sexually arousing fantasies, sexual urges, or behaviours involving sexual activities with a prepubescent child or children (generally aged 13 years or younger)' (APA 2013: 302.2 (F65.4)). The individual must be at least age 16 years and at least 5 years older than the child or children and have acted on these sexual urges or the sexual urges have caused marked distress or interpersonal difficulty. The World Health Organisation (WHO) defines paedophilia as 'a sustained, focused, and intense pattern of sexual arousal – as manifested by persistent sexual thoughts, fantasies, urges, or behaviours – involving pre-pubertal children' (WHO 2019).

Despite these distinctions in UK law and medical classification, nonsensical references are used in the media, such as the 'convicted paedophile': 'Convicted paedophile who dressed as Santa and offered to pose for pictures with children is sent back to jail' (Giordano 2019); 'Convicted paedophile, 34, travelled 500 miles to abuse schoolgirl, 14, he met in online self-harm support group after seven transport police officers failed to stop him' (Riley 2019). 'Paedophilia' and 'paedophile' are expressions which are widely recognisable, and have 'popular, cultural currency in the media and more generally' (Jewkes and Wykes 2012: 948).

In the 1960s and 1970s child sex offenders or 'molesters' used to have the image of the simple old man in the grubby raincoat standing on street corners near schools. Today child sex offenders are viewed as highly intelligent in their methods to gain children's trust through forms of electronic communication and such behaviour as grooming. They are often referred to as predatory. The nature and rationale of such a movement in imagery could be the subject of a study in itself. The use of the term 'predatory' is problematic as it suggests that individuals who commit child sex offences are not executing agency and portrays wild animals rather than human beings, essentially dehumanising the suspects and encouraging hate and violence toward them.

It is also worth noting that the terminology of the professionals and practitioners engaged in childcare has changed and expanded since the 1960s. In those early days the term 'battered babies' was used in the USA and came over to be used in the UK. During the early 1970s the terminology changed to that of children suffering 'non-accidental injury', or NAI, and by the early 1980s had changed again to that of 'child abuse'. The term 'child abuse' notified a potential expansion in the definition of the children falling under concern, and that it might not be just physical injuries but psychological and emotional injuries. Child sex offenders were inevitably drawn into the definitions of child abuse and by the end of the 1980s the terms 'child protection' and 'safeguarding' were being used (Parton 2006: 29–35).

The Children Act 1989 was the origin of the terms 'child protection' and 'safeguarding' but they were also indicative of a change of focus away from the condition of the child and more towards the activities of those working with them. It was these practitioners and professionals now charged with intervening on behalf of the child that became the centre of attention and not least when they got it wrong and failed to protect and safeguard.

By the end of the 1990s the focus had moved yet again towards those adults who had injured or abused children. This in turn brought us a wider view from child protection to the age of public protection and offender management.

Methodology

This study was based on the creation of the UK sex offender register over the 25–30 years since its inception to the present day. By taking a historical approach the authors have revisited the policy statements made on the register and the laws that were passed over this time period.

The aims of the study have been to focus on the register as an exercise in policy formulation, policy implementation and the reviews and research evaluations that have been produced on that formulation and implementation. The political context in which those statements and laws were made are further examined and the press and media comments that accompanied them. The press and media and the work of non-governmental organisation (NGO)s have been taken to represent a view of public opinion but sometimes that public opinion has been made more directly through bypassing the press and media.

Using primary and secondary sources the authors have:

- examined the evolution of an idea to enhance 'public protection' from known sex offenders living in the community
- examined the political debates on the formulation of laws to create the register
- examined the views of the practitioners and other stakeholders charged with implementing and carrying out the register arrangements
- looked at the experiences of the offenders who are required to notify the police (as custodians of the register) on any changes in their circumstances
- looked at the management of the personal information held on the register
- examined the particular arrangements for young sex offenders (under 18)
- identified the arrangements for 'tracking' the movements of sex offenders across international borders
- identified the arrangements for reviewing the continued status of offenders on the register

- looked at variations in register arrangements in different parts of the UK, the wider British Isles, and British Overseas Territories
- examined the evidence on the effectiveness of the register, the degree of compliance amongst offenders, and the degree of recidivism by those on the register.

Our key contentions are that policy development has been cautious and tentative and with only limited research evaluation. Political debate has sought to reflect public opinion in the creation of new laws and the amendment of these laws, but this has been done without reference to what studies and more considered research evaluations have stated. The question of whether the register contributes to public protection or makes any difference remains a difficult question to answer.

Outline of chapters

This book tells the story of the UK sex offender register from its inception in the 1990s and its subsequent development to today's arrangements. Chapter Two looks at the origins of the idea, the American experience and how policy began to be formulated. The Sex Offenders Act 1997 is examined in Chapter Three including the parliamentary discussion on the Bill, the appointment and role of the police as custodians of the register and the early implementation of the register.

Chapter Four examines the first five years of the register and the 'teething problems' of implementation in the early days. It looks at the need to take into account the requirements of risk assessment and risk management which had been missed out of the 1997 Act, the idea of police offender management and the construction of Multi-Agency Public Protection Arrangements (MAPPA) to form a 'home' for the register. The chapter ends by considering the first evaluations of the register by the Home Office. The new registration law in the form of the Sexual Offences Act 2003 is considered in Chapter Five. The 2003 Act remains the legal foundation for today's register with the 1997 Act having been repealed.

Chapters Six and Seven trace the history of the years 2003 to 2010 and 2010 to 2020 respectively. Offender management of those on the register becomes more embedded, rights of entry to the homes of those on the register is added and legal challenges are made against the registration laws. Chapter Seven effectively brings the story up to date with more amendments and changes made to the Sexual Offences Act 2003 adding new offences that will result in a convicted person's name being placed on the register and adding new requirements in terms of information to be notified to the police. It looks at the continuing legal challenges still being made on the register including the right of review for people required to register indefinitely – a theme taken up more fully in Chapter Twelve.

Chapter Eight takes us through some of the existing research on the lives of those on the register and how registration affects them. Aspects of life including family activities, employment activities, leisure activities and travel activities are considered as well as the attitudes people on the register have to face from the police and other professionals, the public and the media.

Central to the idea of the register is that of managing the personal information on over 60,000 people required to notify their details to the police. Chapter Nine looks at how this is done with the aid of the ViSOR database and in terms of exchanging information between agencies that maintain our public protection arrangements and how that information might be made available to some members of the public through disclosure arrangements.

The special circumstances of the young sex offender are outlined in Chapter Ten. These are the offenders convicted or cautioned between the ages of 10 and 18 years of age. It has been argued that these offenders should have their own separate register away from adults and maintained by a non-police agency, but no one has taken up that proposal. The chapter looks at the differences that have been made and the position of parents, as well as some of the legal challenges that have been based on the age of the person on the register.

Chapter Eleven focuses in on the control of registered sex offenders who wish to travel across international borders. This movement of people is divided into the 'outgoing' offenders who wish to leave the UK and the 'incoming' offenders who wish to come into the UK. The chapter describes the various legal barriers that can be mounted against this movement and how they have changed over the years.

Chapter Twelve examines ways to come off the register. It looks at the 2010 Supreme Court finding that the register was in breach of the European Convention on Human Rights by giving no right of review to those on the register required to notify the police of their details indefinitely. It goes on to look at how this breach was remedied by new laws that had to be passed to make the register compatible with the European Convention.

The way in which the sex offender register varies in the different parts of the UK other than England and Wales are considered in Chapter Thirteen. Variations that have been made in Scotland, Northern Ireland, the Channel Islands, the Isle of Man and other British Overseas Territories are discussed.

As the reader will have already realised by now there are many different facets to the idea of a sex offender register and different angles from which to approach it. In that sense it is an 'organic' and diffuse policy holding together 60,000 people, rather than a 'mechanistic' and easy to see policy. All of which makes drawing conclusions together in the final chapter far from easy.

2 The origins of the UK register

Introduction

The idea for a UK sex offender register emerged from a number of sources. In the 1980s child protection social workers wondered why we kept registers of children assessed as being 'at risk' of abuse but not on the adults who might commit sexual crimes against them; initiatives from the USA were looked at with interest, where the idea of the sex offender register had taken hold. The UK's Police Superintendents Association made out the case for a UK sex offender register and ultimately the Home Office brought these various strands of thought together in a 1996 Consultation Document. The UK register was introduced in its initial form by the 1997 Sex Offenders Act and started its operations on 1 September 1997.

Developments in the UK

Police, probation officers and social workers in the 1980s and 1990s had only child protection registers of children assessed as being at risk. As far as the adults who had committed offences against children were concerned, these professionals had tended to refer only to the concept of the 'Schedule One Offender'. This was anyone who had committed an offence against a child – sexual or physical – that was listed in Schedule One of the Children and Young Persons Act 1933.

No national lists of these Schedule One Offenders actually existed, but some local authorities did try to produce their own written lists of them. The Home Office was ambivalent about such activities:

> Some local authorities and other agencies have found it helpful for general social work and child protection purposes to maintain a list of all offenders in the area of offences listed in Schedule 1 of the Children and Young Persons Act 1933. Such a list has its limitations because it is difficult to keep it up to date.
>
> (Home Office et al. 1991: para.6.52)

A legal case at this time appeared to suggest that local authorities should be keeping such lists. In Devon, local social workers had been notifying people about a man only *suspected* of having committed offences against children. He challenged their right to do this in the courts and suggested they were breaching his right to privacy. He lost the case but the implication of the ruling was that the local authority should be doing this dissemination of information in the interests of child protection and therefore should be keeping lists of adults to enable them to carry out this task (*R v Devon CC ex. parte L [1991] 2 FLR*; see also Hayes 1992).

In 2005 the Home Office recommended dropping the term 'Schedule One Offenders':

> it is becoming clear that the term 'Schedule One Offender', which is used by a variety of agencies, is ill defined and, to a certain extent, unhelpful since it defines people by their offending history rather than the ongoing risks they pose. It is with this in mind that the term should be replaced with 'a person identified as presenting a risk, or potential risk, to children'. Obviously offending history is an important factor in such assessments but it is not the only one … Many practitioners are unsure of which offences are included in Schedule One, and whether there are other offences, not included in Schedule One, which may indicate that a person poses a risk to children.
>
> (Home Office 2005a: para.4)

The idea of a national sex offender register had started to gain more currency by the mid-1990s. Pressure in particular came from the Police Superintendents Association (PSA); David Maclean, Minister of State at the Home Office, later told the Commons: 'the suggestion that sex offenders should be required to register was first put forward by the Police Superintendents Association of England and Wales, and I am grateful to that organisation for its assistance in developing our proposals' (*Hansard House of Commons Debates 27 January 1997 cols. 23–4*).

In fact the Police Superintendents Association were not the first to come up with the register idea and the British Association of Social Workers (BASW) had passed a resolution at their AGM calling for a sex offender register as early as 1988 ('Controversy of motion on registers' *Social Work Today* 31 March 1988) and later started to campaign for a register ('Sex offenders list' *Community Care* 18 April 1991).Two MPs tried unsuccessfully to introduce Private Members Bills (the Sexual Offences against Children (Register of Offenders) Bill (27 March 1996) and the Paedophiles (Registration and Miscellaneous Provisions) Bill 1996 (12 June 1996) *Hansard House of Commons Debates 12 Jun 1996: cols. 324–326)*).

The national newspaper *Sunday Express* ran a front-page story headlined 'Will Your Child be Next?' asserting that there were 6,000 convicted paedophiles roaming free in Britain and no one knows where they are ('Will Your Child be Next?' *Sunday Express* 19 May 1996). Some regional newspapers talked about publishing the whereabouts of known offenders in their localities in the interests of public protection. One such newspaper was the *Manchester Evening News* who proceeded to publication of photographs and details. The argument was made that if the government would not do this then we – the newspapers – would, and that child protection trumps all other arguments: 'Once a paedophile, always a paedophile … we are well aware that our action creates a civil rights problem, but we believe the safety of children overwhelmingly outweighs the rights of a convicted paedophile' ('Why we did it' *Manchester Evening News* – Editorial 30 August 1996; see also King 1996).

In a more measured vein, the Home Office commissioned research from the University of Manchester to collate the views of the police on their ability to track sex offenders. The research did not specifically look at the question of a register but it did highlight some of the difficulties the police had in carrying out such tracking:

> The system is haphazard and it is very easy for offenders to become invisible … there are no clear systems for tracking the individual and monitoring his movements. The information is rarely updated and, if it exists at all, often consists of a box file of outdated letters at the back of a filing cabinet.
>
> (Hughes et al. 1996: 34; see also Parker et al. 1996)

One of the authors of this research – Beverley Hughes – would find herself in a few years on the frontline for the Labour government taking questions on the register as a junior Minister at the Home Office.

The American experience

Sex offender registers had already started in the USA and the first one is attributed to the State of California where a register was instituted from 1947. The registers of this time were based on even earlier pre-War registers of organised and serious criminals that had started in the 1930s. During the 1950s these old registers of serious criminals fell into disuse and some States followed California in turning them into sex offender registers. The use of these registers, however, remained patchy and some of them also fell into disuse (Logan 2009: chapter 2).

The turning point for the Americans came in 1989 with a particularly nasty assault in Washington State on a seven-year-old boy by a former offender already known to the police. The State legislature responded with a new law called the Community Protection Act 1990. This law revitalised their existing sex offender register and added the innovation that the register would be open and accessible to the public; the latter policy was to be known as 'community notification'. The essence of the argument, this time, was that 'if you, the professionals know where these people are – then so should we – the public' (see e.g. Boerner 1992; Logan 2009: 49–53).

Other States followed suit and to that extent local communities would in future have open access to a register of offender's names and know the whereabouts of sex offenders living in their vicinity. In New Jersey a law forming a register with open access was passed in 1994 and informally known as 'Megan's Law' after seven-year-old Megan Kanka who had been sexually assaulted and killed by a man living in the same street as her in Mercer County, New Jersey.

By 1994 a Federal law had been passed in Washington DC encouraging all 50 US States to introduce a register; the word 'encouraging' is used here because the law was not mandatory but States not complying could lose Federal funding for other policing and criminal justice matters. Every State was allowed to create their own individual form of register and in 1996 President Bill Clinton passed a new law to require all States to allow public access to registers. The parents of Megan Kanka joined Clinton at the White House for the signing of the national 'Megan's Law'. Federal Guidelines were offered on how States might like to organise the details of their registers (Federal Register Vol. 62 Number 139, 21 July 1997).

One thing that was missing in the USA was any hard evidence that these registers and community notification policies were going to be effective. Did registers make any difference to public protection? Professor Wayne Logan made the point:

> Remarkably, given the ostensible public safety premise of registration and notification, it largely remains an untested article of faith that the laws tangibly contribute to community safety ... In Washington State and Iowa researchers tracked registrant and control groups for over four years. Neither study found a statistically significant difference in recidivism.
>
> (Logan 2003)

The Washington State research Logan referred to examined their Community Protection Act 1990 and its register and community notification policy. The community notification law was viewed by its proponents as having two objectives. The first was crime prevention, through the communities' enhanced awareness of known sex offenders in their neighbourhoods. The second was to enhance the ability of law enforcement agencies to investigate crime by providing them with information regarding convicted sex offenders residing in their jurisdictions. The findings suggested that community notification had little effect on sex offender recidivism as measured by new arrests for sex offences or other types of criminal behaviour; what differences existed with a comparative group were statistically insignificant (Schram and Milloy 1995). The Iowa Research report that appeared five years later also compared two groups – one pre-registration policies and one post-introduction of a register. Once again differences in recidivism were found to be not statistically significant (Adkins et al. 2000).

Policy transfer

The idea of countries watching the development of policies in another country to see what they might use is not new. In the UK the Home Office had clearly been looking at the idea of the American sex offender register. Countries are not necessarily closed circuits in which policies are made in isolation especially with the improved international communication systems now available to enable the exchange of ideas and policies. Increasingly the practice of international policy transfer has come into being whereby one jurisdiction adopts a policy from another jurisdiction.

The ability to 'copy' one policy from another country, and 'enacting a more or less intact program' (Rose 1993: 27), has been observed in various areas of welfare reform (Dolowitz and Marsh 1996) and criminal justice (Earle et al. 2002), and has long been marked out as a 'growing phenomenon' (Dolowitz and Marsh 2000: 5). In practice, policy transfer is a more complex activity than simply copying.

Rose (1993) identifies a number of ways in which policies may be adopted from another country which can include: copying; emulation; hybridization; synthesis; and inspiration:

- *Copying* can be seen when a country adopts a programme without making any changes.
- *Emulation* occurs when a country 'reject(s) copying in every detail, [but] accepts that a particular program elsewhere provides the best standard for designing legislation at home' (ibid: 21).
- *Hybridization* and *synthesis* involve combining elements of policies found in other countries.
- *Inspiration* involves the expansion of ideas and development of a policy with ideas taken from other policy contexts.

Dolowitz and Marsh (2000: 12) suggest that the transfer of policy can be situated on a continuum from coercive transfer to lesson drawing. Coercive policy transfer can take place when, for example, a supra-national institution such as the European Union (EU) and the European Court of Justice impose the transfer of policies onto member states (Dolowitz and Marsh 1996). It was such perceived impositions that contributed to the 2016 successful Brexit campaign in the UK and the slogan 'to take back control'.

Voluntary transfer is seen to arise from instances where, for example, there may be public or government dissatisfaction with how government policies are not functioning properly and thus look for lessons from other countries to provide a solution for this perceived policy failure (Dolowitz and Marsh 1996). Examples of this can be seen in the UK's adoption of US style 'welfare-to-work' policies in the 1980s to tackle rising levels of unemployment (Dolowitz and Marsh 2000).

Policy transfer is sometimes described as lesson drawing, which implies that political decision makers in one country draw lessons from other countries, which is then applied to their own political system. Lesson drawing is sometimes distinguished from policy transfer because rather than transferring or emulating a policy, lessons are learnt about the potential negative consequences of adopting that policy, and thus institutional change does not always take place (Dolowitz and Marsh 1996).

It has also been argued that:

> Just as each policy is unique, different areas of public policy pose their own distinct challenges for transfer. This is certainly true of criminal justice. There are considerable variations among different nations in their views about the origins of crime, and about how the state and the community should respond to offenders ... It is increasingly recognised that the trajectory of criminal justice policy development depends upon a wide range of political, economic, social, cultural and emotional influences, interacting with each other in uncertain ways.
>
> (Canton and McFarlane 2014: 1–2)

The importation of policies from the US to the UK, although the policy transfer may appear straightforward, when we look more closely it is much more complex.

In the UK the Home Office prepared to take on the idea of the sex offender register.

'Sentencing and supervision of sex offenders: a consultation document'

Home Secretary Michael Howard formally announced that the government was proceeding with a UK sex offender register in March 1996 (Bennetto 1996). Further confirmation came in the March 1996 White Paper *Protecting the Public: The Government's Strategy on Crime in England and Wales* where the government stated its belief that 'there is a strong case for strengthening the arrangements for supervising convicted sex offenders following their release from custody to provide greater protection for the public' (Home Office 1996a: para.8.2). In particular change was needed because it was believed that some sex offenders left custody even though they might still be an active threat. When formal supervision was ended, there was no way of monitoring or controlling their activities and short supervision periods were sometimes unable to accommodate Sex Offender Treatment Programmes (SOTP) (ibid: para.8.9). Overall, the government were turning to the idea of a register and considering suggestions that convicted sex offenders living in the community, should be required by law to notify the police of any changes of address (ibid: para.8.11).

A follow-up consultation document three months later, entitled *Sentencing and Supervision of Sex Offenders*, outlined 'the Government's proposal that convicted sex offenders should be required to notify the police of any change of address' (Home Office 1996b: para.41). The aim was stated, quite simply, that this was a means to ensure 'that the information on convicted sex offenders contained within the police national computer was fully up to date' (ibid: para.43). This would make certain that if a convicted sex offender moved into their area the local police would be aware of it. In the past mobile sex offenders could turn up anywhere unannounced. It enabled the police to make the known but 'invisible' offender 'visible' in their area; visible at least to the police if not to the general public.

Apart from keeping police records up to date, other reasons to start a register were noted. A register held by the police could 'help them to identify suspects once a crime had been committed, but could also *possibly* help them to prevent such crimes. It *might* also act as a deterrent to potential re-offenders' (Home Office 1996b: para.43 emphasis added). Emphasis has been added to the words 'possibly' and 'might' to illustrate the hesitant nature of just what the Home Office thought the register might achieve. The idea that the register might help identify suspects *after* a new crime had been committed was considered useful to the police but it would not have fulfilled the register's 'public protection' aims in preventing a new victim being made. As for the idea that the register might be considered a deterrent, this put the register forward almost as a form of punishment which the Home Office had always said was not its purpose (ibid: para.51). One thing that was not mentioned in *Sentencing and Supervision of Sex Offenders*, was that the information gathered might be used to assess and manage any risk posed by sex offenders.

Annex A to the Consultation Document carried the sexual offences in England and Wales that would lead to registration with no mention of the different offences that could occur in Scotland and Northern Ireland. Some pedants spotted that one of the sexual offences that was listed had been repealed two years earlier (Sexual Offences Act 1967 s.2 – homosexual acts on merchant ships). The Home Office received 238 formal responses to the Consultation Document with 87% of respondents supporting the idea of a register (*Hansard House of Commons 25 October 1996 WA 956*).

The North Wales case

Running in parallel to these 1996 policy developments was another court hearing about the authorities disseminating information about two known child sex offenders to people living near them. The couple in question had moved from the Burnley area to North Wales where they lived in a caravan. Unlike the *Devon* case it was the police, rather than the local authority, who were informing the neighbours; the offenders sought remedy in the courts claiming breach of Article 8 of the European Convention on Human Rights (the right to privacy) and the prevention of the information being distributed on them (Jenkins 1997).

Stephen Solley QC for the couple said that they were in danger of being made 'outlaws' with no protection from the law; he added that 'it is self-evident that no one is above the law, but it is also self-evident that no one is below it'. The High Court ruled that the police were acting correctly by informing the people living near them because the two people concerned posed a high risk to any children in the area. The Court said such disclosures should be exceptional and did not see them as being used on a 'blanket basis'; each person needed to be the subject of a risk assessment and '[d]isclosure should only be made when there is a pressing need for that disclosure' (*R v North Wales Police ex p. AB and CD The Times Law Report 14 July 1997*). An appeal against the decision was also dismissed (*AB & Anor, R (on the application of) v North Wales Police Area [1998] EWCA Civ 486 (18 March 1998)*).

The significance of the *North Wales* case was that it came at the same time as policy makers were still discussing exactly what the purpose of the register was going to be. To start with the collation of information by the registration process was going to be simply for the police to know where people lived and to keep their records up to date. The *North Wales* case had drawn attention to the way in which disclosure of information about sex offenders to the public should be carried out. What was important, and at the heart of such dissemination, was going to be the need to make a risk assessment. The Home Office recognised the significance and said it welcomed the judgement because it reinforced the approach they were taking:

> We will be studying the [*North Wales*] judgement very carefully and we are already working on guidance to the police and other organisations on the use of information about the whereabouts of sex offenders collected when the Sex Offenders Act is implemented.
>
> (Home Office 1997a)

The case would directly affect the Home Office guidelines then being drawn up (see Chapter Three).

A survey carried out for ACPO and made available in February 1997, entitled *Disclosure of Information – Sex Offenders*, saw the register as something that could only provide 'a warning system' to communities or particular institutions. Thirty-six police forces had responded to the survey and the majority of them thought a warning system should itself only be used 'in extreme circumstances'; another three forces were not in favour of a warning system at all. The belief was that, in future, registered offenders would go underground and not comply with their notification obligations thereby making more work for the police (ACPO 1997a: 2). The survey was later referred to in the House of Lords Debate on the Sex Offenders Bill where there was general agreement with its findings (*Hansard House of Lords Debates 20 March 1997 col.1136*) (we return to this subject in Chapter Nine).

Summary

Here we have traced the development of the thinking behind the Sex Offenders Act 1997 and the first manifestation of the UK sex offender register. As we shall see the Bill went through Parliament at a fast pace set by the forthcoming general election and with both the two main parties wanting to be seen to be 'tough on crime'. Maybe insufficient thinking went into this first attempt. Nothing was said about assessing risk, and managing risk, at this early stage and there appears to have been a simplistic assumption that simply having the information would at least allow the police to know where these people on the register were.

3 The Sex Offenders Act 1997

Introduction

This chapter starts by tracking the publication of the Sexual Offences Bill and through its parliamentary stages that followed. The Sex Offenders Act 1997 provided the initial legal framework for the first version of the UK sex offender register. It would be followed the next year by the Crime and Disorder Act 1998 and the Criminal Justice and Court Services Act 2000; both Acts had an impact on the 1997 Act.

The Sex Offenders Bill

With the various announcements and media reports about the forthcoming sex offender register it was something of a let-down to have no formal mention of a Bill in the Queen's speech opening Parliament (23 October 1996) for the final session before the next general election. Normal practice was that the Queen's speech listed the Bills that the government were going to introduce; now two of them, including the one on the sex offender register, had gone missing. Tony Blair, then Leader of the Opposition, asked the question:

> Where, in the Queen's Speech, are the Bills on stalking and a register of paedophiles -those Bills that were made so much of in the conference speeches of Conservative Members? Let me make them this offer now: produce those Bills on stalking and paedophiles, as Government Bills, and we will co-operate to take them through the House without delay. It could be done. The Conservatives should stop playing politics and point scoring. It could be done; let us do it, and do it without delay.
>
> (*Hansard House of Commons Debates 23 Oct 1996: col.17*)

The Prime Minister, John Major, explained that the Bills had 'never been in the Queen's Speech. They were intended to be Private Members' Bills because we judged that the House would pass them speedily'. The Leader of the Opposition and the Liberal spokesperson having now both offered support to the Bills, the Prime Minister added that 'I accept that deal. We were determined to put the Bills through. We shall now get them through, and I hope that Opposition Members will facilitate their speedy passage' (*Hansard House of Commons Debates 23 October 1996 col.*28; see also Jones 1996).

The Sex Offenders Bill was duly published on 18 December 1996 and the same purpose was noted as in the Consultation Document, that this Bill 'require[s] the notification of information to the police by persons who have committed certain sexual offences'. The Bill, once again, contained no mention of using this information to risk assess and to manage that risk. The Bill divided into two Parts with Part One covering the 'register' and Part Two covering the committing of sexual offences outside the UK; for present purposes we are focusing on Part One.

The Sex Offenders Bill Part One was made up of just six clauses that would provide the legal basis for the register:

- Clause 1 described the offenders who would be subject to the notification requirements and the time periods those requirements would last for.
- Clause 2 described the nature of the information that they would have to give to the police within 14 days.
- Clause 3 made failure to supply that information an offence in itself.
- Clause 4 outlined the position of persons under the age of 18 (i.e. children and young people) who had been convicted or cautioned.
- Clause 5 provided for certificates if a person had been found not guilty by reason of insanity or if they had been cautioned by the police.
- Clause 6 provided for the interpretation of Part One and defined certain terms used in it.

The remaining Clauses 7 and 8 made up Part Two of the Bill regarding sexual offences committed overseas. Schedule 1 of the Bill listed the offences to which registration would apply; unlike in the Consultation Document the *Sentencing and Supervision of Sex Offenders*, the offences for Scotland and Northern Ireland were now included. It was noted that the offences for England and Wales listed in the *Sentencing and Supervision of Sex Offenders* had numbered 32 (Home Office 1996b: Annex A) but that this number had now been reduced to 14 in the Bill Schedule 1.

On the wider front the Bill reassured everyone that there would be no cost consequences: 'There will not be any significant financial burden on public expenditure arising from the Bill. Any additional costs will be met from within existing resources. The Bill is not expected to have any effect on public service manpower' (Sex Offenders Bill page ii).

One addition to the Bill not mentioned in the Consultation Document was the inclusion of police cautions alongside convictions as being criteria leading to registration. The Consultation Document had, indeed, proposed that registration should: 'probably best be targeted on those who are convicted of any sexual offence which is sufficiently serious to attract the possibility of custody' (Home Office 1996b: para.46).

In complete contrast the Bill now declared that notification requirements could be made of anyone 'cautioned by a constable in respect of such an offence which, at the time of when the caution is given, he has admitted' (Sex Offenders Bill Clause 1(c) and Clause 5(4)).

Cautions meant there was no need for a court appearance. It is not clear who decided that cautions should be included in the Bill. The idea of the police caution was that the offenders had to admit to the offence, which was considered less serious, and that the behaviour was out of character and unlikely to be repeated. The idea of the register was that the behaviour was the opposite – that the behaviour was endemic and was likely to be repeated. As news of this inclusion became known, others suggested cautions were unjustified because they were not public information and should therefore not be used in a register (*Daily Telegraph* 'When Inquiries are abused' (Editorial) 14 June 1996) and that cautions should, in any event, not be being used for sexual offences (Liberty 1997: para.1.5; see also Soothill et al. 1997).

The parliamentary debate

The parliamentary debate was based very much on the topic of 'paedophiles'. As we have noted the term paedophile has emerged from the clinical and medical fields and been taken up by journalists and politicians as anyone who offends against a child. Some would argue – including the present authors – that it is a term used far too loosely and not adhering to the tighter medical definitions (Harrison et al. 2010).

Much of the parliamentary debate on the Sex Offenders Bill was otherwise centred around three themes.

Suspects

MPs wanted to know what could be done about people suspected of sexual offences; could they be registered? The answer was no. Attention was drawn once again to the 1991 case of *R. v. Devon County Council ex parte L* that stated social services have a duty to maintain surveillance of suspected child abusers, even if they have not been convicted; the implication was that there is, therefore, a clear duty on the government to maintain the best possible information systems and to assemble an overall list that will pull all that information on adult suspects together.

Debates at this time may have been influenced by the Children Act 1989 which was implemented on 4 October 1991. The Act stated that Care Orders on children could be made if the court was satisfied 'that the child concerned is suffering or *is likely to suffer*, significant harm' (Children Act 1989s31(2), emphasis added). Similar wording covered Emergency Protection Orders (s44 (1) (a)). The rationale being that we should not have to wait for a child to suffer before we intervened.

The campaign group ACHE (Action on Child Exploitation) was one group that wanted to see 'suspects' registered:

> if we have evolved measures with appeals and representation, for registering victims, then a similar mechanism should be worked out concerning suspected perpetrators. This addition would allow child protection agencies greater opportunities to be preventative instead of having to wait for men to offend again.
>
> (Niven 1996)

The other problem with registering suspects was the question of how to compel people to notify details to the police: people who had not actually done anything in the eyes of the law.

In Parliament one MP raised a case from his constituency (Knowsley South) when the police were alerted to the fact that a man was abroad in the community with a bag of colouring books and pens with which he evidently wanted to lure a child. He was arrested for a breach of the peace and, subsequently, under the Mental Health Act 1983, detained in a psychiatric unit for 28 days. In that unit, he was diagnosed as a psychopathic paedophile, and as such not amenable to treatment (*Hansard House of Commons Debates 7 July 1997 col.745*).

This led to a debate outside of Parliament on those with dangerous personality disorders who were untreatable; if they had done nothing the police could not intervene – if they were not treatable the medical services could not intervene under the 1983 Act. The term Dangerous and Severe Personality Disorder (DSPD) came to be used (Home Office/DoH 1999) and proposals made for reform of the mental health laws (DoH/Home Office 2000). The proposals were for more detentions and compulsory treatment in the community (Community Treatment Orders) and were eventually introduced through the Mental Health Act 2007 which amended the 1983 Act. In the USA they approached the same problem with their 'civil commitment' schemes which had resulted in people being detained for years with no crimes having been committed and no real illness diagnosed (Janus 2000).

The 2007 Act also changed the definition of mental disorder in the 1983 Act. The original 1983 Act had excluded 'promiscuity or other immoral conduct, [and] sexual deviancy' from the definition (1983 Act s.1(3)). The 2007 changes deleted this wording from the definition and thereby effectively reintroducing the wording 'promiscuity or other immoral conduct, [and] sexual deviancy' back into the definition (Mental Health Act 2007 s1).

Retrospective offences

MPs also wanted to know what could be done about people who had offended in the past. What good would the register be if these 'old' offenders were not on the sex offender register? The Home Office had published statistical evidence to show that as many as 125,000 offenders in the 1993 population had a conviction that would have required them to be on the register (Marshall 1997); as it was none of these 125,000 would be on the register. Again, the answer was 'no' because it was not possible for laws to be retrospective (Blackhurst 1997).

A later report from the Metropolitan Police suggested the numbers of unconvicted and unregistered sex offenders living in the community could be even higher:

> The statistics have been compiled by Det Chief Insp Bob McLachlan, the head of the Yard's paedophile unit, who sees them as a 'conservative estimate' … Mr McLachlan explained: 'Working on prevalence of victim to victimiser, what we are saying is that 110,000 convicted would extrapolate to 250,000 known and unknown people who have a sexual interest in children.'
>
> (Lusher et al. 2000)

In one way, the registration requirements would apply to those convicted of relevant offences in the past. These would be on those offenders still in contact with the criminal justice system on 1 September 1997, the day the register started – because they were already in prison, detained in hospital or on probation. They would be required to register even though their offences may have been committed years before the register became law. As for all the other former offenders, David Maclean for the Home Office stated that:

> It would be a vast undertaking to track the many thousands who would be involved and then to calculate who should still be subject to registration having regard to the length of sentence originally imposed upon them. It would be a still greater exercise to subject all those persons to a fresh risk assessment, as some have suggested. We concluded that it would be impracticable to place such an obligation at large in that way.
>
> (*Hansard House of Commons Debates 27 January 1997 col.31*)

Community notification

There was still the unknown factor of just what this information collated on the people required to register would be used for. It was as though this information would just self-evidently be available to the police to make these 'invisible' offenders 'visible' and that in itself was going to be sufficient.

The amount of information to be provided was originally just name and address, but David Maclean for the government said that the police had already argued that they wanted more information than this:

> in the light of further views put to us by the police, who have argued that in practice they will need fuller information, to ensure the proper identification of the offender furnishing the information. We shall therefore be tabling an amendment to require a person to notify his name and address at the time of

> conviction, his last notified name and address, his date of birth and the information which he is notifying the police has changed.
>
> (*Hansard House of Commons Debates 27 January 1997 col.30*)

Alun Michael for the Opposition questioned the wider position:

> I think that it is only fair to the police to make it clear what they are expected to do with that information, and also in the interests of the public for everyone to be clear about the way in which that information is to be used and acted on
>
> (*Hansard House of Commons Debates 27 January 1997 col.34;* for further parliamentary debate on how register information might be used see *Hansard House of Commons Debates 25 February 1997 cols. 214–219*)

MPs were also wanting reassurance that the information on sex offenders by being on the register was not going to go to waste and metaphorically gather dust on a shelf. In particular they wanted to know if information was going to be given out to the public in a manner comparable to the 'community notification' policies of the USA. The answer was, again, that 'no', it was not.

Earl Russell in the House of Lords said:

> I also have misgivings about the use that is made of the notification. The Bill has practically nothing to say on that subject. Notification is to be made to the police. What happens to the notification thereafter is left wide open.
>
> (*Hansard House of Lords Debates 20 March 1997 col.1136*)

Also, in the House of Lords one member suggested how the information could be used:

> the police are quite likely to make a habit of stopping the car of the individual on the register more often than they stop other people's cars, or to question him and require him to submit to DNA tests every time any sex crime occurs in the area, even if the sex crime for which the person was convicted is a trivial one. If it was a matter of no more than a trivial offence, one does worry about the *de facto* punishment inherent in being placed on any black list being disproportionate to the crime.
>
> (*Hansard House of Lords Debates 20 March 1997: col. 1133*)

This was part of a debate in the Lords on whether the notification requirements in Clause 1 constituted punishment. The answer to that question was – once again – that it was not intended to be punitive even though it could be experienced as such in practice (ibid).

The parliamentary summing up

Alun Michael for the Opposition demonstrated the lack of interest in further scrutiny of the Bill:

> I welcome the Bill, and give an assurance that we will work with the Government to get it through as quickly as possible – although I hope that we can improve it in some respects during the process. We promise to do what we can to work positively, particularly in Committee.
>
> (*Hansard House of Commons Debates 27 January 1997 col.34*)

There was little concern about the addition of the cautions slipped into the Bill. Labour MP John Hutton said:

> I welcome the Government's inclusion of cautions in the Bill. We must operate along the lines of a precautionary principle. If someone is evidencing behaviour that gives rise to serious concern that he may offend against innocent children and others, he should be on the register: we should know where such people are, and the police should know about their movements.
>
> (*Hansard House of Commons Debates 27 Jan 1997: Col. 63*; see also Soothill et al. 1997)

Another unspoken possibility was that once police cautions were known to lead to registration then more people might not admit to their crimes which meant they could not be cautioned and would prefer to go to court for a formal hearing.

The same hesitancy that was in the Consultation Document *Sentencing and Supervision of Sex Offenders* was present in the parliamentary discussions:

> I do not regard the Bill as a panacea to prevent all sexual offences against children; no measure can do that. No measure can control all paedophiles, but the Bill is a significant step in helping the police to track down the whereabouts of those who may be offending against children. If the police are armed with the information provided under the Bill, it will not only help them to identify suspects once a crime has been committed; it will act as a deterrent to some re-offenders.
>
> (David Maclean, Minister of State, Home Office *Hansard House of Commons 27 January 1997 col.26*)

There was no real debate on how simply being on a register would stop a person from reoffending and ensure public protection and still no mention of risk assessment and risk management becoming an integral part of the register.

Mclean for the Home Office recognised at this early stage that:

> the police will have the administrative burden of dealing with the large number of paedophiles who will register under our proposals – we might be trying to run before we can walk if we try to go much further before we have a successful paedophile register in place.
>
> (*Hansard House of Commons Debates 27 January 1997 cc23–72*)

In the Lords Earl Russell wondered about the pace that the Bill was moving at:

> Inevitably this Bill has been prepared in haste. It is a Bill on a rather complicated subject which is difficult to get right at any time. I am not quite certain that the Bill is yet in a form where we can leave it in peace. It will require some attention in the next Parliament.
>
> (*Hansard House of Lords Debates 20 March 1997 col.1135*)

Other commentators later noted the speed that the Bill went through Parliament:

> The [Sex Offenders] Bill went through Parliament with, if not undue haste, a certain degree of alacrity. It was, perhaps understandably driven, by a desire for some action to be seen to be taken in respect of increasing alarms about activities of paedophiles.
>
> (Selfe and Burke 2001: 171)

There was little or no debate on Human Rights and in particular Article 8 of the European Convention on Human Rights which states that 'everyone has the right to respect for his or her private and family life' and that interference with this right should only occur for serious reasons such as 'for the protection of health or morals, or for the protection of the rights and freedoms of others.' Article 7 of the International Covenant on Civil and Political Rights also asserted that:

> privacy must be respected and a person should have the right to remain free from damaging or harmful interference. The balance to be struck is therefore between the right to privacy and the need to protect the most vulnerable in our society.
>
> (Article 7(2))

External critique did come from a column in *The Times* written by Matthew Parris who linked the register to the forthcoming general election. Parris pointed out that we are all on the electoral rolls, and the police keep details of all our convictions on the centralised Police National Computer and that therefore, on that basis:

> There is no reason for this Bill. No reason at all. It is simply a piece of electioneering … It does nothing achieves nothing, helps nobody, protects nobody. It demeans and discourages … But it raises a saloon-bar cheer … It is shameful. It will have all party support.
>
> (Parris 1997)

The Sex Offenders Act 1997

The Sex Offenders Act 1997 received its Royal Assent on 21 March 1997. This was the first attempt at devising a UK sex offender register and it was still noticeable for making no reference to how the information collated would be used and no mention of a need for risk assessments and risk management plans to be made.

Section 1 – Sex offenders subject to notification requirements

Section One outlined how people might become subject to notification requirements by being convicted of a sexual offence as designated in Schedule One of the Act or cautioned in respect of such an offence.

It would also include those found not guilty of any of these offences by reason of insanity, those found unfit to plead but found to have still carried out the act they were charged with. The Act would apply to those sentenced since 1991 who were still in contact with the criminal justice system meaning they were still in prison or subject to other community orders. These obligations to notify the police of addresses etc. would continue for time periods related to the severity of sentence and by assumption the seriousness of the offence as described in Table 3.1

A 'person of any other description', as the last entry in Table 3.1, refers to a person subject to a community punishment, fine or caution. There were no appeals allowed against the length of time a person was to be on the register. The only way of coming off was when the time period came to an end or the original conviction was appealed against and quashed; anyone on the register for an 'indefinite period' had no means of coming off the register, until the introduction of a review system in 2012.

No real thought appears to have gone into these time periods. They simply replicate the time periods used in the 1974 Rehabilitation of Offenders Act after which certain criminal records could be considered 'spent'. Young sex offenders between the ages of 10 and 18 were liable to inclusion on the register and the concession they got as juveniles was that their time periods for notification were half that of those given to adults; an argument could have been mounted that they should get twice as long as adults because they may have been more amenable to change as young offenders, and with appropriate work from offender managers with a knowledge of young sex offenders (see also Section 4 below).

Table 3.1 Time periods for notification requirements (Sex Offenders Act 1997 s.1(4))

Description of person	*Applicable period*
A person who, in respect of the offence, is or has been sentenced to imprisonment for life or for a term of 30 months or more	An indefinite period
A person who, in respect of the offence, is or has been admitted to a hospital subject to a restriction order	An indefinite period or finding
A person who, in respect of the offence, is or has been sentenced to imprisonment for a term of more than 6 months but less than 30 months	A period of 10 years beginning with the relevant date
A person who, in respect of the offence, is or has been sentenced to imprisonment for a term of 6 months or less	A period of 7 years beginning with that date
A person who, in respect of the offence or finding, is or has been admitted to a hospital without being subject to a restriction order	A period of 7 years beginning with that date
A person of any other description	A period of 5 years beginning with that date

Section 2 – Effect of notifications

People leaving a police station, courts, prisons and hospitals with a caution or a conviction for a sexual offence were now required to report to the police to make an initial notification. They had 14 days to do this. The information they had to provide was:

- name; or where he or she used any other names, each of those names
- his or her home address
- date of birth
- name being used on the day and any other names that might be being used
- home address being used on the day.

Any changes in these items of information had also to be notified to the police within 14 days (s2(2)). These notifications could be done by a visit to any police station in his or her local area or by a written notification (s2(5)). Anyone who was homeless had to report to the police the address of any premises which he or she regularly visited (s2(7)).

Section 3 – Offences

Section Three rules that any offender failing to meet their notification requirements or providing the police with false information was committing an offence. On summary conviction the person could be fined an amount not exceeding Level 5 on the standard scale (£5000) or sentenced to a maximum of six months imprisonment, or both (s3(1)).

The Bill as originally published had said the amount was to be not exceeding Level 3 on the standard scale (£1000) and the imprisonment period not longer than a month. David Maclean for the Home Office said he had changed it after publication: 'After receiving further representations from the Police, I have decided that tougher penalties are needed to stop sex offenders from flouting the registration requirements' (Home Office 1997b).

Given that registration had not yet started it is hard to know what evidence there was that suggested the penalties needed to be increased to stop 'flouting' of the notification requirements. The standard scale was a system whereby fines in legislation have maximum levels set against a standard scale. When inflation makes it necessary to increase the levels of the fines the legislators need to modify only the scale rather than every individual piece of legislation.

Section 4 – Young sex offenders

Section Four outlined the law on the registration of sex offenders aged 10 to 18. These children and young people were liable to registration in exactly the same way as adults except that their time periods of registration were half the length of those imposed on adults. Parents may be directed that for some young sex offenders they maintain 'parental responsibility' for them and can notify on his or her behalf and also be liable for any failure to comply. The subject of young sex offenders is returned to in more detail in Chapter Ten.

Section 5 – Certificates for purposes of Part 1

Section Five authorises the certification of certain facts concerning a person's conviction status, a finding of 'not guilty' by reason of insanity or found to be under a disability but to have done the act charged against him or her. Similar certificates could be produced to verify a police caution. A Statutory Instrument was produced, for example, containing a Certificate of Caution that the offender could take away with them known as the Sex Offenders (Certificate of Caution) Order 1997 no.1921.

Section 6 – Interpretation of Part 1

Section Six defined such phrases as 'admitted to a hospital', 'detained in a hospital', 'community order', etc.

Schedule One – Sexual offences to which Part One applies

Schedule One divided into three separate lists of the sexual offences that would lead to registration in England and Wales, Scotland and Northern Ireland.

The general election of May 1997

Over the summer of 1997 a general election was followed by a change of government. The Conservative government that had steered the Sex Offenders Act through Parliament stood down leaving the new Labour government with the task of implementing the new Sex Offenders Act. The Home Office produced circular guidance to assist the police and other agencies with that implementation.

Home Office circular guidance quoted Alun Michael, now a Home Office Minister, as stating that 'The information contained on the register will need to be carefully handled. Each case will need to be assessed for the risk that the individual may pose' (Home Office 1997c) and the Home Office circular itself did now refer to the need for risk assessment:

> Ministers have made it very clear that the information must not merely be recorded or filed: it is essential that risk assessment should be undertaken by the police working with other child protection agencies, in order to protect children and vulnerable adults … and assessment of risk is at the heart of the process which should be adopted.
>
> (Home Office 1997d: Appendix A para.1)

Both of these references are still only about risk assessment and say nothing about risk management. The suggestion is that the speed of getting the Act into law before the general election on 1 May 1997 meant these requirements on the use of information had simply been over-looked. A Home Office circular now stating that risk assessment was 'at the heart of the process' seems a bit late in the day and was even now, information only being conveyed in a circular rather than the law itself.

Implementing the register

The Sex Offenders Act 1997 was implemented from Monday 1 September 1997. There was no great fanfare in the media about the fact that the UK now had a sex offender register because other events took precedence. In the early hours of Sunday 31 August Diana, Princess of Wales had been killed in a traffic accident in Paris and all other stories in the press and on television were relegated to second place or non-existence.

Various forms of guidance and advice were issued to the police and other authorities to help them with implementation of the Sex Offenders Act 1997. By now a number of commentators were pointing out that registration in itself could not deliver child or adult protection; such protection could only be achieved through effective risk management plans and their competent implementation (see e.g. Bean 1997a and Cobley 1997).

The Home Office guidance (August 1997)

Home Office circular guidance was published on 11 August 1997 a matter of weeks before the register was due to start on 1 September 1997. The circular described itself as just 'draw[ing] attention to the provisions of the Sex Offenders Act 1997' (Home Office 1997d: para.1). The circular outlined the requirements to be imposed on the designated sex offenders who had to report to the police and provide certain information; two appendices gave more specific guidance to the police on their role.

The circular seemed to be trying to make up for the omission from the Act of anything to do with risk assessment and management. The message now was that '[T]he Guidance contained in this Appendix is, principally, directed towards assessing the risk posed by offenders at the time of their registration' (Home Office 1997d: Appendix A para.12).

The Home Office guidance on actual risk assessment was that the following factors should be taken into account:

a the nature and pattern of previous offending
b compliance with previous sentences or Court Orders
c the probability that a further offence will be committed
d the harm such behaviour would cause
e any predatory behaviour which may indicate a likelihood that he will reoffend
f the potential objects of the harm (and whether they are children or otherwise especially vulnerable)
g the potential consequences of disclosure to the offender and their family
h the potential consequences of disclosure in the wider context of law and order.(ibid: para.13)

Item (c) in this list seemed a bit self-contradictory as, presumably, the whole risk assessment was precisely to answer this question. Appendix B had more detailed guidance geared to the operational requirements of the police and focused in on the cautioning of offenders, and the treatment of mentally disordered offenders.

The Association of Chief Police Officer guidance (ACPO) (August 1997)

ACPO produced its own guidance which was more about the mechanisms and procedures required to fulfil police responsibilities under the Act but again reasserting the message about 'the expectations' of risk assessment and management:

> There is a public expectation which is shared by ministers that the process of assessing and managing the risks posed by sex offenders should apply to all sex offenders generally and therefore, the police will continue to

> assess those offenders who pose a risk, whether registered or not, so as to minimise the risk to children and other vulnerable people.
>
> (ACPO 1997b: para.3)

> There is an expectation by the public, and Parliament has expressed in the debates that surrounded the passage of the Sex Offenders Act 1997, that the Police Service will use the register as an additional means to promote the protection of children and vulnerable people from the activities of sex offenders … there is an expectation of the Service that we will integrate the information from the Sex Offender Register into existing and developing systems of risk assessment and risk management.
>
> (ibid: para.22)

Seven action points were identified as a minimum to get the register up and running:

i identify a lead officer to oversee implementation

ii identify a single point of contact to enter convictions on to the Police National Computer (PNC)

iii ensure local courts, probation, prisons and mental health units could liaise smoothly

iv training for PNC operators

v officers authorised to caution offenders need information about the registration consequences to pass on to the offender; reception staff need briefing on people coming in regarding notification

vi where no such arrangements exist to assess and manage risk, forces will need to determine how they will assess and manage the risk posed by registered sex offenders.(ibid: para.31)

Home Office commissioned research on registers in the USA (November 1997)

The purpose of this research was to see what lessons the British police could learn from experience of registers in the USA and was structured around a number of key issues that had been identified. These related to the operational arrangements of a register; the way in which inter-agency work relates to registration; the impact that registers have on police investigation, detection and prevention of sexual offences; the maintenance and updating of registers; and the disclosure of information from registers (Hebenton and Thomas 1997).

The authors made a number of recommendations which included having a single agency being responsible for the register, adequate advance notice of release given to the police, clear information given to those required to register, agreed access to registration information, appropriate time periods for registration and affective procedures for de-registering. Registration in the USA was inevitably found to be a much bigger project, with far more numbers involved, than anything in the UK.

What was notable was the finding of a 'dearth of good research studies' and:

> with few exceptions, no substantial effort has been devoted to examining base-rates for offending and the scientific literature on long-term reconviction data, nor even to looking at the career path of offenders and the efficacy of all (as opposed to some) sexual offenders.
>
> (Hebenton and Thomas 1997: 34)

Alun Michael stated that:

> There is no magic wand – so we will be open to new ideas and initiatives. In the autumn I will be working with Ministerial colleagues across Whitehall to see what else can be done to tackle this evil activity.
>
> I want to see how the sex offender register operates and if changes are necessary then I will look at how it can be developed and improved. We owe it to our children to make sure that the system put in place to protect them actually works in practice.
>
> (Home Office 1997e)

Summary

There was little opposition mounted against the Sex Offenders Bill as it went through its parliamentary stages. As Soothill and Francis put it, the Bill went through 'with quite remarkable speed – and no significant opposition' (Soothill and Francis 1998). The two principal political parties were both vying for being the party of 'law and order' in the belief that that was the ground on which the pending general election of May 1997 would be won. Nobody wanted to be seen to be 'soft' on crime. The result was a rather unseemly race to the finishing line with other punitive laws being unopposed by New Labour.

4 The first five years (1997–2002)

Introduction

With the Sex Offenders Act 1997 and its accompanying guidance now in place the police were still left with the task of implementing the register as an administrative arrangement that could receive sex offenders in for completion of their notification requirements. The need for risk assessment and risk management was being increasingly discussed, all of which would lead more directly to the new police role of offender manager. The police were also going to be working more closely with the probation service and other agencies.

One police officer recalled the early days:

> So, in 1997 the register came in and the police had no idea what to do with it and they didn't do anything with it. People who had to sign up to it did so and were probably never visited again. It was a complete and utter shamble. No records were kept, it was awful, not just here, it was the same everywhere … I was the only one at that point doing all the visits to sex offenders in [city] and all the nitty-gritty.
>
> (Thompson and Thomas 2017: 165)

Concern for protection against sexual offenders continued to have a high priority amongst the public, sometimes described as a 'moral panic' or even a 'paedophile panic' (Burrell 1998). An atmosphere of 'something must be done' was in the air and politicians knew they had no choice but to make public protection a priority. The Crime and Disorder Act 1998 now introduced a new route on to the register through Sex Offender Orders, and the Criminal Justice and Court Services Act 2000 made further adjustments that impacted on the register and created a framework for offender management.

In 1999 a complete review of the law on sexual offences had been started alongside a review of the workings of the sex offender register. Together these two reviews would become the basis of the Sexual Offences Act 2003 that would replace the Sex Offenders Act 1997.

The Crime and Disorder Act 1998

The Crime and Disorder Act 1998 was the new Labour government's flagship policy on criminal justice. It had several links to the sex offender register. It created the Sex Offender Order, renewed the law on 'Extended Sentences' and introduced the Home Detention Curfew scheme.

Sex Offender Orders

The Sex Offender Order (SOO) was first proposed by the Home Office in November 1997. Originally, they were to be called Community Protection Orders but the new name was brought in before the Bill was published (Home Office 1997f). From the outset the SOO had always been portrayed as a way of retrospectively adding names of sex offenders to the register, although they had committed their crimes before the register was implemented; the idea was, the higher the number of people on the list the more effective the register would be. During parliamentary debate on the Bill, Home Office Minister Alun Michael had explained: 'We are trying to address the fact that the Sex Offenders Act 1997 left those who had offended previously entirely outside the reporting requirements that can be useful in combating offenders' (*Hansard House of Commons Debates Standing Committee B on the Crime and Disorder Bill 5 May 1998 – pm session*).

Later in discussions on the 2001 Home Office/Scottish Office *Review of the Sex Offenders Act* the same point was made:

> One potential solution mooted in the consultation groups to the problem of retrospection would be to amend the Crime and Disorder Act 1998 so as to make it possible for a Sex Offender Order to contain no restrictions, but simply to trigger the application of the Sex Offenders Act's notification requirements. On reflection, we have concluded … that such an amendment to the Crime and Disorder Act would not add to the measures already available.
>
> (Home Office/Scottish Executive 2001: 37–38; see Chapter Five for more on this Review)

Both a previous conviction or a caution could trigger an application but the argument was made that the SOO should be about the current risk the defendant posed to the community, and not the past conviction; to that extent how the offender was dealt with at the time of the original offence was not a material factor in the subsequent assessment of risk.

The Sex Offender Order (SOO) came into force on 1 December 1998. The term 'sex offender' was defined as anyone committing an offence listed in the Sex Offenders Act 1997 Schedule 1 that would now lead to registration. The Chief Officer of Police could apply to the magistrates' court for a SOO if it appeared to him or her that:

the following conditions are fulfilled with respect to any person in his police area, namely—

a that the person is a sex offender; and
b that the person has acted, since the relevant date, in such a way as to give reasonable cause to believe that an order under this section is necessary to protect the public from serious harm from him.

(Crime and Disorder Act 1998 (s2) (1))

This meant a person could be made subject to a SOO without any current offence having been committed as long as they met the criteria that (a) they had previously committed sexual offences (even if those offences had been committed prior to the start of the register) and (b) they had been acting in such a way that measures of 'public protection' were now required. The SOO described the behaviour that the subject of the Order was prohibited from engaging in and breach of the prohibitions could lead to further criminal sanctions. If the person subject to the SOO was not already on the register he or she was now automatically included and required to notify the police of any changes in their circumstances (Crime and Disorder Act 1998 s2(5); see also Home Office 1998a).

In parliament the opposition had tried unsuccessfully to have the word 'serious' removed from the term 'serious harm' in section 2(1)(b) (*Hansard House of Lords Debates Standing Committee B 5 May 1998 – am session*) and had also tried to get a new Sex Offender Supervision Order introduced that would be available to the probation service and be an add-on to the SOO; again this was unsuccessful (*Hansard House of Lords Debates Standing Committee B 5 May 1998 – pm session*).

In her research on SOOs Knock interviewed some police officers who 'saw the advantages of SOOs as a means of ensuring that offenders who would not otherwise be subject to the provisions of the Sex Offenders Act were placed on the register' (Knock 2002: 56). She also found some police officers who did not know it led automatically to registration and one prohibition was found in an Order required the offender to 'register under the provisions of the Sex Offenders Act' (ibid: 16).

The implication was, again, that the register would benefit from as many names as possible being added in these early days before it would become useful; SOOs would be one way of doing that. In reality a total of only 96 SOOs were made between 1 December 1998 and 31 December 2001 (*Hansard House of Commons 8 May 2003 col.233W*). This was a disappointingly low number if SOOs were intended to add to the numbers on the register and was something that plagued the SOOs and subsequent forms of civil orders. The police complained that the law was complicated and the applications time consuming.

The Sex Offender Order, itself, had a short life of only five years and was then replaced by a series of civil orders in the Sexual Offences Act 2003 Part Two, and then later still by the Sexual Risk Orders (SROs) and Sexual Harm Prevention Orders (SHPOs) in the Anti-Social Behaviour, Crime and Policing Act 2014 ss.113–115. As we shall see all of these Orders provided a route on to the sex offender register (this story is taken up further in Chapters Five and Seven).

Some adjustments were made to the law on SOOs by the Police Reform Act 2002 ss67–74. The police were enabled to apply for a SOO before an offender arrived in their area and prohibitions that were effective only in England and Wales were now widened to cover the whole of the UK. The Act also made it possible for the police to apply for 'interim orders' and easier to apply for variations or discharges of the SOO (Home Office 2002b).

Extended sentences

The Crime and Disorder Act 1998 ss58–60 allowed a criminal court intent on imposing a custodial sentence on a sexual or violent offender to pass an 'extended sentence'; this built on the original concept of 'extended sentences' to be found in the Criminal Justice Act 1991 s2(2) (a). The idea now was that this would lead to a longer licence period in the community when the custodial sentence had ended. This, in turn, enabled more work to be done with the offender for purposes of preventing further offending. The 'extended sentence' was then made up of 'the custodial term' and a further period known as 'the extension period'.

The difficulties arose for the convicted sex offender as to what constituted the length of sentence that would indicate the length of time a person would be subject to registration. Was it just the 'custodial term' or both the 'custodial term' plus 'the extension period'?

In 2001 the Court of Appeal ruled that the correct length was just that of 'the custodial term'. It was argued that in plain English a term of 'imprisonment' denoted actual and immediate imprisonment. It did not include a sentence of 'extended licence' during which he or she was liable to be imprisoned, but not necessarily to be imprisoned. This meant that the total periods of 'extended sentences' should not be considered when assessing whether or not a sentence threshold for registration had been met (*R v Graham (S) [2001] 1 Cr App R(S) 335*).

This ruling was followed for three years until another Court of Appeal decision said it was wrong. This time the Court ruled that a 'custodial sentence' was to include both elements of the 'extended sentence' – the 'custodial' and 'the extension' (*R v Wiles [2004] 2 Cr App R (S) 88*). By this time the 'extended sentence' had been repealed from the Crime and Disorder Act and was to be found in the Powers of Criminal Courts (Sentencing) Act 2000 s.85.

How quickly this change in ruling by the decision in *Wiles* was acted upon by police and courts across the country remains uncertain; nobody appears to have the role of keeping any records on such matters. The Home Office took a year to write to all Chief Constables pointing out the change:

> I know that many courts and police forces have been aware of this issue and have already been applying the effects of this judgement. This letter is intended to encourage those who have not been aware of *R v Wiles* to make sure that they have applied the effects of this judgement from at least 1 April 2005.
>
> (Home Office 2005b)

By this time the law had changed again and 'extended sentences' were now to be found in the Criminal Justice Act 2003 ss227–8 where the wording had been made clear that it was the whole term – 'the custodial' and 'the extension' – that had to be taken into account for purposes of registration (s227(2)).

Commentators noted the confusion:

> Wiles was actually decided on the 4th March 2004 but because it went below the radar it didn't dawn on anybody (including the Home Office) of the consequences until over a year later. But even then, Judges were still not aware of it for years afterwards and were telling Defendants they were subject to ten year [register] notifications, when in fact it was life … As unfair as that seems, matters were further confused that not every police force in England and Wales enforced the ruling in *Wiles* for convictions dated prior to the 1 April 2005. So dependent on where you lived in the country would depend on whether you were subject to the [register] notification requirements.
>
> (Olliers Solicitors n.d.)

The problem of the 'extended sentence' rumbled on. In the case of *Minter* a man receiving an 'extended sentence' was told by the Court and by the prison that he would be on the register for ten years when released from prison. He was then told by the local police that he would be on for life because the 'custodial period' and the 'extension' had not been added together. The High Court determined that the police were correct in their reading of the law (*Minter (on the application of) v Chief Constable of Hampshire and others [2011] EWHC 1610)*.

In 2012 the Home Office received a Freedom of Information request by someone asking fairly pointed questions about the register and 'extended sentences'. Had there been any cases of offenders needing to restart notification when they believed they had finished? If an offender had moved between police forces whilst under notification, would they have seen a reduction or increase to their notification dependent on that particular force's policy? The Home Office gave no specific details but said, 'the *R v Wiles* [2004] judgement applied to that legislation as from 25 August 2000 across all police forces in England and Wales'; its response is still on their website (Home Office 2012a).

Home Detention Curfew

The Crime and Disorder Act 1998 (ss99–100) also introduced the Home Detention Curfew (HDC) that started from 28 January 1999, and allowed prisoners to leave prison in advance of their formal discharge date if they agreed to wear an electronic tag for a given period of time. Originally the curfew period varied from 14 days to 60 days dependent upon the length of the original sentence; later it would be extended to as many as 90 days. Early discharges would help both the former prisoner adjust to life outside the prison and relieve the overcrowding in prisons. Since 1999, a number of prison and probation instructions had been published in relation to the HDC process (see latest statement at MoJ/HM Prisons and Probation Service 2019). The only people where doubts existed about this policy from the start were when registered sex offenders were involved.

In the early days registered sex offenders had to obtain specific authorisation for HDC from their prison governor which would only be given 'in exceptional circumstances' (Home Office 1998b: Annex B para.1; Home Office 1998c: paras.7–9). The Home Office was quite explicit about this: 'In recognition of the particular type of risk they represent, there is a strong presumption, against considering for HDC those offenders who will be required to register with the police under Part 1 of the Sex Offenders Act' (Home Office 1998c: para.7). What exactly a 'type of risk' meant, as opposed to an actual risk assessment, and why it needed 'recognition' was left unsaid.

Later the prisoner on the sex offender register applying for HDC was obliged to get authorisation from both his local prison governor *and* the national Director General of the Prison Service. The 'full assessment' procedure, as it was called, was still available only 'in exceptional circumstances', as outlined in Prison Service Order 6700 (HM Prison Service 2000: para.2.4.1–2.4.3).

Three people on the register had been allowed to leave prison in this way having claimed the 'exceptional circumstances' (*Hansard House of Commons Debates 7 November 2000 cols.203–4W)* even though in some cases prison governors appeared to have made the decision rather than the Director General of the Prison Service; the Home Secretary explained to the House of Commons how this might have happened (see *Hansard House of Commons Debates 23 June 2000 cols.337–8W*).

Although the three people released had not reoffended and no doubt arguments for increased – rather than decreased – use of the HDC scheme for sex offenders could have been mounted, the general public hostility towards sex offenders was such that the restrictions were to be increased. By the end of 1999 the Home Secretary announced that this form of authorisation for sex offenders would be coming to an end: 'We have no plans or intention whatever to provide for electronic tagging to facilitate the early release of serious or sexual offenders. Let me make that clear, with a full stop – none whatever' (Hansard House of Commons Debates 29 November 1999 col.27).

The Criminal Justice and Court Services Bill was then amended to the effect that anyone on the sex offender register was to be statutorily excluded from the HDC scheme (Criminal Justice and Court Services Act 2000 s65). The same law to this effect is now to be found in the Criminal Justice Act 2003 s246 (4)(e).

Case study 4.1

An offender was convicted of unlawful sexual intercourse with a 14-year-old girl and was sentenced to 12 months' imprisonment. He was considered as a candidate for Home Detention Curfew in view of the exceptional circumstances that he was a registered blind person and it was his first offence. He had a suitable address and was judged at an enhanced risk assessment board to pose a low risk of reoffending. He was placed on the scheme on 11 July 2000 until his conditional release date of 8 September 2000. He successfully completed the curfew and is not known to have been arrested, charged or convicted of any further offence since.

Under existing arrangements, sex offenders subject to the 1997 Act may be released only in exceptional circumstances and then only with the personal authorisation of the Director General of the Prison Service. In this case, as in the other cases previously notified, I regret that this requirement was not followed by the establishment. Although I am satisfied in this particular case that the risk to the public was remote, I have asked the Director General for a report into the circumstances of the release.

(Paul Boateng Minister of State (Home Office) cited in *Hansard House of Commons Debates 7 November 2000 cols. 203–4W*)

A similar policy of exclusion for sex offenders was followed during the coronavirus pandemic of 2020 when plans were drawn up to release some prisoners from prison early; the Ministry of Justice reported: 'Public protection is paramount. No high-risk offenders, including those convicted of violent or sexual offences, anyone of national security concern or a danger to children, will be considered for release' (MoJ 2020b). Any greater rationale for not giving HDC to sexual offenders was never given.

Early problems

The hospital discharge problem

One area of concern was that of getting information from hospitals about the date of discharge of someone detained in a hospital following sexual offences. The medical and health care professionals seemed reluctant to notify the police that there was a new person to add to the sex offender register and to give notice that the offender should be coming in to make their initial notification. ACPO gave early indication of this reluctance:

> the Department of Health will be issuing guidance to hospital managers which advises that routine notification to the police will not be made in every case. The decision has been the subject of considerable debate and

> has been taken despite arguments which were presented by the Police Service.
>
> (ACPO 1997b: para.15)

The phrase 'considerable debate' sounds like polite language for something quite intense. In essence the hospital managers and health care professionals wanted to first get the patients' consent to notify the police, and if they did not get it they said they would not pass the information on. The police thought that the public interest and public protection justified the overriding of the refusal to consent (ibid: para.17).

A consultant forensic psychiatrist, at the time, elaborated on some of the difficulties with the simple statement that 'psychiatrists have not traditionally considered public protection to be one of their duties' (Kaul 2001) and that as psychiatrists they held a superior professional view on confidentiality compared to many of the agencies involved in public protection: 'one is repeatedly struck by the low priority given to confidentiality by non-health agencies … agencies that do not necessarily have a tradition of giving confidentiality the degree of primacy that doctors and allied mental health professionals do' (ibid).

The Department of Health and Home Office both produced guidance on the subject of discharges and both were diplomatically and similarly worded. Hospital managers were advised that:

> The patient should be asked to consent to the disclosure [to the police], and the terms of it. If the patient refuses consent … it is anticipated that the need to protect the public means that the balance will generally come down in favour of notification.
>
> (NHS Executive 1997: Part A (8))

> they should give serious consideration to notifying the local police when a patient is no longer detained. The patient's consent for this will be sought and if not forthcoming managers will be expected to consider whether public interest justifies overriding the refusal … there will be no automatic decision to notify [but] it is anticipated that the need to protect the public means that the balance will generally come down in favour of notification.
>
> (Home Office 1997d: Appendix B para.17)

The Home Office said that its Mental Health Unit would step in and advise the police if the detainee being discharged was a 'restricted patient' (ibid). Restricted patients are those subject to special controls by the Secretary of State (Mental Health Act 1983 Part 3).

An Early Warning System (EWS) was introduced in April 1999 to alert the Home Office and other agencies to potentially violent or sexual offenders being released from prison or discharged from hospital. The Early Warning System was generally considered a useful, if not 'invaluable', addition to helping the safe management of high-risk offenders in the community (Home Office 1999a; see also Home Office/Scottish Executive 2001:12).

The Criminal Justice and Court Services Act 2000 introduced the possibility of new Regulations creating a statutory duty for health services to alert the police (Criminal Justice and Court Services Act 2000 Schedule 5 para.7 inserting a new s5B into the 1997 Sex Offenders Act).

The 'conditional discharge' problem

An omission in the Sex Offenders Act 1997 had also come to light. Anyone convicted for a sexual offence but only given a conditional or absolute discharge did not have to go on the register. This was clearly wrong when people with only police cautions, who had not even gone to court, did have to go on. The press referred to it as a 'loophole' and a Home Office spokesman used the same language: 'We are certainly aware of the loophole in the law which allows people with conditional and absolute discharges to escape registering. We will act as soon as possible to close it' (cited in Bamber 2000).

Two legal cases illustrated the problem. First *R v Malone* (2001) concerned a man who was given a discharge but still went on the register (see also Gillespie 2002) and secondly, in 2003, *R v Oliver and others* concerned another man who was given a discharge but did not go on the register.

The Criminal Appeal Court looked at the matter again in the case of *R v Longworth [2004] EWCA Crim 2415* and decided that the man in question should go on the register. This was now seven years after the 1997 Act causing one commentator to speculate on what would happen if the man then refused to comply with this ruling:

> it would be a brave Crown Prosecutor that would seek to prosecute in these circumstances on the basis that a defence would surely exist that the law has been in flux for such a period of time that it would be irrational to suggest that a lay person should know the law when the appellate courts did not.
>
> (Gillespie 2004)

The 2003 Sexual Offences Act s82(1) changed the law and closed the 'loophole'.

The 'For Sarah' campaign

During the summer of 2000 considerable media attention followed the police search for a missing eight-year-old girl in Sussex named Sarah Payne. Her body was eventually found in a field on 17 July 2000 and the attention now turned to the search for the perpetrator of the crime. At this point the Sunday newspaper *News of the World* joined forces with Sarah's parents and started its 'For Sarah' campaign to allow open access to the sex offender register so that everyone could find out where anybody convicted for sexual assaults on children lived. The newspaper's opening salvo was a front-page headline saying 'Named, Shamed' (23 July 2000) and the decision that it would publish the names and photographs of all the convicted sex offenders that it could find and would continue to do so, until the authorities took action. The following week (30 July 2000) the *Sunday People* newspaper started a similar campaign for tougher sentences on child sex offenders called the 'Hang them Campaign'.

The result was a degree of street protest and vigilantism which interrupted police and probation service work with sex offenders and resisted politicians' attempts to calm everything down (O'Neil 2000). Sarah's mother would later describe a situation in which 'all hell broke loose. The country was divided in its reaction [and] … there seemed to be no middle ground. On the one hand the so-called "ordinary British public" were overwhelmingly behind us' (Payne 2005: 95).

The emotionally charged turmoil and public disorder that followed tied the police up in restoring public order and prevented probation officers from carrying out their work with sex offenders and others. Paulsgrove near Portsmouth became notorious for their demonstrations (Perry 2000). Nothing short of an American style 'community notification' policy and a *Sarah's Law* was demanded. Eventually talks took place between the various parties and the campaign was stopped (Moyes and Bennetto 2000).

Home Secretary Jack Straw decided there could be no blanket community notification if the public could not handle this information in a more considered way but agreed to look at tightening the registration laws (Bennetto 2000). For many the 'For Sarah' campaign, demonstrated the limitations of open access to police files on sex offenders. Reports from South Wales suggested a paediatrician had had her home vandalised because the word 'paediatrician' had got confused with 'paedophile' (Allison 2000; Silverman and Wilson 2002: chapter 8).

The favourite headline of these times was 'Name and Shame', which itself betrays a degree of laziness on the part of journalists. The word 'shame' is, if anything, a word connected to the sentence and punishment of offenders rather than public protection. For many the only worth of the couplet 'Name and Shame' was that it made for an easy journalistic headline because the two words rhymed.

The *News of the World* had been well prepared in the approach it took to its 'For Sarah' campaign and had commissioned a telephone MORI poll on community notification before starting. The results suggested that the idea would play well with their readership (MORI Polls 2000a). A second one was completed a month later (MORI Polls 2000b) and the newspaper reported in triumph that '82% of Britain wants "Sarah's Law and thereby "community notification" comparable to the USA's "Megan's Law"' (*News of the World* 20 August 2000).

This figure of 82% was challenged by the journalist Alan Travis of *The Guardian* newspaper who looked more closely at the second MORI Poll. He challenged the newspaper report on three grounds:

> The MORI Poll had found 51% (the majority) of their poll did not think the newspaper was right to proceed with its naming and shaming policy; this had not been reported in the *News of the World*;

1 The MORI Poll had produced a large list of people's fears about community safety and what could be done about it; 24% wanted more policing, 23% wanted more traffic speed control and 16% wanted safe areas/parks for children to play in. A further 13% wanted better parenting and responsibility for child safety, 11% wanted more places to keep teenagers off the streets. The list continued down to where only 3% of the people polled wanted the public naming of convicted paedophiles; this had not been reported in the *News of the World*;

2 Finally, the '82% of Britain wants "Sarah's Law"' statement itself was challenged. The *News of the World* suggested that this was in answer to the short and simple question 'Do you support "Sarah's Law"'? But as Travis pointed out the question posed was actually far longer:

> The 'Sarah's Law' campaign wants to introduce a new law in Britain that would ensure every parent's right to controlled access to information about individuals in their neighbourhood who may pose a risk to their children. Sarah's law would also include severe penalties for misuse of this information. The campaign is endorsed by the NSPCC, the Association of Chief Police Officers and the Association of Chief Officers of Probation. Do you support or oppose the introduction of 'Sarah's law'?
>
> (quoted by Travis 2000)

A 'heavily loaded question' in the view of *The Guardian* (ibid); the 82% was made up of 52% strongly supporting and 30% tending to support (MORI Polls 2000b: Question 12).

Travis's conclusion was that 'Even in the dismal history of newspaper coverage of specially commissioned opinion polls, this must stand out as one of the most remarkable pieces of selective reporting and amnesia in the cause of self-justification' (ibid).

After Roy Whiting's conviction for the murder of Sarah Payne it became known that he was already on the sex offender register for assaulting a nine-year-old girl. The *Daily Express* ran a front page headline 'He's done it before' (13 December 2001) and the *News of the World* started another 'Named, Shamed' campaign (16 December 2001). Beverley Hughes went on Radio 4 for the Home Office to declare that full 'community notification' was still 'unworkable' (BBC News 2001). Sarah's parents met with Home Secretary David Blunkett on 18 December to push the case for a 'Sarah's

Law' but the Home Office stand against 'community notification' held firm (Home Office 2001a).

At this point it is worth noting that the Sussex police as part of their search for Sarah had made a nationwide appeal to all forces in the UK: 'The request was for ALL registered sex offenders to be visited at their homes in an effort to find Sarah alive. In addition, the offender should be interviewed and eliminated from the inquiry' (West Yorkshire Police 2000: 2).

West Yorkshire Police were probably not the only force who considered this request to be impossible to fulfil given the numbers involved; at that time, they had 1,134 offenders on their local register. What they could do was use the expertise of the police officers monitoring these sex offenders to identify those most likely and able to commit such an abduction. On this basis, 'over 100 registered offenders were made subject of a home visit within days of Sarah Payne being abducted. All were interviewed and eliminated from the enquiry. They also submitted to a full house search' (ibid: 2).

Nobody was detained and nothing found. The West Yorkshire Police recorded that 'there is no doubt that the course of action adopted by Sussex Police will form the benchmark in all future inquiries of a similar nature' (ibid: 2).

A social work review of the register

The journal *Community Care* commissioned a survey of social worker attitudes to the sex offender register after one year of its operation. The general feelings coming across were negative. Almost 60% of the social workers surveyed thought that its biggest fault line was not having people on the register with offences committed before September 1997. Forty per cent thought the register had not made it any easier to do their work involving sex offenders and 35% said it had made no difference. Almost 80% believed that the government had diverted public attention to 'stranger danger' when there was a much greater threat to children from their own families and from people they knew (Valios 1998).

'Where are they now?'

The first 18 months of the sex offender register were evaluated for the Home Office in the report *Where Are They Now?* This research started in August 1998 and was completed in April 1999. It was published on 2 August 2000 right in the middle of the 'For Sarah' campaign. The study consisted of a survey of all the 43 police forces in England and Wales with interviews in each force with the senior officer responsible for overseeing implementation of the Sex Offenders Act, and the officer designated as the point of receipt of registration information; further visits were made to six forces and interviews conducted with selected officers (Plotnikoff and Woolfson 2000).

The report covered five main areas:

- the current picture; where notification was reported to be 94.7% compliance
- force policies and organisational structures; 'few forces referred to the management of sex offenders in policing plans, crime and disorder audits or crime reduction strategies. This omission was seen as having a significant impact on the status of work and had consequences for resource allocation' – 'most forces reckoned that implementation of the Act had resulted in a significant increase in their workload, but only 17 (40%) had provided additional manpower'
- information flow and the registration process/information management; 'significant problems relating to the timeliness and quality of information flow from courts, prisons and hospitals' were reported. 'Most forces ... were unsure about being informed about hospital releases because they had no formal lines of communication' and experienced information management as fragmented
- monitoring sex offenders; 'to be effective, registration must be a dynamic process in which sex offenders are monitored in the community according to their level of assessed risk'. This may include home visits – 30 forces (70%) visited all their people on the register
- the utility of sex offender registration information varied; some officers did introduce risk assessment and management – others did a minimum. There were poor links to register information as intelligence (ibid: v–vii).

Most police officers noted the improved quality of information and working relationships with other agencies. Seven out of the 43 police forces did not send an officer to visit any registered sex offenders during the first year of the register. Another six visited only some (ibid: 40–41). The other 30 visited all of them. Only 13 police forces could give examples in which they had actually used the register to prevent sex crimes, and only ten had used their registers during investigations (ibid: 48).

Where Are They Now? warned that the register may create 'unrealistic expectations' from the public, since some police forces were still doing only 'the minimum compatible with their obligations, namely maintaining a library of register information' (ibid).

A series of recommendations were drawn up for consideration by the Home Office, including reviewing the scope of the law, clarifying the status of sex offender monitoring in relation to other policing priorities; whether guidance is needed for those sentencing offenders for failure to register; and liaising with the Department of Health to improve communications between hospitals and the police in respect of offenders with a registration requirement. It was suggested that ACPO should consider convening a national meeting of officers involved in sex offender monitoring to address issues including risk management strategies, the development of intelligence on sex offenders, the exchange of information about home visit checklists, the contribution of databases to monitoring and crime detection, and the development of relevant training programmes (ibid: vii–ix).

The Criminal Justice and Court Services Act 2000

All the media publicity, arguments, street demonstrations and general chaos that surrounded the 'For Sarah' campaign had prompted the government into some immediate action. The Criminal Justice and Court Services Bill had been published on 15 March 2000 and was passing through its parliamentary stages during the year. In its original form it had no clauses in it concerning the sex offender register. This position changed after the disruptions caused by the campaign and the government decided to add a series of amendments to the Bill in September 2000.

Home Secretary Jack Straw explained:

> The tragedy of Sarah Payne's death touched everyone's lives. We have I believe recognised the very strong public concern which her murder has evoked. This has been brought home to us very strongly in the discussions we have had with Mr and Mrs Payne about how the law could be improved.
> (Home Office 2000a)

The timing of the September additions to the Bill was inconvenient because a complete Review of the register had only been announced on 26 June 2000 just days before the 'For Sarah' campaign events took place (Home Office 2000b). Some of the provisions of the register due to be part of this Review were now simply transferred straight into the Bill without the benefit of any Review, discussions or public consultation. According to the Home Office looking back on these times:

> Several important measures to strengthen the Sex Offenders Act have already *been brought forward* in advance of the consultation paper in response to public concern … following the tragic death of Sarah Payne. These were contained in the Criminal Justice and Court Services Act …
> (Home Office 2001b: Editor's Note 1 emphasis added)

This move no doubt did allay 'public concern' but it also meant there would be no repeats of the earlier disruptions that politicians would have to sort out. The Review would be left with the residual non-urgent aspects of the register to look at (see also Home Office/Scottish Executive 2001: 4 para.8).

The primary purpose of the Criminal Justice and Court Services Act was about forming two new services – the new National Probation Service and the new Children and Family Court Advisory and Support Service (CAFCASS). The Act also brought in Disqualification Orders to prevent certain people from working with children, and sought to rename some community sentences. Tucked away in Part 3 of the Act entitled 'Dealing with Offenders' and under a sub-heading called 'Miscellaneous' were amendments to the Sex Offenders Act 1997 and the sex offender register. The Act received its Royal Assent on 30 November 2000.

The relevant sections in the Criminal Justice and Court Services Act were as follows.

Section 66 – Amendments of the Sex Offenders Act 1997

Section 66 and Schedule 5 together amended the Sex Offenders Act 1997 in respect of the register. New duties were placed on those required to notify their details to the police. Initial notification had to now be within three days (reduced down from 14 days) and their initial notification had to be in person; previously it could be done by letter. This new requirement seemed to run against the grain of the *Where are they now?* findings only published 2 August 2000. That study had specifically made the point that the courts were often slow to serve registration notices and even failed altogether to serve notices to the police. The implication was that people turning up within three days for an initial notification would be even more likely to be simply unknown to the police, than when they had had 14 days in which to notify.

Schedule 5 altered the meaning of Section 3 in the 1997 Act concerning non-compliance of any notification requirements or by giving false information. This was done by substituting the words 'he is guilty of an offence' for the existing terminology that the person would be liable on conviction for various punishments. This change also gave the police the power of arrest for non-compliance.

Sanctions for non-compliance were increased by further amendments to Section 3 raising them to imprisonment for a maximum five years (from a maximum six months), or a fine or both, on indictment, or imprisonment for a maximum six months or a fine or both on summary conviction. Compliance rates had been put at 94% by the *Where are they now?* evaluation (Plotnikoff and Woolfson 2000: 22). Most criminal justice policy projects would probably have regarded 94% as implying a very successful policy that required little or no changes, let alone more deterrence to get it up to a 100%. These changes all came into effect on 1 June 2001.

Schedule 5 introduced new sections 6A and 6B into the 1997 Act giving the police powers to take fingerprints and photographs of someone on the register and to check them against any database of fingerprints and photographs available to the police. The *Where are they now?* report had said this practice was already going on voluntarily in many police force areas (ibid: 35); now it was on a statutory footing.

A new Section 6C empowered the Secretary of State to use regulations to authorise notifications to be made only at police stations prescribed in name by those regulations. These duly appeared in the form of the Sex Offenders (Notification Requirements) (Prescribed Police Stations) Regulations 2001 no.

1708 and the Sex Offenders (Notification Requirements) (Prescribed Police Stations) (Scotland) Regulations 2001 no. 173. The list of prescribed police stations has been updated annually ever since.

New Sections 6D to 6G empowered the Secretary of State to make further regulations concerning the registered sex offender who was going abroad for more than eight days, and requiring him or her to notify the police of their date for leaving the UK, the country they are going to and their point of arrival; they should also give information about their return to the UK. This was all about notification and there were no powers to stop the travel. It was the first form of control imposed on people convicted or cautioned for sex offences regarding their international travel. The regulations appeared in the Sex Offenders (Notice Requirements) (Foreign Travel) Regulations 2001 (SI 2001 no.1846) which came into force on 1 June 2001 for England, Wales and Northern Ireland and the Sex Offenders (Notice Requirements) (Foreign Travel) (Scotland) Regulations 2001 (SSI 2001 no.188); this subject is returned to in Chapter Eleven.

The restraining order and 'Information about release or transfer'

New Sections 5A and 5B were inserted into the 1997 Act by Schedule 5 introducing the Restraining Order (s5A) and potential new laws on 'Information about release or transfer' of sexual offenders (s5B).

The Restraining Order was another innovation for those on the register and could be imposed if a court was satisfied that it was necessary to do so in order to protect the public in general, or any particular members of the public, from serious harm. The Order prohibited the offender from doing anything described in it, but in particular to stay away from certain people or areas; if the offender did anything which he or she was prohibited from doing they were guilty of an offence. Restraining Orders were subsequently merged into other civil orders by the Sexual Offences Act 2003 (see Chapter Five).

The new laws on 'Information about release or transfer' of sexual offenders created by the new s5B in the 1997 Act required anyone defined as being responsible for a registered sex offender serving a sentence of imprisonment or detention in a hospital, to notify details of his or her release from that detention or when a different person becomes responsible for them (s5B(2)). This was designed to avoid the need for the Early Warning Systems.

Section 67 – Arrangements for assessing etc. risks posed by certain offenders

The Criminal Justice and Court Services Act also sought to make amends for the omissions in the Sex Offenders Act on the need to risk assess and risk manage the men and women on the register. It was one thing to have Home Office circulars and even press releases talking about the expectations of risk assessments and management coming into play but the Act was now quite prescriptive in putting this expectation into statutory law:

> s.67(2) The responsible authority for each area must establish arrangements for the purpose of assessing and managing the risks posed in that area by—
>
> a relevant sexual or violent offenders, and
> b other persons who, by reason of offences committed by them (wherever committed), are considered by the responsible authority to be persons who may cause serious harm to the public.
>
> (3) The responsible authority for each area must keep the arrangements established by it under review with a view to monitoring their effectiveness and making any changes to them that appear necessary or expedient.
> (Criminal Justice and Court Services Act 2000)

'Responsible authority' was defined as the police and probation service acting jointly (2000 Act s67(1)); the Prison Service would later become a third 'responsible authority' (Criminal Justice Act 2003 s325(1)). 'Relevant sexual offender' meant anyone falling under the notification requirements of the Sex Offenders Act 1997; i.e. a registered sex offender (see also Home Office 2001c).

The Criminal Justice and Court Services Act 2000 s67 would also form the basis of what soon came to be known as the Multi-Agency Public Protection Arrangements or MAPPA. The Home Office now issued guidance to all local police and probation services on how these 'working together' arrangements could be set up, and outlined six minimum requirements that would be needed by the first year starting from 1 April 2001:

> a to establish Strategic Management Arrangements to keep everything under review;
> b to establish systems and processes for sharing information;
> c to establish systems and processes to ensue only the critical few that require additional consideration are referred to a Multi-Agency Public Protection Panel;
> d to establish systems and processes for a Multi-Agency Public Protection Panel for the highest risk cases, including young offenders;
> e to consider resource allocation and multi-agency training; and
> f to build community and media communications.
> (Home Office 2001d: para.9)

The 'critical few' referred to at (c) above were those offenders where there was:

- imminence of serious harm;
- a possible requirement of unusual resource allocation;
- serious community concerns;
- media implications; and
- a need to involve other agencies not usually involved (ibid: para.9(c)).

Today the term 'critical few' has been replaced by that of Critical Public Protection Cases (see NPS 2007).

At the end of the first year the Act required the production of local reports from all MAPPA areas to keep the local community informed of what they were doing (2000Act s67(4); Home Office 2003a); this report would become an annual report and further guidance was issued on how these should be prepared and produced (Home Office 2003b). The Act also permitted the Secretary of State to issue guidance to 'responsible authorities' on general matters of MAPPA (2000 Act s67(6)); the first such Guidance was issued in March 2003 (Home Office/NPS 2003).

The importance of getting the idea of risk assessment and management to the fore of policing and probation work was confirmed by Professor Hazel Kemshall:

> The effective and reliable assessment and management of sexual and violent offenders is a pressing issue. Both offence types, but particularly violent sexual crime and paedophilia, are attracting increasing public and media attention. In this climate it is essential that police personnel can fulfil their duties to identify, assess and register sex offenders, and where appropriate, contribute to the effective assessment and management of dangerous offenders.
>
> (Kemshall 2002: para.6.1)

We should recall that many police and probation services were already doing this work relating to risk and to that extent 'the MAPPA legislation confirmed and consolidated what was already good and emerging practice: it did not create something entirely new' (Bryan and Doyle 2003).

Section 68 – Section 67: interpretation

Section 68 offers an interpretation of s67 and in particular the meaning of a 'relevant sexual or violent offender' which primarily means anyone on the register as formed by the Sex Offenders Act 1997. It also included anyone convicted of a sexual or violent offence as defined by the Powers of Criminal Courts (Sentencing) Act 2000, subject to them receiving a sufficiently serious sentence or hospital order.

Section 69 – Duties of local probation boards in connection with victims of certain offences

Section 69 of the 2000 Act placed duties on the probation service to talk to victims of sexual offences and ask them their views on any licence conditions or requirements that should be placed on offenders when they were released from prison. They were also asked whether they wished to receive any information about any conditions or requirements which the offender may be subject to on release; if they did then the probation service had to take all reasonable steps to provide it.

Offender management

A direct consequence of the Criminal Justice and Court Services Act was the need for the police to form special units to carry out all the risk assessment and management work that was now coming their way by law. Some forces were ahead of the game and had started doing risk assessment and management work (see e.g. Kemshall 2001). This was to be a new form of policing. Officers originally trained to prevent crime, keep public order and investigate crime now found themselves in a role more akin to a probation officer assessing and managing risk and supervising offenders living at home in the community. The term 'polibation officers' was used by some (Nash 1999); others avoided the word supervisor in favour of the term 'offender manager'.

Probation officers acted as offender managers if sex offenders were on statutory supervision arrangements as well as the register with the police taking over when the statutory work ended. Otherwise the offender management was undertaken by the police.

As noted above, the 2001 'further guidance' that was issued to the police on how they should organise themselves based on the Criminal Justice and Courts Services Act 2000 section 67 was mainly about linking with the Probation Service, establishing arrangements for assessing and managing the risk posed by offenders, devising information sharing protocols and establishing Strategic Management Arrangements, and later a Strategic Management Board (SMB) to oversee the work of the Multi-Agency Public Protection Panel (Home Office 2001d).

These arrangements became the Multi-Agency Public Protection Arrangements and their workload divided into categories:

Category 1 – registered sex offenders
Category 2 – violent and other sex offenders
Category 3 – other potentially dangerous offenders.

Other offenders were added later.

The SMB would also produce an annual report that would be 'a clear and accessible document that informs and reassures the public about the work of taking place for their protection' (ibid: para.9(g)).

The first MAPPA annual reports were published during the summer of 2002.

The police started to organise themselves into suitably named Offender Management Teams, or Registered Sex Offender Management Units or teams, or MOSOVO teams (Managing Sexual Offenders and Violent Offenders). It was becoming clear that the wishful thinking that the register was going to have no financial consequences as suggested in the original Sex Offenders Bill was going to be far from the truth.

Early reports suggested that the lack of staff engaged in offender management could even lead to poor police practices:

> if resources are continually stretched, strategies to 'encourage' offenders to move to a different area could be an attractive safety valve … certain areas were known to deliberately make sex offenders feel as uncomfortable as possible, and in some cases, were even suspected of 'leaking information' in the hope that they would be 'hounded out' and hence move on elsewhere.
>
> (Maguire et al. 2001: 22)

Following implementation of the Criminal Justice and Court Services Act, a joint inspection report looked at how risk assessment and management was coming together. Some initial problems were uncovered including some police offender managers trying to risk assess without even knowing details of the original offence that had put people on the register. As the report said '[t]his information is critical if a comprehensive risk assessment is to be undertaken' (Chief Inspector of Social Services et al. 2002: para.9.23) and:

> The actual management of offenders also varied from area to area visited. Some forces had prescriptive visiting timetables depending on the risk of harm posed by the offender. In other areas, the MAPPP determined how often an offender would be visited. Very high and high risk of harm offenders were given priority, but in some areas, there was little or no supervision being conducted with medium and low risk of harm offenders, which caused inspectors some concern.
>
> (ibid: para.9.24)

As the new Home Secretary, one of the first things David Blunkett did after his appointment was to write a short article for the *News of the World* telling its readers that he knew the issue of protecting children was a 'massive concern' to them all, and that he would be looking at ways to give 'controlled access to information about sex offenders' (Blunkett 2001)

Case study 4.2

British Airways move men away from sitting next to children if the child is alone – *A spokeswoman for British Airways said flight crew and ticket staff were under instructions to keep men away from unaccompanied children wherever possible because of the dangers of paedophiles.*

(Smith 2001)

Legal challenges

The register was soon subjected to legal challenge. Mostly these challenges were to question the laws underpinning the register and their compliance with the European Convention on Human Rights (CoE 1950). Any non-compliance by the Member States could be contested by the European Commission on Human Rights and the European Court of Human Rights in Strasbourg.

The British government had been involved in the writing of the European Convention in the 1950s but once it was in place, they showed little interest in it. The British traditions and culture of civil liberties were seen as more important than the concept of 'rights'; British citizens were not even allowed to petition the Strasbourg Court until 1966. Most European countries incorporated the Convention and its 18 Articles into their own national laws in the 1950s but the British had to wait until 1998 before the UK government did so with the Human Rights Act 1998. Under the Human Rights Act the UK courts must have regard to the Convention and its jurisprudence when determining cases involving public authorities' acts and omissions.

An early UK appeal to the European Court of Human Rights argued that being on the sex offender register was an additional and covert punishment that fell outside the criminal law. Article 7 of the Convention held that:

> 7(1) No one shall be held guilty of any criminal offence on account of any act or omission which did not constitute a criminal offence under national or international law at the time when it was committed. Nor shall a heavier penalty be imposed than the one that was applicable at the time the criminal offence was committed.
>
> (CoE 1950)

In the case of *Ibbotson v UK (Application No. 40146/98)* the automatic nature of the obligations placed on those convicted of sex offences to register their names, without judicial discretion or involvement, only helped the European Commission of Human Rights in its conclusion that the measure was not a penalty but a 'public protection' measure.

Article 8 of the European Convention was seen as particularly pertinent to matters relating to the register because it created a qualified right to privacy. According to Article 8:

1 Everyone has the right to respect for his private and family life, his home and his correspondence.
2 There shall be no interference by a public authority with the exercise of this right except such as is in accordance with the law and is necessary in a democratic society in the interests of national security, public safety or the economic well-being of the country, for the prevention of disorder or crime, for the protection of health or morals, or for the protection of the rights and freedoms of others.(ibid: Article 8)

The European Commission of Human Rights quickly established that the sex offender register did 'engage' Article 8 but did not actually breach it; the sex offender register was deemed 'necessary and proportionate' (*Adamson v UK (1999) Application 22293/98*).

At home in the UK courts the law was clarified concerning the independence of the sentencing decision from the obligations of being on the register. In particular that the length of time a person was to be on the register was not a relevant factor to be taken into account in the sentencing decision. In the case of *AG's Ref. No. 50 of 1997 (David Victor V) [1998] 2 Cr. App. R.(S) 155* the Appeal Court held that it was not appropriate for a sentence to be reduced to limit the offender's obligation to register under the Sex Offenders Act 1997. The provisions of the 1997 Act should not be regarded as a 'penalty' within the provisions of the Criminal Justice Act 1991s.28 (now Powers of Criminal Courts (Sentencing) Act 2000 s.158).

This division between the sentence and the registration time period occurred again in another legal case. The defendant was sentenced to two years imprisonment for offences of indecent assault and gross indecency with a child; the registration period should have been ten years but the trial judge incorrectly said that it would be five years. The Court of Appeal said that the court had not been under a legal duty to inform the defendant of how long his registration might be and upheld it at ten years (*Rawlinson* (1999) *The Times* 27 October).

The Sexual Offences (Amendment) Act 2000

It was during this period that the Sexual Offences (Amendment) Act 2000 was passed with further repercussions for the register. The two main innovations brought in by the Act were:

a the equalisation of the age of consent for same-sex activities with that of heterosexual activities; the age came down from 18 to 16 years of age (2000 Act ss1–2)
b the new offence of 'abuse of trust' – whereby teachers and others working in positions of trust with 16–18-year olds could be prosecuted, and thereby criminalised, for consensual sexual activities with those children they were working with. In other words, the age of consent was effectively raised from 16 to 18 for some children in these workplace circumstances. Teachers could be jailed for up to five years for consenting relationships with pupils, under the 'abuse of trust' laws (2000 Act ss3–4). Offenders were to have their names added to the sex offender register (2000 Act s5).

Home Office Minister Charles Clarke MP stated that, even after the equalisation of the age of consent, men previously convicted of consenting gay sex with 16- and 17-year olds would remain on the register (Outrage 2000).

Two reviews

Two reviews, both involving public consultation, threw light on the need for further change. A review of the law on sexual offences had been set up by the government in 1999, resulting in the consultation paper, *Setting the Boundaries: reforming the law on sex offences*, published in July 2000; a further public consultation closed in March 2001. In addition, the government carried out a Review of the Sex Offenders Act Part One and proposals were published for public consultation in July 2001 (Home Office/Scottish Executive 2001). During the period of this second review ongoing changes were being planned to the criminal justice system and legislation. The two reviews fed into a White Paper: *Protecting the Public* published in November 2002 (Home Office 2002a) which ultimately led to the Sexual Offences Act 2003.

Summary

Despite some teething problems the sex offender register as first conceived was up and running. The proposed Review of the first three years had been disrupted by the 'For Sarah' campaign. In the face of angry public protests demanding community notification, the Home Office decided to take some of the Review ideas out of the Review and implement them without further discussion in the Criminal Justice and Court Services Act 2000. The critical White Paper *Protecting the Public* outlining a new Sexual Offences Bill and the way forward for the register was published in 2002.

5 The Sexual Offences Act 2003

Introduction

The Sexual Offences Act 2003 repealed and replaced the original Sex Offenders Act 1997 and remains, to this day, the legal basis of the sex offender register arrangements; as with the 1997 Act the word 'register' is never used in the 2003 Act. Here we trace the nature of the new Act by looking at the two reports that preceded it, in the form of *Setting the Boundaries: reforming the law on sex offences* (Home Office 2000c) and the *Review of Part One of the Sex Offenders Act 1997*(Home Office/Scottish Executive 2001).These reports provided the grounds for debate on the Sexual Offences Bill and its passage through Parliament. In the same year the Criminal Justice Act 2003 became law repeating and strengthening the provisions in the Criminal Justice and Court Services Act 2000 on how risk posed by sex offenders was to be assessed and managed.

Two reviews

Setting the Boundaries: reforming the law on sex offences

A review of the law on sexual offending was completed in the *Setting the Boundaries* report. This was the first time the law on this subject had been looked at in a comprehensive way since the 1950s. The report had little to say on the register as such, other than confirming that any new offences recommended in the report should lead to registration unless they were more akin to 'public order offences'. They also declined to comment on the question of children being put on the register deferring that matter to the *Review of Part One of the Sex Offenders Act 1997* (see Home Office 2000c: para.9.5).

The Review of Part One of the Sex Offenders Act 1997

The Home Office first gave notice of a Review of the Sex Offenders Act 1997 in June 2000. Junior Minister Charles Clarke established a small steering group 'to direct the Review and undertake a consultation process' and 'I anticipate that the steering group will report to Ministers at the end of the year' (*Hansard House of Commons Debates 26 June 2000 cols.395–6W*). The aim of the Review was stated to be 'To strengthen the operation of the Sex Offenders Act 1997 in contributing to the protection of the public from sex offenders' (Home Office 2000b).

The Consultation Paper for the Review appeared in July 2001 (Home Office/Scottish Executive 2001); in the 'Forward' Home Secretary David Blunkett reaffirmed that this was part of a 'strengthening' exercise:

> We are determined to take every opportunity of building on and strengthening the steps already taken to protect the public from these offenders. The Sex Offenders Act has proved a valuable tool in helping protect the public and has been the focus of much discussion since its introduction. Experience in implementing it has suggested that some aspects could be strengthened.
>
> (ibid: Forward)

Journalists described the Consultation Paper as offering a means to 'tighten up loopholes in the law' (Tempest 2001).

The Home Office was aware of the human rights element of the register and more so since the Human Rights Act 1998 had been passed, to incorporate the European Convention on Human Rights into UK law. This was clearly noted in the Consultation Paper:

> Challenges to the SOA [Sex Offenders Act 1997] on human rights grounds have been successfully resisted because the registration requirement has been seen as an administrative consequence of a sentence passed by the court, rather than being a separate sentence in its own right. Were the registration requirement to become more onerous, there could come a point at which the Act could no longer be seen as an administrative requirement. A balance has, therefore, to be maintained between maximising the contribution of the SOA to protecting the public and ensuring that individual rights under the HRA [Human Rights Act] are not infringed. The current review of the SOA was conducted within this frame of reference.
>
> (Home Office/Scottish Executive 2001: 13)

The range of offences covered by the 1997 Act

The Consultation Paper was in favour of a new discretionary power for courts. It suggested a list of violent offences be drawn up with respect to which the court should have discretion to decide whether, in an individual case, an offence was sexually motivated. If the court decided it was, it could order the offender to be subject to the requirements of the register. The list of offences would include murder, manslaughter, malicious wounding, grievous bodily harm, kidnapping, false imprisonment, abduction and attempts to commit these acts. The defendant would have the right to appeal against such a decision.

It was also suggested that the offence of burglary with intent to rape should be added to the offences leading to registration and varying thresholds should be introduced for young offenders. Where the offender was below the age of 20, registration should not be required for offences of:

- unlawful sexual intercourse with a girl aged between 13 and 16
- buggery
- indecency between men
- abuse of trust unless the sentence is imprisonment of any length, community supervision of 12 months or more or admission to hospital subject to a restriction order. Where the offender was over 20 years of age, anyone committing these offences should be liable for registration automatically.

How the Register should apply to children and young people who sexually abuse

The Consultation Paper presented the idea that the current registration regime for those aged under 18 should be continued but also asked for views that only those over 16 be on a register unless those under this age had been sentenced to a custodial sentence of any length or admitted to hospital subject to a restriction order. Even more adventurous was the idea of registering children and young people who sexually abuse with an agency other than the police which had a remit to address both their abusive behaviour and their wider needs.

Penalties available for children and young people in non-compliance with the register requirements were re-examined with the suggestion that they be increased to include Detention and Training Orders of a maximum of two years' duration, Action Plans and Curfew Orders should be available to the courts as penalties for those under 18 who fail to comply with the requirements. It was also suggested that Parenting Orders should be available to courts to ensure that advice and support can be made available to those with parental responsibility for children and young people failing to meet the requirements of the legislation.

These ideas and the response to them will be returned to in more detail in Chapter Ten.

Sex offenders who travel

The need for UK sex offenders travelling overseas to notify the police of their plans had already been dealt with by the Criminal Justice and Court Services Act 2000. What was now proposed was some form of putting UK and foreign nationals convicted of sex offences overseas on to the register when they returned to the UK if the offence was equivalent to one under Schedule 1 of the 1997 Act; this subject will be returned to in more detail in Chapter Eleven.

The power to arrest people in non-compliance with the Register

Views on this subject were not required because it had been dealt with by the Criminal Justice and Court Services Act 2000.

Cautions and conditional discharges

It was proposed that cautions and conditional discharges for relevant offences should trigger registration where the victim was under 18 and the offender was aged 20 or over for a period of 12 months. Absolute discharges should not trigger registration (Home Office/Scottish Executive 2001: 36).

Responses to the Consultation Paper were published in 2002 and were nearly all supportive of the Home Office recommendations – some unanimously and some overwhelmingly (Home Office 2002c).

The 2002 White Paper – *Protecting the Public*

The White Paper *Protecting the Public* published on 19 November 2002 was subtitled *Strengthening Protection against Sex Offenders and Reforming the Law on Sexual Offences.* On the question of *Setting the Boundaries*, it regarded the current law to be archaic and discriminatory, and legal clarification and revision was long overdue. The proposals sought to strike a balance between protecting individuals from abuse and exploitation, whilst recognising the personal, private relationships of consenting adults.

Home Secretary David Blunkett had already announced that he wanted to tighten the register with annual visits by the registered sex offender to the police, and to ensure that known sex offenders entering the country from abroad would be put on the register on arrival. He also wanted lay representatives of the community to be included into multi-agency arrangements. With respect to the last item he said there would be no wider 'community notification' as long as we had 'vigilantes who do not understand the difference between "paediatrician" and "paedophile"' (Blunkett 2002; see also Home Office 2002d).

When it appeared a month later the White Paper contained all the proposed changes to the register plus more general reforms to the law on sexual offences:

- Tightening the notification requirements of the sex offenders' register. Establishment of multi-agency risk management plans to cover sex offenders assessed as a serious public risk who cannot be held in custody. Including powers to disclose information to schools, voluntary groups and others.
- Clarifying the law on consent, including specifying circumstances where consent is presumed most unlikely to have been given, and introducing a test of reasonableness in rape cases where the defendant claims an honest belief that consent was given.

- New measures to give special protection for children and the vulnerable, particularly in the light of increased use of the internet by child sex offenders, including a new crime of sexual grooming.
- New offences involving commercial sexual exploitation, including those who buy or control the sexual services of a child under 18 years old.
- A new public order offence dealing with sexual behaviour in a public place which causes alarm to others, which covers both heterosexual and homosexual activity.
- The maximum penalties for a number of offences were to be increased in order to take account of the long-term harm caused by sexual abuse, particularly in childhood.
- Under 13s will not be capable in law of giving consent to any form of sexual activity. Any sexual intercourse with a child under 13 will be charged as rape.
- A new offence of adult sexual activity with a child – which will capture behaviour such as inappropriately persuading children to undress.
- New offences with severe penalties against those who sexually exploit children for their own gain (Home Office 2002a: *passim*).

The Sexual Offences Bill

The Sexual Offences Bill was published on 28 January 2003. The Bill as a whole divided into two parts concerning the sexual offences (Part One) and the sexual offenders (Part Two). It is Part Two that concerns the operation of the sex offender register. Apart from the discussions on the Bill during its passage through Parliament the Bill was also examined by the Joint House of Lords/ House of Commons Committee on Human Rights and the House of Commons Home Affairs Committee. On 6 October 2003 a number of amendments were added to the Bill 'to further tighten sex offender monitoring'; in particular the law was to be changed to allow the police to cross-check offenders' details with passport, National Insurance, and driving licence records to confirm identities provided were correct (Home Office 2003c).

The notification requirements

The Bill now created three levels of notification requirements ranging from an initial notification at the start of the registration period to a notification concerning any change in circumstances, through to a periodic – or annual – notification. All had to be made in person at a prescribed police station. See below in the section covering the Act for full details.

Civil Orders

The Sexual Offences Bill contained proposals for four new Preventative Civil Orders – the Notification Order (NO), the Sexual Offences Prevention Orders

(SOPO), the Foreign Travel Orders (FTO) and the Risk of Sexual Harm Orders (RSHO). These Orders would replace the Sex Offender Order (SOO) and will be discussed more fully below. Here we might just note that these civil orders were now bound by the *McCann* judgment that proceedings in court for certain civil orders should be conducted at criminal justice levels with findings 'beyond all reasonable doubt' rather than the lower levels of civil procedures being 'on the balance of probabilities' (*R v. Crown Court of Manchester ex parte McCann and others [2002] UKHL 39*).

The Parliamentary Joint Committee on Human Rights (JCHR) expressed concern at the proposed Risk of Sexual Harm Orders (RSHO), and whether the safeguards against unjustified orders were sufficient. They believed that such orders had the potential 'to have a catastrophic effect on people's lives and reputation' and to engage Article 8 of the European Convention on Human Rights (House of Lords/House of Commons 2003: para.40). Apart from some matters concerning Part One of the Bill, the committee declared themselves otherwise satisfied with the Bill reporting that it 'raises no human rights issues requiring to be drawn to the attention of either house' (ibid: para.42). It might be pointed out that the Joint Committee completely overlooked the breach of the European Convention that would be upheld by the UK Supreme Court in 2010 (see Chapter Twelve).

The House of Commons, Home Affairs Select Committee examined the Bill and expressed more concern about the proposed RSHO and in particular the fact that the Order may be obtained against persons over the age of 18 who had no previous convictions for any offences, let alone sexual offences. The person had to have, on at least two occasions, engaged in sexually explicit conduct or communication with a child or children, and there was reasonable cause to believe that the order was necessary to protect that child or children from harm arising out of any future such acts. The RSHO would list behaviour the defendant was prohibited from engaging in aimed at protecting the child or children. Breach of the Order would lead to registration (House of Commons 2003: paras.53–62).

The campaign group Liberty described the proposed RSHO as 'an affront to any notion of traditional British justice', in that they 'permit the badge of paedophilia and accordingly broad and ill defined "prohibitions"… to be placed upon a person who has never been convicted of any criminal offence' (cited in ibid: para.55).

A Police Federation representative also described the RSHO as possible 'overkill,' adding that 'when you start looking at human rights legislation and the like, for people not having any prosecution and conviction, to have an order of this nature I think would probably be against human rights legislation' (ibid: para.57).

The Sexual Offences Act 2003

The new law was implemented from 1 May 2004 and remains in place to this day subject to amendments.

The notification requirements

Part 2 of the Sexual Offences Act 2003 outlined the notification requirements on people convicted of, or cautioned for, designated sexual offences. As with the 1997 Act registration is an automatic add-on to a sentence and the courts have no discretion in the matter except in Scotland (see below); people required to register originally had no right of appeal against being made subject to the registration period.

The offences leading to registration

The designated offences that lead to registration are listed in Schedule 3 of the 2003 Act and includes the old offences from the 1997 Act Schedule 1 and the new sexual offences contained in Part 1 of the 2003 Act. In Scotland the courts did have some discretion about registration with the inclusion of paragraph 60 to Schedule 3 permitting registration if the courts determine a case included a significant sexual aspect to the offender's behaviour in committing the offence.

The registration time periods

The registration notification time periods remain mostly the same as in the 1997 Act. The time period of five years for a police caution was reduced down to two years, and the 'conditional discharge' problem was resolved by making the notification period the same as for the period of time that the 'conditional discharge' lasts for. The new sentence of 'imprisonment for public protection' leads to an indefinite period of notification (see Table 5.1).

Young people aged 10 to 18 still only spent half the time on the register compared to adults (2003 Act s82(2)).

Anyone convicted of any of the sexual offences listed in Schedule 3 of the Sexual Offence Act 2003 was automatically subject to the notification requirements, meaning they must notify their local police force of their name, address and certain other personal details.

Sexual offenders required to register were now referred to as 'relevant offenders' (2003 Act s80(2)) and, as noted above, they were required to make three notifications to provide certain initial basic personal information, any subsequent change in their circumstances to the police and to make an annual verification notification to the police:

1 *Initial notifications* – were to be made at the start of the registration notification period and within three days of a conviction or caution decision or on leaving prison or hospital; the information required is:

   a the 'relevant offender's' date of birth;
   b his or her National Insurance number; this was an innovation not required by the earlier law; people already on the register had to provide such information when they first notified a change to their

Table 5.1 Time periods for notification requirements (Sexual Offences Act 2003 s82(1))

Description of relevant offender	*Notification period*
A person who, in respect of the offence, is or has been sentenced to imprisonment for life, to imprisonment for public protection under section 225 of the Criminal Justice Act 2003, to an indeterminate custodial sentence under Article 13(4)(a) of the Criminal Justice (Northern Ireland) Order 2008 or to imprisonment for a term of 30 months or more	An indefinite period beginning with the relevant date
A person who, in respect of the offence, has been made the subject of an order under section 210F (1) of the Criminal Procedure (Scotland) Act 1995 (order for lifelong restriction)	An indefinite period beginning with that date
A person who, in respect of the offence or finding, is or has been admitted to a hospital subject to a restriction order	An indefinite period beginning with that date
A person who, in respect of the offence, is or has been sentenced to imprisonment for a term of more than 6 months but less than 30 months	10 years beginning with that date
A person who, in respect of the offence, is or has been sentenced to imprisonment for a term of 6 months or less	7 years beginning with that date
A person who, in respect of the offence or finding, is or has been admitted to a hospital without being subject to a restriction order	7 years beginning with that date
A person within section 80(1)(d) (cautions)	2 years beginning with that date
A person in whose case an order for conditional discharge or, in Scotland, a community payback order imposing an offender supervision requirement, is made in respect of the offence	The period of conditional discharge or, in Scotland, the specified period for the offender supervision requirement
A person of any other description	5 years beginning with the relevant date

details after commencement of the 2003 Act or at their first 'periodic notification' (see below);

c his or her name on the 'relevant date' and, where they used one or more other names on that date, each of those names; the 'relevant date' is the date of conviction or for those with a 'sentencing threshold' the date of sentencing (2003 Act s82(6));

d his or her home address on the 'relevant date';

e his or her name on the date on which notification is given and, where they used one or more other names on that date, each of those names;

f his or her home address on the date on which notification is given;

g the address of any other premises in the United Kingdom at which, at the time the notification is given, he or she regularly resides or stays (Sexual Offences Act 2003 s83(5)).

2 *Change notifications* – if any personal circumstances change. The notification of changes should be within three days of the change; this was in line with the Criminal Justice and Court Services Act 2000 amendment to the original 1997 Act and a tightening up of the 14 days allowed under the 1997 Act. The information required is:

a using a name which has not previously been notified to the police under section 83(1);
b any change of home address;
c having resided or stayed, for a qualifying period, at any premises in the United Kingdom the address of which has not previously been notified to the police under section 83(1); or
d his or her release from custody pursuant to an order of a court or from imprisonment, service detention or detention in a hospital (Sexual Offences Act 2003 s.84(1)(a)–(d)).

3 *Periodic notifications* – all registered sex offenders must make annual reports to the police to confirm their notified details (Sexual Offences Act 2003: ss83–5). Periodic notifications had been recommended by the 2001 Review of the register:

> Currently, the police may only discover that the offender is not at the registered address if they undertake a periodic visit there or if he is discovered living elsewhere. It has been argued that the onus should lie on the offender periodically to confirm the registered information about them is accurate. If they do not have to register a change to their name or address, there is currently no mechanism for achieving this. In the consultation groups, there was a clear consensus in favour of requiring periodic re-registration.
>
> (Home Office/Scottish Executive 2001: 23)

These three forms of notification have to be carried out by a personal visit to a prescribed police station as required by the Criminal Justice and Court Services Act 2000 (see Chapter Four). 'Prescribed police stations' for England and Wales are listed in a Statutory Instrument which is updated at regular intervals; at the time of writing (August 2020) the most recent list may be found in the Sexual Offences Act 2003 (Prescribed Police Stations) (England and Wales) (Amendment) Regulations 2019 no. 1055. It is permissible to notify changes in advance of the three day period, but to get them corrected if, for some reason, they do not go ahead.

The police were given the power to request fingerprints, and may take a photograph of the 'relevant offender' at any one of these three notification arrangements (2003 Act s87); as noted in the last chapter, these powers appear to be giving legal authority for a police practice that had been going on, on a voluntary basis, in some police stations for the last six years (Plotnikoff and Woolfson 2000: 35). New requirement to give details of passports, bank accounts, and credit cards and details of any residence with a child were added on from 13 August 2012 (see Chapter Seven).

A person subject to the notification requirements commits a criminal offence if he or she fails, without reasonable excuse, to:

- make an initial notification in accordance with 2003 Act s.83(1);
- notify a change of details in accordance with s.84(1);
- make an annual re-notification in accordance with s.85(1);
- comply with any requirement imposed by regulations concerned with the notification of foreign travel (s.86(1));
- notify the fact that a change did not happen as predicted when it had been notified in advance in accordance with s.84(4)(b);
- allow a police officer to take his photograph or fingerprints (s.87(4));
- ensure that a young offender on whose behalf he is required by a parental direction to comply with the notification requirements attends a police station when a notification is made (s.89(2)(b)); and
- in the first four cases set out above, if he or she knowingly provides false information

(Sexual Offences Act 2003)

An offender convicted of such an offence on summary conviction (in a magistrates' court) will be liable to a term of imprisonment of up to six months or to a fine or both; an offender convicted on indictment (in a Crown Court) will be liable to a term of imprisonment of up to five years. Breach of the requirements is an arrestable offence (2003 Act s91).

The Civil Orders

The Sexual Offences Act 2003 replaced Sex Offender Orders (Crime and Disorder Act 1998 s2) and Restraining Orders (Sex Offenders Act 1997 s5A as inserted by the Criminal Justice and Court Services Act 2000 s66 Schedule 5 para.6); they were replaced by four new preventative orders.

The Notification Order (NO) and the Foreign Travel Order (FTO)

The Notification Order (NO) and the Foreign Travel Order (FTO) were concerned with people with convictions for sexual offences and international travel. The NO was for those arriving in the UK and led to their inclusion on the sex offender register; the FTO was to prevent some of those already on the UK register from leaving the country. Both of these Orders will be considered separately in Chapter Twelve on the 'travelling sex offender'.

The remaining two were the Sexual Offences Prevention Order (SOPO) and the Risk of Sexual Harm Order (RSHO) and both had links to the sex offender register.

The Sexual Offences Prevention Order (SOPO)

The Sexual Offences Prevention Order (SOPO) was the nearest to the Sex Offender Order and the Restraining Order that had been available under the old laws. The SOPO could be made on someone with a criminal record for a sexual offence but whose continuing behaviour makes the Order necessary. Application was made by the police 'for the purpose of protecting the public or any particular members of the public from serious sexual harm from the offender' (2003 Act s.104). The 'sentencing thresholds' set out in Schedule 3 would continue to apply for the purposes of determining whether an offender would be made subject to the notification requirements.

The SOPO made a list of prohibited behaviour, that the man or woman must adhere to in the interests of protecting the public (2003 Act s.107 (1–2)). If not already on the sex offender register then the subject of the SOPO was automatically included on the register for the duration of the SOPO (2003 Act s107 (3–4)). Breach of a SOPO was an offence which could lead to a fine or imprisonment depending on the seriousness of the behaviour (2003 Act s113(2)).

The appropriate length of time a SOPO should last for should be equal to the length of time for which the individual is subject to the registration notification requirements. In some cases, a SOPO has been imposed 'until further order' despite the subject only being required to register with the police for a determinate period of between five to ten years. This was clarified in the ruling of *Hammond.* Hammond's offences led to sentences that meant he was on the register for five years. At the same time, he was made subject to a SOPO which was to last 'indefinitely'. On appeal the court ruled that.

> In general terms, when imposing a Sexual Offences Prevention Order at the same time as imposing the requirement to register under Schedule 3 of the 2003 Act, it will normally be important to ensure the terms of the Sexual Offences Prevention Order are consistent with the duration of the notification requirements.
>
> (*R v Hammond [2008] EWCA Crim 1358*)

To vary a SOPO the applicant must show a change of circumstances. There cannot be an attack on the grounds for the original order (*Sadler v Deputy Chief Constable of West Mercia Police 2014 EWHC 1715 (Admin)).*

In the North East a man made subject to a SOPO took exception to the local police deciding to impose the wearing of an electronic tag to enforce the prohibitions he was made subject to. The man sought judicial review on the grounds that (i) there was no express provision in the Sexual Offences Act 2003 authorising electronic tagging; (ii) the requirement was a positive obligation and not a negative requirement; and (iii) it breached his rights to a private and family life under Article 8 European Convention on Human Rights. The Court of Appeal disagreed and concluded that the requirement was lawful (*R (on the application of Richards) v Teesside Magistrates Court [2015] EWCA Civ 7*). For a general overview of the law on SOPOs see *R v Smith and Others [2011] EWCA Crim 1772.*

The Risk of Sexual Harm Order (RSHO)

The Risk of Sexual Harm Order (RSHO) was the fourth of the Civil Orders and was imposed on adults who had been involved in at least two incidents of explicit sexual conduct or communication with a child (2003 Act s123 (3)). No offence needs to have been committed and the application for a RSHO was made to magistrates by the police. We noted some earlier concerns about the RSHO and human rights during debate on the Bill.

The RSHO again listed behaviour that was now prohibited and gave the length of time the Order would last for. If the person concerned did have earlier convictions, and was already on the sex offender register, his or her registration period would be extended until the end of the RSHO. If they had no earlier convictions for sexual offences and they breached the prohibitions listed in their RSHO, they would face a fine or period of imprisonment; at this point they would also have their name included on to the sex offender register (2003 Act ss128–9).

The Order seeks to prevent adults from initiating contact with children to 'groom' them in order to initiate the sexual abuse of a particular child or group of children (Craven et al. 2006). Mostly grooming takes place face to face but the new law was also to reduce growing fears that adults were grooming children over the internet in chat rooms and similar social media spaces. At this point in time internet grooming was not as common as face-to-face grooming but it had received a great deal of publicity (Craven et al. 2007). The RSHO was an attempt to prevent preparatory interactions between adult and child from taking place whether online or offline.

In more detail the application for a RSHO had to demonstrate that a person had on at least two occasions been:

a engaging in sexual activity involving a child or in the presence of a child;
b causing or inciting a child to watch a person engaging in sexual activity or to look at a moving or still image that is sexual;
c giving a child anything that relates to sexual activity or contains a reference to such activity;
d communicating with a child, where any part of the communication is sexual.(Sexual Offences Act 2003 s 123 (3))

The first two items on this list of required evidence – (a) and (b) – were actually offences as documented in the Sexual Offences Act 2003. Critics of the RSHO believe that this list, therefore, represents behaviour that could have led to a prosecution but had not done. In effect the civil RSHO is then being used as a 'softer' alternative to criminal prosecution (Craven et al. 2007).

The need for evidence of 'sexual communication' (item (d)) also suggested that internet grooming was getting a greater priority in the law than its lower rate of incidence warrants, compared to face to face grooming (Sexual Offences Act 2003 s 123 (3)).

The same critics also suggested that RSHOs could have offered a more exact definition of 'grooming' and pointed out that: 'it is extremely difficult to distinguish between sexually motivated grooming behaviours and perfectly normal child/adult interactions that have no sexual motivations' (Craven et al. 2007).

A new offence of 'sexual communication with a child' became law in the Serious Crime Act 2015 s67 (for more on this see Chapter Seven).

A RSHO could be made on *anyone*; there was no necessity that the person already be 'known' and convicted for earlier sexual offences, as is the case with the SOPO. Applicants had only to demonstrate the behaviour patterns listed above at (a) to (d); it was a tacit further widening of the scope of just who might be a potential sex offender.

All four of the preventive orders were used for the next ten years. There was then a Review of their usefulness and they were replaced by two new Orders in 2014 (see Chapter Seven).

Miscellaneous provisions

Sections 94 and 95 of the Sexual Offences Act 2003 introduced a new power that would help the police to verify that an offender had notified the correct details and that he or she was not omitting any details (such as another name or address being used) in compliance with sections 83, 84 and 85. This would be done by comparing the details received at notification against those details offenders will have registered with other agencies:

- The various agencies which perform social security, child support, employment and training functions on behalf of the Secretary of State for the Department of Work and Pensions (DWP) and the equivalent Northern Ireland Department.
- The agency which issues passports on behalf of the Home Secretary (i.e. the UKPS (UK Passport Service)).
- The agency which performs functions under Part 3 of the Road Traffic Act 1998 on behalf of the Secretary of State for the Department of Transport (i.e. the Driver and Vehicle Licensing Agency) or Part 2 of the Road Traffic (Northern Ireland) Order 1981. The DVLA holds details on everyone with a driving license. In addition, it is an offence not to inform the DVLA of a change to these details.

The details the police may provide to the DWP, UKPS and DVLA are the offenders':

- date of birth
- national insurance number
- any names he or she has notified
- home address and any other addresses notified.

This information may have been supplied by an offender at his initial notification, when notifying a change or at his periodic notification.

This information could only be shared for the purpose of verifying that the information supplied to the police, etc. by the offender was accurate. It could not, for example, be used by DWP to pursue someone for a child support payment. The information supplied by the police, etc. will be compared against the information held by the DWP, UKPS and DVLA and a report of discrepancies compiled. Any transfer of data must still comply with the Data Protection Act 1998 (2003 Act s94(6)); or the later Data Protection Act 2018.

The Sexual Offences Act 2003 s93 and Schedule 4 introduced new procedures to end registration requirements for offences that had been abolished. In practice this referred to the Sexual Offences (Amendment) Act 2000 which had lowered the age of consent for homosexual men from 18 to 16. The Sexual Offences Act 2003 now abolished the old offences of consensual buggery and indecency between men that had led to registration. This had left some men still on the register for activities that were no longer offences. This subject is returned to in Chapter Twelve.

The Criminal Justice Act 2003

The MAPPA arrangements initiated by the Criminal Justice and Court Services Act 2000 were repeated and enhanced by the Criminal Justice Act 2003. The 'responsible authorities' which were the police and probation service now had the prison service added to their number (2003 Act s325(1)). Why the prison service was not included in by the Criminal Justice and Court Services Act 2000 remains a mystery, but here it was – three years on – now added in.

The Act also placed a new duty on other agencies in the local MAPPA area to cooperate with these three 'responsible authorities':

> In establishing those arrangements, the responsible authority must act in co-operation with the persons specified in subsection (6); and it is the duty of those persons to co-operate in the establishment by the responsible authority of those arrangements, to the extent that such co-operation is compatible with the exercise by those persons of their relevant functions.
>
> (2003 Act s3)

The 'duty to cooperate' agencies concerned were duly listed as:

a every youth offending team established for an area any part of which falls within the relevant area,
b the Ministers of the Crown exercising functions in relation to social security, child support, war pensions, employment and training,
c every local education authority any part of whose area falls within the relevant area,
d every local housing authority or social services authority any part of whose area falls within the relevant area,
e every registered social landlord which provides or manages residential accommodation in the relevant area in which persons falling within subsection (2)(a) or (b) reside or may reside,
f every Health Authority or Strategic Health Authority any part of whose area falls within the relevant area,
g every Primary Care Trust or Local Health Board any part of whose area falls within the relevant area,
h every NHS trust any part of whose area falls within the relevant area, and
i every person who is designated by the Secretary of State by order for the purposes of this paragraph as a provider of electronic monitoring services.

(Criminal Justice Act 2003 s325(6))

The Act permitted the Secretary of State to issue guidance to 'responsible authorities' on the discharge of the functions conferred by sections 325 and 326; the first version was published in 2003 (Home Office/NPS 2003) and subsequent versions produced in 2007, 2009 and 2012.

Although MAPPA was established in 2001, the Criminal Justice Act 2003 introduced Schedule 15 as the comprehensive new list of offences that would qualify an offender as subject to MAPPA. This new legislation cited new offences captured in the Sexual Offences Act 2003, and expanded the violent offences included under MAPPA. These changes came into force in April 2004.

Lay advisers

Another innovation of the Criminal Justice Act 2003 was the idea that 'lay advisers' could be added to the Strategic Management Board (SMB) of each MAPPA area: 'The Secretary of State must appoint two lay advisers under subsection (2) in relation to each responsible authority' (2003 Act s326(3)). This was taken as a concession to the 'For Sarah' campaign for more public access to the register and MAPPA arrangements. Whether it would be enough for the campaigners remained to be seen. The lay advisers were not, for example, going to be able to discuss their MAPPA work with anyone and to that extent they did not represent the community as a councillor or MP might represent a community.

Before the Act was introduced lay adviser pilot schemes were run in eight areas to see how they worked; these were in Durham, Cumbria, Greater Manchester, Dorset, Hampshire, Surrey, South Wales and the West Midlands, starting from 15 April 2004. The schemes reportedly went well and were generally welcomed and positively reviewed (Hebenton and Thomas 2004).

The lay advisers had found the appointment process itself quite onerous but at the same time 'strangely reassuring in that it indicated to them the worth of the post for which they were applying'. Induction at local level was a bit more 'unstructured' and the advisers felt they were rather left to their own devices and might have benefitted from having mentors (ibid).

There was some 'confusion and uncertainty' about (a) engagement with the public and (b) the extent to which the lay advisers identity should be made known. They felt they were supposed to 'engage with the public' but that the term was too loose and needed to be made more explicit and 'there exist wide disparities in the … experience of Lay Advisers' (ibid). Three action points were put forward by the reviewers for consideration:

- it is important that the SMBs are given time and support to develop a clear understanding of their role within the wider MAPPA …
- the process of clarifying the SMB role might be usefully assisted by providing all SMB members (including lay members) with nationally consistent training about what it means to be operating at the strategic level …
- consider providing national guidelines on broad terms and conditions for lay members (ibid).

The Strategic Management Board (SMB) of each MAPPA area would now have two – or sometimes even more – lay advisers sitting alongside the professionals. According to Terry Grange the ACPO lead on Child Protection at the time:

> Lay advisers will play an important part in the review and monitoring of the MAPPA. They represent a community interest in public protection and bring a different perspective from that of the professional interests in the MAPPA. This gives a freshness of view, a disinterested opinion which can, as the pilots showed, provide a reality check. I believe that lay advisors offer a real opportunity to enhance public confidence in public protection work.
>
> (Home Office 2004a)

The lay adviser's role was to act as unpaid voluntary consultants, informed observers and as posers of questions that the professionals, closely involved in the work, might not necessarily think of asking. In short, they were to be 'critical friends'. They did not have a role in decisions about, or the management of, individual cases assigned to MAPPA.

In 2007 the Home Office still had residual concerns about lay advisers:

> their activities vary between MAPPA areas. Lay advisers form an essential link between the authorities and the public, and should play a key role in communication. We need a clearer definition of the lay adviser role, and to ensure it is applied across all areas.
>
> (Home Office 2007a: 16; see also Action 11)

The problem with having a 'key role in communication' is having no constituency for the lay adviser to communicate with, meaning their role as representatives of the community is curtailed at best or reduced to tokenism at worst.

Today the more detailed tasks of the lay advisers are listed as being to:

- Contribute to the monitoring and evaluation of the operation of MAPPA in their area.
- Act as a critical friend in challenging professionals.
- zParticipate in reviewing the SMB Business Plan and broader communication strategy.
- Confirm that the SMB has created effective links with other multi-agency forums, e.g. local Community Safety Partnerships, Criminal Justice Boards, Safeguarding Children Boards and Safeguarding Adults Boards.
- Support the SMB to ensure that MAPPA adhere to the duties under equalities legislation.
- Participate in any SMB sub-groups, working parties or projects.
- Participate in reviewing and questioning local MAPPA statistics.
- Assist in the preparation of the MAPPA annual report.
- Attend local and regional events with the agreement of the Responsible Authorities (NOMS 2012 para.5.6).

The lay advisers serve initially for a maximum of four years with the possibility of a second term going on for another three years subject to a satisfactory performance appraisal; two terms is usually the maximum length of an appointment.

Comments on the role of the lay adviser have generally been positive, with SMB chairs and MAPPA coordinators commenting on 'their ability to ask difficult questions and to provide a helpful independent and external perspective' (CJJI 2015: para.7.11).

Summary

The Sexual Offences Act 2003 modernised all the law on sexual offences and included the new laws covering the register and the civil orders aimed at 'public protection' into Part 2 of the Act. The Act created four new civil orders ranging from the Notification Order through the Foreign Travel Order, the Sexual Offences Prevention Order and the Risk of Sexual Harm Order. Running alongside the 2003 Act was the Criminal Justice Act 2003 that enhanced and clarified the Multi-Agency Public Protection Arrangements and introduced the idea of having lay advisers on the Arrangements. The Sexual Offences Act 2003 forms the legal basis for the register today.

6 2003–2010

Introduction

Once the Sexual Offences Act 2003 was in place arguments simmered as to who exactly was leading the way on public protection policy formulation. These arguments had been heard before during the 'For Sarah' campaign (see Chapter Four). The protagonists were again the Home Office, the media and some of the practitioners charged with implementing the policies. The particular policies included those on home visits and rights of entry to the addresses of those on the register and the re-emergence of arguments for more community notification. John Reid, the Home Secretary at this time, defended himself with two important reports which appeared in 2007 and 2008 on the subjects of child protection and wider public protection matters with implications for those on the register.

Media driven policy?

In the summer of 2006, a public argument took place over who exactly was running the UK's public protection policies. Was it the government or was it the media? Did the media really act on behalf of the public?

John Reid replaced Charles Clarke as Home Secretary on 5 May 2006. He inherited a growing concern about overcrowded prisons, the deportation of overseas prisoners, people being allowed to leave prison 'too early' and going on to re-offend (see e.g. *Hansard House of Commons Debates 20 April 2006 cols.244–256*). Within a matter of weeks, he had expressed his concern about the state of the Home Office and infamously declared it 'not fit for purpose' (Mulholland and Tempest 2006). Reid's comment was not particularly directed at sex offenders and public protection policies but the press started to home in on this aspect of his responsibilities and questioned how public protection could be maintained while known (and unknown) sex offenders lived in the community and overcrowded prisons were reluctant to take them.

Within weeks of Reid's appointment, the case of Craig Sweeney acted as a catalyst for a minor moral panic. Sweeney, a registered sex offender, was in court for abduction and sexual assault of a three-year-old on 12 June 2006.

He received a life sentence at Cardiff Crown Court and was told he would not be considered for parole for five years – and only then if he did not pose a significant risk of re-offending. Family members of the victim described the sentence as an 'insult' and Home Secretary Reid agreed and decided to write to the Attorney General describing the sentence as unduly lenient (BBC News 2006a).

Case study 6.1

In July 2004 Craig Sweeney was released on licence from a three-year custodial sentence for indecent assault on his six-year-old step-daughter. He had served almost 15 months of the sentence. He was made subject to the Notification Requirements under Part 2 of the Sexual Offences Act 2003 (placed on the Sex Offender Register), and managed by South Wales Probation Area as a MAPPA Level 2 case in approved premises in Swansea.

Sweeney was recalled to prison in August 2004 for breaching his licence by consuming alcohol and engaging in violence. This behaviour led to his accommodation being withdrawn and he was consequently in breach of three of his licence conditions (to be of good behaviour, not to consume alcohol and to reside at the approved premises).

He was re-released on licence as a Level 2 MAPPA offender on 1 April 2005, again under the supervision of South Wales Probation Area, to an address in Newport, Gwent, which had been finalised one day prior to his release. This arrangement had not been communicated to Gwent Probation Area until the day before his release and South Wales Probation Area continued to have contact with Craig Sweeney in Newport. A MAPPA meeting was held in Gwent on 14 April 2005 to discuss Craig Sweeney's management in the area. His management was officially transferred from South Wales Probation Area on 22 April 2005.

Two significant incidents occurred during Craig Sweeney's second licence period. One was an allegation of violence towards an adult man by Sweeney at his accommodation in July 2005, and the other consisted of Sweeney allegedly making inappropriate comments towards three children and touching one of them on the bottom while he was in Avon and Somerset.

His licence expired on 31 December 2005 and he abducted and sexually assaulted a three-year-old girl on 2 January 2006. In June 2006 he was sentenced to life imprisonment for these offences.

An article in The Times newspaper on 14 June was critical of Reid for saying the sentence was 'too lenient' when the sentence appeared to have been caused by the government's own policies. Headlined 'Get Some Policies Mr Reid, and stop hiding behind an Odious Sex Offender' The Times article said that:

> In speaking out so quickly, our new Home Secretary engaged his mouth before his brain, and not for the first time ... Mr Reid is railing against government policy. It is the Government that decided to formalise the introduction of an automatic discount for a guilty plea, which is what has made Sweeny's sentence so potentially low.
>
> (Miles 2006)

On the same day as The Times outburst another child sex offender was given a very light sentence. This was picked up by the Daily Mail in the headline 'Outrage over Five Week Sentence for Paedophile' (Rayner and Koster 2006) who followed it up, the very next day, with 'Blair in Panic over Sentencing'; Downing Street immediately denied there was any 'panic' at all (Chapman 2006).

By the weekend there were more stories about the Home Office sending a representative to the USA to look again at American-style community notification for those on the sex offender register and further stories about chemical castration being planned for some sex offenders. John Reid had asked Gerry Sutcliffe, junior minister at the Home Office, to go to the USA and take another look at how community notification – Megan's Law – was working after ten years of operations. Mr Reid declared that his 'starting point' was 'that information should no longer remain the exclusive preserve of officialdom' (BBC News 2006b). On his return Sutcliffe did not recommend the American model, but made another visit to the USA in November 2006 to look at more selective and targeted forms of information disclosure.

Earlier in the year while Charles Clarke was still Home Secretary, the News of the World had picked up on the number of child sex offenders living in probation 'approved hostels' that were directly adjacent to schools. The News of the World was, of course, the bête noire of the Home Office going back to the 'For Sarah' campaign of June 2000. John Reid now decided that something had to be done about these hostels and responded by instructing the National Offender Management Service to move the relevant sex offenders elsewhere; a policy of 'restricted admission' was to be implemented at eleven such hostels and involving about 60 people who would be moved (BBC 2006c). Harry Fletcher from the National Association of Probation Officers pointed out that this move would lead to treatment programmes being disrupted and that there was no research that showed sex offenders located in hostels had ever offended against children in nearby schools (ibid).

An opposition MP suggested that 'John Reid is proving very adept at capturing headlines, whilst ignoring the difficult decisions that must be taken to provide the most appropriate protection for the public' (Nick Clegg quoted in BBC 2006b). Another sex offender expert added his opinion that:

> it just worries me that a new home secretary comes and doesn't appear to know what his department, his government has been doing for years and years, and why they came up with sex offender register, multi-agency public protection panels.
>
> (Ray Wyre quoted in BBC News 2006c)

Terry Grange, Chief Constable of Dyfed-Powys Police, and ACPO lead on sex offending, said he thought the government's policy in this area was now being led by the media and especially the News of the World. According to Grange the Home Office had surrendered power over policy to the News of the World and in doing so abandoned any coherent strategy for the management of sex offenders:

> Mr Grange accused the Home Office of responding to pressure from the News of the World, allowing the newspaper to dictate a shift in government policy … [and] accused Home Office officials of 'attending meetings at the behest of a newspaper to discuss what the newspaper wants and then surrendering to their wishes – altering their whole approach overnight'.
>
> (BBC News 2006d)

Downing Street immediately denied that this policy was media led (BBC News 2006e; see also Mulholland 2006).

Much of this was reminiscent of the 'For Sarah' campaign during August 2000 when senior police officers and probation officers needing to talk to the Home Secretary frequently found themselves in second place in the queue, after Rebekah Wade, the editor of the News of the World. Gill Mackenzie the spokesperson on sex offending for ACOP said that:

> There were times during meetings when Rebekah Wade talked of the home secretary as though he was a puppet whom she could manipulate. In fact, there was something frighteningly contemptuous of politicians and democracy as a whole in the News of the World's attitude.
>
> (Silverman and Wilson 2002: 154)

This conflict between the politicians, the professionals and the media will be returned to in our final chapter – Chapter Fourteen.

Offender management

Within the world of MAPPA, arguments had persisted about the best way to assess and manage the risk posed by sex offenders. One concerning issue was the home visits that were made by offender managers; what were their purpose, what should the frequency be and what rights of entry did offender managers have to the homes of the registered sex offenders they were visiting?

Home visits

From the early days of the register offender managers had made home visits. Before they left their office, they were advised to make 'pre-visit checks' on the records held and an up-to-date risk assessment was also to be made. Personal cars were not to be used and civilian clothes were to be worn. Police officers were to go in pairs and ideally one of them should have been before to note any changes on the most recent visit.

Initially home visits were to be based on the degree of risk posed by the registered sex offender; the higher the risk posed the more frequent the visits. The MAPPA Guidance produced in 2007 suggested the following frequency for visits to registered sex offenders:

- risk assessed as high/very high risk of serious harm offenders to be visited by police monthly
- risk assessed as medium offenders to be visited quarterly
- risk assessed as low to be visited at least annually, but preferably every six months (NOMS 2007:82 section 15).

But this frequency changed in the version of the same Guidance published two years later in 2009 (Version 3). The frequency of home visits was now to be reduced as follows:

- Very high risk – monthly
- High risk – every three months
- Medium risk – every six months
- Low risk – every twelve months.(NOMS 2009:183 section 21)

The new regime of visits took the high-risk offenders visits from monthly to three monthly, and the medium risk offenders from four visits a year down to two a year. The low risk offenders where it had been preferable to visit every six months dropped down to one visit a year. Nobody knew if this was down to the lack of availability of police officers or whether this would make communities less safe. In the absence of any overt explanation the press started asking questions. A Ministry of Justice spokesman responded:

> The sections of the Guidance which relate to home visits to registered sex offenders were drafted in consultation with ACPO and suggest best practice to police forces on how regularly they should undertake home visits and the place which such home visits have in the overall scheme of supervising and managing the risk presented by registered sex offenders.
>
> Such home visits are but one means available to the police, within MAPPA where registered sex offenders are also subject to licensed supervision, to manage the risk which such offenders present and to protect the public. It is the quality of supervision and not the number of visits that is the critical issue.
>
> (cited in Whitehead 2009)

The following year in 2010 an internal Ministry of Justice document was leaked to the press giving details of their thoughts on yet more reductions in home visits to people on the register and perhaps even stopping some visits all together:

> Officials are looking at whether the monitoring of some convicted sex offenders can be reduced, including stopping home visits and keeping meetings to just ten minutes. They are also examining whether some more serious offenders can have their risk assessment downgraded so supervision can be lightened.
>
> (Whitehead 2010)

According to the leaked document the reason for the possible reductions in visits to the low risk offenders was to see if they 'could be managed in a defensible way whilst enabling the effective use of resources' (ibid). A Ministry of Justice spokeswoman said the document was an internal draft and no decisions had been made. She added: 'We are constantly looking to improve the management of known high-risk offenders in the community and ensure MAPPA is as effective a set of arrangements as possible … public protection is the priority' (ibid).

Formal guidance outlined the purpose of these home visits. They were to assist risk assessment and management but also for a number of other purposes:

- to check compliance with legislation and court orders
- confirm the registered sex offender is at the address he or she says they are
- manage the risk
- review the risk and note changes
- gather information for risk review
- detect offences
- fulfil duty of care to the offender (ACPO/NPIA 2010: para.7.4).

MAPPA's latest guidance at this time still suggested home visit frequency should be based on the degree of risk posed:

- Very High Risk – monthly
- High Risk – every three months
- Medium risk – every six months
- Low risk – every twelve months.(NOMS 2012: para.2.5)

Home visits and arguments for rights of entry.

The original Sex Offenders Act 1997, and the later Sexual Offences Act 2003, gave the police no automatic rights of entry to the home of anyone on the sex offender register; officers making home visits had to ask for permission to enter. The police always had the right of entry by force if necessary, using other parts of police law; an example would be where there was risk to life and limb, or by using the Police and Criminal Evidence Act 1984 s17.

Inevitably it was not always possible to make a home visit due to the registered person not being at home to allow the visit. If these 'no reply' visits continued, or the police had other difficulty gaining access to a home, the question of a 'right of entry' using force if necessary, was raised.

Research on the Sex Offenders Act 1997 had reported that:

> Although the Sex Offenders Act confers no right of entry to the offender's home, almost all offenders co-operated with home visits. Thirty forces (70%) visited all offenders with a requirement to register. A further ten (23%) only visited those assessed as higher risk or who met some other condition. In 31 forces (78% of those conducting visits), frequency depended on the outcome of a risk assessment.
>
> (Plotnikoff and Woolfson 2000: vi–vii)

The Home Office Review of the register a year later took a similar view:

> We have concluded that a power of entry cannot be justified. Observing an offender and their belongings at an address one day does not mean that they will be there the next. Moreover, there are other means of confirming that an individual is living at their stated address.
>
> (Home Office/Scottish Executive 2001: 38)

Some people still thought that having no 'right of entry' for the police to the homes of registered sex offenders was an omission in the law. Conservative MP Sir Paul Beresford had described it as a 'loophole' in the law:

> it is my belief that we, like many western nations, should allow right of entry to the police when they knock on the door to risk-assess such individuals. Unusually in the western world, British police do not have that opportunity.
>
> (*Hansard House of Commons Debates 17 December 2003 col.1691*)

Sir Paul had tried to get an amendment made to the Sexual Offences Bill to remedy this 'loophole'. His amendment would have changed the law by giving the police the power to visit the offenders' home, to ascertain that all details were correct and to enable them to complete a risk assessment; a duty would be placed on the registered sex offender to cooperate with the police attending their home. For the Home Office Paul Goggins had counter-argued that:

> First, in clause 86, we are introducing a new requirement for offenders to go to their local police station annually to confirm their notified details. Failure to make that annual notification is a criminal offence, in the investigation of which the police may, of course, under existing powers, visit the offender's home. If an offender does not make that annual visit to restate their details, that failure could become the subject of a criminal investigation, and the police would have the power to enter that offender's home.
>
> Secondly, in new clauses 15 and 16, we are proposing to provide a new power that will enable the information notified by registered sex offenders to be regularly checked against information held by other Government

> agencies. That will involve cross-referencing with the Driver and Vehicle Licensing Agency, for example. Any discrepancies noticed in that process will be passed to the local police for further investigation.
>
> Thirdly, the police already have a general power to apply for a search warrant when investigating whether a crime has been committed. That would include a breach of the registration requirements. There are already a number of circumstances in which police may enter an offender's home.
>
> (*Hansard House of Lords Standing Committee (B) 14 October 2003* cc343–4 (Sexual Offences Bill 2002–03))

Sir Paul's amendment was withdrawn. The Sexual Offences Act 2003 still gave no right of entry to the homes of registered sex offenders.

Sir Paul later tried to get a Private Members Bill through Parliament to amend the Sexual Offences Act 2003 and give the police the right of entry. The Bill focused only on those adults on the register who had committed crimes against children and those who had been convicted and not just cautioned (The Sexual Offences Act 2003 (Amendment) Bill [Bill 26 of Session 2004–5]). Amongst those still disagreeing were ACPO:

> The Association of Chief Police Officers (ACPO) is opposed to the Bill, and considers that it risks breaching the Human Rights Act 1998 … As it stands today, ACPO and the Home Office feel that these amendments are a 'step too far' and there is a very real risk that this new power could make the notification requirements onerous that they may become disproportionate in terms of Article 8 of the Human Rights Act.
>
> (Terry Grange, Chief Constable of Dyfed Powys and ACPO lead on sex offenders cited in House of Commons 2005: 23)

Without government support and in the face of the arguments against him Sir Paul withdrew his Bill.

Using SOPOs as a 'right of entry'

Some police officers who did regard 'rights of entry' as a problem sometimes used the wordings of Sexual Offence Prevention Orders (SOPOs) to give them that right of entry. As we have seen, anyone subject to a SOPO was automatically on the register and the SOPO contained negative prohibitions describing the sort of behaviour the person concerned should desist from; SOPOs were not allowed to include any positive requirements of the sex offender.

But it only required a bit of semantic creativity to re-write the prohibitions of a SOPO in a manner to get the result the police wanted. A positive requirement that the person on the register always had to allow the police to enter a home would not be permitted, but a negative prohibition that the he or she should *not* prevent a police officer from entering a house might get round that problem.

When the courts came across such twisted negative prohibitions becoming mandatory positive requirements, they expressed their dislike and said they should not be used:

> We have come to the clear conclusion that in the particular circumstances of this case the provision in Clause 6 of the [Sexual Offences Prevention] Order cannot possibly be justified. It confers on the police an extremely wide power to enter the applicant's home for the purpose of checking his use of the computer and his use of the Internet. It amounts to the grant of a continuing search warrant which may be executed repeatedly and without the need to demonstrate any further justification over a period of 5 years. That is truly a Draconian measure.
>
> (*R v Edward Thompson [2008] EWCA Crim 3258* paras.24–5)

> This prohibition is further an impermissible attempt to confer extensive powers of search and seizure upon the police, pursuant to a statutory provision which only enables an order preventing something from being done to be made. SOPOs should not create a situation in which police powers of search and seizure are extended with none of the procedural safeguards which usually and importantly regulate the exercise of such powers.
>
> (*R v Hemsley [2010] EWCA Crim 225* para.5)

New law on rights of entry

The matter of forced entry to the homes of registered sex offenders was finally resolved with a change in the law. In 2005 an Inspectorate report returned once more to the subject of rights of entry to the homes of those on the register. The report accepted that a 'right of entry' might only be necessary in 'exceptional circumstances' but this was still 'an area of police practice that *needed to be supported by legislation*' (HMIP and HMIC 2005: para.7.16 emphasis added).

The Violent Crime Reduction Bill published in November 2005 had no mention of any 'rights of entry' to the homes of registered sex offenders, but new powers were introduced by a House of Lords amendment in 2006. The amendment was described as giving the police:

> significant additional powers … giving the police a pre-emptive power to enter premises and search the homes of the sex offenders who are on the register, even in circumstances that fall short of suspecting that an offence of whatever kind has been committed.
>
> (*Hansard House of Commons Debates 30 October 2006 col.63*)

Sir Paul Beresford welcomed the amendment but wondered why it had taken so long. He described it currently as a 'loophole in the law [that] offers them an opportunity. When the police knock on their door, and ask for admittance so that they can risk-assess them, they just close it'. He did wonder if a forced 'right of entry' would mean the person on the register might then refuse to cooperate with any ensuing risk assessment (*Hansard House of Commons Debates 30 October 2006 col.66*). For the government Tony McNulty, Minister of State at the Home Office accepted that the amendment dealt with matters of substance, and had 'received ample debate in both the Lords and the Commons' and commended it to the House.

The Violent Crime Reduction Act 2006 became law in November of that year. Most of the Act was about disorder and violence coming from excessive alcohol consumption, the use of dangerous weapons and football spectator violence, but its s.58 gave the police the new powers of entry and search – using force if necessary – of the home address of a registered sex offender. Section 58 inserted a new s96B into the Sexual Offences 2003 which was implemented from 31 May 2007.

This was not a new blanket power for the police to enter all homes of people on the register and required an officer of Superintendent rank or above to apply to a magistrate to sign a warrant giving approval. The magistrate had to satisfy him or herself that the offender was a registered sex offender, and that the address was the address last notified to the police, that the risk assessment and search was necessary and that two unsuccessful attempts to enter on a voluntary basis had been made; the latter might include a house being found empty (see also Home Office 2007b).

A Home Office follow-up report five years later suggested that:

> This power provides police with a valuable tool in assessing the risk posed by an offender. We consider that the current thresholds surrounding the use of this power ensures that it contains sufficient safeguards.
>
> (Home Office 2012b: 23)

In Scotland a new section (96A) to the same effect was inserted into the 2003 Act by the Police, Public Order and Criminal Justice (Scotland) Act 2006 s80.

One registered sex offender in September 2011 began legal proceedings to challenge s96B by means of a judicial review. His argument was that a right of entry should only be used if:

a there was a reasonable suspicion of offending
b the person whose house was to be searched was given notice of the proceedings.

He claimed that section 96B was incompatible with Article 8 of the European Convention on Human Rights (the right to privacy) and that even informal visits to his home breached his Convention rights. The argument was made that the very existence of s96B hung over any request from the police, and any refusal to allow the police in was always backed up by a right of entry using force if consent was withheld; this consent was therefore not a freely given consent. The appeal was dismissed (*R (M) v the Chief*

Constable of Hampshire Constabulary and Secretary of State for the Home Department [2014] EWCA Civ 1651).

Case study 6.2

Pete Townshend of the music group The Who was cautioned for offences of paying for and accessing a website containing child abuse images. His offence took place in 1999 and came to light as part of Operation Ore, an international anti-child pornography police operation. His defence was:

> As I made clear at the outset, I accessed the site because of my concerns at the shocking material readily available on the internet to children as well as adults, and as part of my research towards the campaign I had been putting together since 1995 to counter damage done by all kinds of pornography on the internet, but especially any involving child abuse.

Townshend was cautioned in May 2003. The police said 'As a routine part of the cautioning process fingerprints, a photograph and a DNA sample will be taken; additionally, in these cases, the person concerned will be entered on the sex offenders register for a period of five years'.

(cited in Wilson 2003)

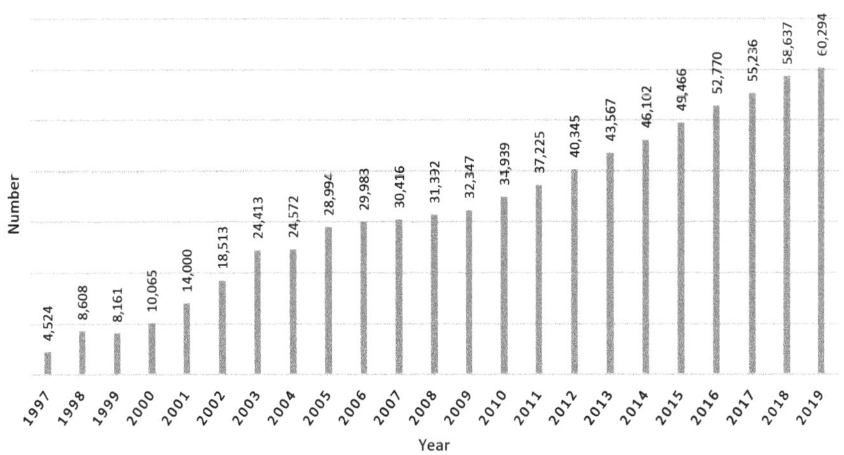

Figure 6.1 Numbers on the register in England and Wales

A review and an action plan

Review of the Protection of Children from Sex Offenders

After the minor 'moral panic' of June 2006 and arguments between the media, the police and the Home Office, the Home Office published its Review of the Protection of Children from Sex Offenders in the summer of 2007 (Home Office 2007a). The Review had been requested by Home Secretary John Reid in June 2006 in the middle of the media 'firestorm' that had surrounded him, and now on publication a year later the Review contained 20 Actions for improving the protection of children from sex offenders; most of these 20 Actions had implications for the register:

> ACTION 2 Increase public awareness of how sex offenders are managed in the community, by ensuring easy-to-use information is widely available, and by ensuring strong local communication of MAPPA's work.
>
> ACTION 3 Introduce a legal duty for MAPPA authorities to consider the disclosure of information about convicted child sex offenders to members of the public in all cases. The presumption will be that the authorities will disclose information if they consider that an offender presents a risk of serious harm to a member of the public's children.
>
> ACTION 4 Pilot a process where members of the public can register their child protection interest in a named individual. Where this individual has convictions for child sex offences and is considered a risk, there will be a presumption that this information will be disclosed to the relevant member of the public. We want to pilot the new policy in order to work through the details of implementation and to ensure we have a system of two-way disclosure that is as effective as possible without increasing the risk to children. It will be important for people who register an interest to receive a timely response. In all cases they should be given generic information on how best to protect their children. Following the pilot, we will consider whether this principle of two-way disclosure should be extended.
>
> ACTION 6 Develop the use of drug treatment to support existing psychological treatment.
>
> ACTION 8 Develop national MAPPA structural and management arrangements to be applied in each area to ensure consistent, auditable processes.
>
> ACTION 9 Develop national standards for MAPPA and ensure each area has strong central co-ordination and administration and is able to provide a single point of contact for general public enquiries about the work of MAPPA, support the roll-out of ViSOR, facilitate the duty to consider disclosure and support the key processes of risk assessment, recording of decisions and follow-up.

ACTION 10 Develop robust performance management arrangements for MAPPA.

ACTION 11 Establish a defined and consistent role for MAPPA lay advisers, which includes increasing public awareness.

ACTION 12 Develop the current process for managing cross-border MAPPA cases.

ACTION 13 Take a power to amend sex offender notification requirements by secondary legislation, and consider changes to the information registered to strengthen public protection.

ACTION 14 Revise MAPPA guidance to provide direction on managing young offenders.

ACTION 15 The Youth Justice Board to ensure all Youth Offending Teams have appropriate guidance and training on MAPPA, and all Youth Offending Teams have a policy on public protection that includes reference to engagement with the local MAPPA.

ACTION 16 Develop guidance on compulsory programmes of purposeful activity for residents in approved premises

ACTION 17 Implement standard rules of residence for all approved premises.

ACTION 18 Maximise the use and awareness of the Child Exploitation and Online Protection Centre website's 'most wanted' list of non-compliant and missing high-risk sex offenders.

ACTION 20 Review the potential to expand the use of satellite tracking to monitor high-risk sex offenders.

(Home Office 2007a: Annex 3)

Actions 3 and 4 on the increased disclosure of information on sex offenders will be considered further in Chapter Nine. Action 6 caused the tabloid press to run amok with headlines about chemical castration and Action 13 would enable the government to expand the list of notification requirements on registered sex offenders by use of Statutory Instruments. The *Review* suggested this expanded list might include a change in the law so that all registered sex offenders might in future be required to:

- provide a DNA sample where one has not been given previously
- notify the police of any email addresses
- notify the police of passport numbers
- notify the police of any bank account numbers
- notify the police if they are living in the same household as a child under the age of 18
- notify the police of *any* foreign travel (at present only trips of three days or longer must be notified)
- report regularly to a police station if they register as homeless (ibid: 18)

Actions 8 to 12 and 14 and 15 concerned changes to MAPPA including a clearer role for the lay advisers (Action 11). Actions 16 and 17 sought to tighten the standards of behaviour in probation hostels or 'approved premises'; this was to address recent revelations by the press about the proximity of 'approved premises' to schools (February 2006) and a BBC *Panorama* programme about lax standards of supervision in 'approved premises' in Bristol (8 November 2006).

Action 18 recommended more use and awareness of the Child Exploitation and Online Protection (CEOP) centre website's 'most wanted' list of non-compliant and missing high-risk registered sex offenders.

Action 19 of the *Review of the Protection of Children from Sex Offenders* recommended the piloting of compulsory polygraph tests as a risk management tool to establish whether they lead to increased disclosure of information. The idea was that the polygraph would collect more information on a sex offender that would assist with making a risk assessment and a risk management plan:

> A polygraph (lie detector) test is designed to support traditional supervision by encouraging offenders to be more truthful in discussing their behaviour, in a way that helps both themselves and those who manage them. The test measures an offender's physical reactions when asked questions: their breathing, their heart rate and how much they are sweating. The offender is asked questions, and the results of the polygraph are used to help assess whether or not they are answering truthfully.
>
> (Home Office 2007a: 23)

A change in the law was going to be required but in fact this had already been carried out. The *Review* was published in June 2007 but steps had already been taken to change the law in February 2007. A new clause was introduced into the Offender Management Bill, in February 2007, at the parliamentary third reading stage, to allow a pilot of mandatory polygraph testing. The Offender Management Act 2007 received its Royal Assent on the 26 July 2007; ss28–30 of the Act included the provisions for polygraph testing for 'a person serving a relevant custodial sentence in respect of a relevant sexual offence' who was now released on licence. The new testing was not directly related to the sex offender register other than that those on licence would already be on the register.

This addition to the Offender Management Bill preceding the publication of the *Review of the Protection of Children from Sex Offenders* and its recommendation in Action 19 was arguably the wrong way round. It was nonetheless symptomatic of the piecemeal way in which the framework for managing child sex offenders in the community was put together.

The use of polygraphs or 'lie-detectors' as recommended started in 2014 (Bowcott 2014). Their introduction followed further consultations (MoJ 2008), preliminary studies (Wood et al. 2010, Gannon et al. 2012), and continuing debate on the value of the polygraph (Marshall and Thomas 2015). At the same time a legal challenge was mounted, alleging that the imposition of a polygraph condition was a violation of Article 8 of the European Convention on Human Rights and was a disproportionate measure that could not be justified in the public interest. The challenge was unsuccessful (*Corbett v The Secretary of State for Justice and the National Offender Management Service* – NOMS [2009*] EWHC 2671*). Early figures revealed some 13% of those tested (63 individuals out of 492 tested) to be potentially in breach of their parole conditions (Ross 2015).

Saving Lives. Reducing Harm. Protecting the Public. An Action Plan for Tackling Violence 2008–11

On 18 February 2008, the government published *Saving Lives. Reducing Harm. Protecting the Public; An Action Plan for Tackling Violence 2008–11.* As its title states this was an 'Action Plan' to set out what the government intended to do along with the police and other delivery partners to tackle serious violence over the next three years. It covered far more than just the sex offender register but did repeat its commitment to the proposed new 'Sarah's Law' (HMG 2008: 26–7; see Chapter Nine).

A follow-up report a year later stated that the Home Office were looking at proposals for sex offenders to register their email address and exploring the possibility, and cost of the monitoring, of computer use for registered sex offenders with the consent of those individuals being made a condition of compliance with a Sexual Offences Prevention Order (SOPO). It did admit that the implementation of some of these other measures 'has been delayed while a High Court case concerning the lack of lifetime review on the restrictions for sex offenders is ongoing'(HMG 2009: 36 and 52).

Legal challenges

Throughout the years 2003–2010 a series of legal challenges to the register were made. In summary they are as follows.

Kevin Gallagher NIQB 26 2003

A case from Northern Ireland where the claimant argued in a judicial review that life-long registration for a sentence of 33 months and no review was disproportionate and incompatible with the ECHR Article 8 – the requirements were considered more onerous than in *Adamson* 1999. The claim was dismissed.

R (Forbes) v Secretary of State for the Home Department [2006] EWCA Civ. 962

In the case of *Forbes v the Secretary of State for the Home Department* the Court of Appeal was asked to rule on the matter of registration being an automatic process and whether or not this made it incompatible with Article 8 because the form and extent of the interference in their lives would vary with different individuals. The court agreed that automatic registration would bear more heavily on some individuals than others but 'to be viable the scheme must contain general provisions that will be universally applied to all within its purview' and therefore automatic registration was a 'necessary and reasonable element of the scheme' (*R (Forbes) v Secretary of State for the Home Department [2006] EWCA Civ. 962* para.18). The case was dismissed.

R v Longworth [2006] UKHL 1

There is no appeal against register time periods for notification – it is consequence of a sentence – not part of the sentence.

R v Odam [2008] EWCA Crim 1087 and R v Davison [2008] EWCA Crim 2795

Mr Odam received a Community Order (with an unpaid work requirement of 120 hours) for his sex offence conviction; the Community Order had to be completed within 12 months and a period of five years on the register was automatically added. Mr Odam completed his Community Order within four months and therefore argued for a shorter time on the register. In law a Community Order containing an unpaid work requirement order comes to an end when the work has been completed.

In those circumstances, therefore, the court judged the applicant had completed the Community Order sentence and he was not subject to the notification requirements. The problem was that no court had jurisdiction to change the registration period. The same thing happened in the case of *R v Davison [2008] EWCA Crim 2795.*

Summary

The struggle between the politicians, the media, the practitioners, the experts and the civil service became visible in the public domain during this time period. The politicians tried to wrest back the situation to show they were in control in two reports – the *Review of the Protection of Children from Sex Offenders* and the *Saving Lives. Reducing Harm. Protecting the Public. An Action Plan for Tackling Violence 2008–11*.

A slow movement toward the register becoming ever more punitive was also noted in what was called 'function creep' (see Thomas 2008a). A senior Ministry of Justice official confirmed that they hoped to start inserting internal chips into offenders through a link-up with satellite-tracking similar to the system used to trace stolen vehicles. 'all the options are on the table, and this is one we would like to pursue,' according to the source. A similar proposal came from Ken Jones, the president of the Association of Chief Police Officers (ACPO), that electronic chips should be surgically implanted into convicted paedophiles and sex offenders in order to track them more easily (Brady 2008). These proposals have not come to fruition.

7 2010–2020

Introduction

In 2010 there was a change in government to what would become known as the Coalition government: a coalition between the Conservative and Liberal Democratic Parties. Theresa May took over as Home Secretary on 12 May 2010 and remained in post until becoming Prime Minister six years later. In the same year the Supreme Court ruled that the sex offender register was in breach of the European Convention on Human Rights because there was no means by which a person on the register for life could ever seek a review of their status; this breach will be dealt with separately in Chapter Twelve. Meanwhile the register itself was strengthened yet again in the sense that people had to notify the police of even more personal information and new offences were created that would lead to registration. This was followed by a new form of risk assessment being introduced and used by offender managers known as Active Risk Management System or ARMS.

Strengthening the register

The register's breach of the European Convention on Human Rights in 2010 was shadowed by the notification requirements being strengthened to reform the register. Home Secretary Theresa May told Parliament that 'we will shortly launch a targeted consultation aimed at closing four existing loopholes in the sex offenders register':

> We will make it compulsory for sex offenders to report to the authorities before travelling abroad for even one day. That will prevent them from being free to travel for up to three days, as they are under the existing scheme. We will force sex offenders to notify the authorities whenever they are living in a household containing a child under the age of 18. We will require sex offenders to notify the authorities weekly of where they can be found when they have no fixed abode. We will tighten the rules so that sex offenders can no longer avoid being on the register when they change their names by deed poll.
>
> (*Hansard House of Commons Debates 16 February 2011 col. 959*)

The Home Office published its *Reforming the Notification Requirements of Registered Sex Offenders (Part 2 of the Sexual Offences Act 2003): A Targeted Consultation* on the proposals on 14 June 2011 and closed it on 8 August 2011 (Home Office 2011a). On the requirement that homeless people should report to the police weekly, instead of annually, the *Targeted Consultation* expressed the Home Office view that 'this change will also encourage registered sex offenders to provide the police with a fixed address, where there is one available, rather than face the increased inconvenience of weekly reporting' (ibid: 12). Possibly an early example of the Home Office's 'hostile environment' to simply remove homeless people from sight by making life inconvenient for them rather than positively helping them.

Mrs May's original four proposals were otherwise only slightly changed and the fourth one, about changing names, was dropped and replaced by a new one requiring people on the register to notify more personal details including financial details. The four proposals in the 'targeted consultation' were now:

- Notification of All Foreign Travel
- Notification of a Place of Residence
- Notification of Residence with a Minor
- Notification of Personal/Identification Details.

The Home Office published a summary of the consultation responses and their conclusions:

> The Home Office has carefully considered all of the comments made in response to this consultation and in light of the views expressed will seek to implement each of the four proposals. This reform is very much intended as a mechanism to strengthen and address potential gaps within the current system.
>
> (Home Office 2011b)

The changes were carried out by means of new Regulations. The Sexual Offences Act 2003 (Notification Requirements) (England and Wales) Regulations 2012 No.1876 were implemented from August 2012 and amended the Sexual Offences Act 2003 (Travel Notification Requirements) Regulations 2004 no.1220 (for more on travel restrictions see Chapter Eleven).

The new Regulations now required registered sex offenders to:

- notify the police of *all* foreign travel (including travel outside of the UK of less than three days)
- notify the police weekly if they have no fixed abode (that is, where a registered sex offender is homeless and has no sole or main residence and instead must notify the police of the place where he can regularly be found)

- notify the police if they are living in a household with a child under the age of 18 for a period of at least 12 hours
- notify the police of bank account and credit card details and notify information about their passports or other identity documents at each notification. This change regarding credit cards and bank account details has been explained by the Home Office as being necessary to tackle internet child pornography being purchased. The information is held securely by the police who are not entitled to examine the details of the account transactions. Police access to bank accounts and transactions is not ordinarily permitted without the intervention of a court order (The Sexual Offences Act 2003 (Notification Requirements) (England and Wales) Regulations 2012 No.1876).

All changes had to be made in person at a prescribed police station within three days.

With this additional information on bank details, passports etc. for registered sexual offenders ACPO decided, that all police ViSOR users should be subject to more rigorous security clearances and police vetting requirements (see NOMS 2014a: para.9.7; for more on ViSOR see Chapter Nine).

A legal challenge soon took place. The new law requiring a person on the sex offenders register to provide details of bank, debit or credit card accounts held by him or her was argued to be incompatible with any rights to respect for private life under Article 8 of the European Convention on Human Rights. The Court considered that though this did amount to an interference with the claimant's privacy, it was not as significant as other notification requirements and dismissed the case (*R (on the application of) Christopher Prothero v Secretary of State for the Home Department [2013] EWHC 2830 (Admin) 18 September*).

New offences

During this time period more sexual offences were identified and appropriate laws brought into being.

Sexual communication with a child

The new offence of sexual communication with a child became law in the Serious Crime Act 2015 s67 which inserted the new s.15A and Schedule 3 para.24 into the Sexual Offences Act 2003. The new law was implemented from 3 April 2017 for England and Wales. The offence was triable either way and carried a maximum two-year prison sentence; conviction led to automatic inclusion on the register (MoJ 2017a).

The offence of making a sexual communication with a child was to enable police to intervene at an earlier stage than the current law allowed. The existing Sexual Offences Act 2003 s15 on 'grooming' required the offender to firstly communicate with a child, and then make arrangements to meet that child. The arrangements to meet were no longer necessary to commit an offence. A communication is regarded as sexual if any part of it relates to sexual activity, or a reasonable person would consider that it is sexual, regardless of the sender's intentions. The law covered both online and offline communication including social media, email and letters.

Up-skirting laws

The Voyeurism (Offences) Act 2019 was introduced to tackle the problem of so-called 'up-skirting'. This is the act of covertly photographing underneath someone's clothing without their consent. It is known to have been performed in crowded public places, for example on public transport or at music festivals, which can make it difficult to notice the perpetrator. The increased numbers of mobile phones now available with integrated cameras no doubt assisted the rise of the problem. The Act became law for England and Wales on 12 February 2019 adding a new section 67A and Schedule 3 para.34A to the Sexual Offences Act 2003; it was implemented from 12 April 2019.

Conviction may lead to inclusion on the sex offender register for the more serious offenders (see Sexual Offences Act 2003 s67A (4)). The register notification requirements would only be imposed if the following conditions were met:

- the offence was committed for the purpose of obtaining sexual gratification
- the 'relevant condition' is met (Sexual Offences Act 2003 Schedule 3 para.34A (1)).

The 'relevant condition' mirrors the current provision for the existing section 67 voyeurism offences:

- if the offender is aged under 18, the relevant condition is that they have been sentenced to imprisonment for at least 12 months
- in any other case, the relevant condition is either that the victim was under 18, or the offender has been sentenced to a term of imprisonment, detained in a hospital, or given a community sentence of at least 12 months (Sexual Offences Act 2003 Schedule 3 para.34a (2); see also MoJ 2019b).

Up-skirting had been covered much earlier in Scotland since 2010 by the Sexual Offences (Scotland) Act 2009 s.9, but an editorial in *The Scotsman* in 2018 bemoaned the fact that only an average of three people a year had been prosecuted ('Scotland's up-skirting law not fit for purpose' *The Scotsman* 9 August 2018).In contrast the CPS had prosecuted ten men in the first year of legislation for England and Wales with one of them – already on the register – getting a custodial sentence (CPS 2019).

Revenge porn

For completeness we might note new laws on 'revenge porn' which is the distribution of sexually explicit images or video of individuals without their permission; it became an offence in 2015 but is not considered a sexual offence. The sexually explicit images or video may be made by a partner of an intimate relationship with the knowledge and consent of the subject, or it may be made without his or her knowledge. The Criminal Justice and Courts Act 2015 s33 made it an offence in England and Wales to disclose these sexually explicit images without the consent of the individual depicted and with the intent to cause distress. In Scotland, revenge porn became an offence in April 2016 when their Abusive Behaviour and Sexual Harm Act 2016 ss.2–4 came into effect; in Northern Ireland, it was made a crime in February 2016 through the Justice Act (Northern Ireland) 2016 ss. 51–53. Registration does not follow automatically because sexual motivation is not considered part of the crime.

Offender management

Inspections of offender by police forces

Starting in 2014 HM Inspectorate of Constabulary (renamed HM Inspectorate of Constabulary and Fire & Rescue Services (HMICFRS) in July 2017) started a series of inspections of police forces throughout England and Wales known as the National Child Protection Inspections. It looked at all aspects of police work with children but included the work of offender managers overseeing registered sex offenders. At the time of writing (August 2020) 31 reports had been written out of the 43 forces (see HMICFRS 2020) Some of these reports are considered below.

Nottinghamshire Police has a dedicated unit to manage registered sex offenders known as the Dangerous Persons Management Unit. Offender managers working in the unit were 'clear about their responsibilities, assessed risk and took action to reduce it' (HMICFRS 2015: 21). The inspection found that the information and intelligence about sex offenders 'was recorded and managed in a timely manner, with accurate monitoring of all the registered sex offenders' (ibid). The force was commended for good communications with neighbourhood teams who 'were generally aware of sex offenders living in their area and knew how to respond' (ibid). They cited the example of a police community support officer noticing a child's bicycle outside the house of a sex offender and immediately alerting the offender managers. Another case of good partnership work was cited when offender managers became aware that a registered sex offender was fitting blinds in a school and were able to work with the school to ensure he had no contact with pupils (ibid).

A National Child Protection Inspections report on Cleveland Police described the work of their dedicated unit – the Sex Offender Management

Unit (SOMU). Staff in the Unit were dealing with a caseload of between 50 and 60 registered sex offenders each, which was considered about right. Staff working in the teams were said to be 'clear about their responsibilities, undertook relevant enquiries, assessed risk and took action to reduce it' (HMICFRS 2017: 39).

Some criticisms were made of the communications systems between offender managers in the Cleveland SOMU and other parts of the force. Incidents involving a registered sex offender were logged and sent to the offender managers but it did not work the other way round. This meant officers attending an incident were unlikely to know that they were dealing with someone on the register and members of neighbourhood policing teams were not routinely informed of people living in their areas who were on the register (ibid: 39).

Criticisms of Merseyside police offender management teams made for some uncomfortable reading. At the time of the inspection, there were 2,256 people on the register in Merseyside and 1,769 of them were being managed within the community. Of those being managed within the community, 277 were graded as high risk and six as very high risk. The police offender managers in the Sex Offender Unit were each responsible for 100 sex offenders which was considered twice the recommended number and in turn this led to a backlog of people not being visited. HM Inspector of Constabulary Matt Parr said:

> At the time of our inspection, Merseyside Police's sex offender unit was seriously overstretched. Offender managers were individually responsible for up to 100 registered sex offenders – double what we would like to see.
>
> This had a serious impact on the force's ability to manage sex offenders. Too often, offender managers were playing catch-up and couldn't prioritise preventative work. Neighbourhood policing teams were often unaware of sex offenders living in their communities. And it was particularly concerning to see that the force's records show a backlog of 98 overdue visits to registered sex offenders.
>
> (HMICFRS 2018a; full report at HMICFRS 2018b)

The report led to adverse headlines in the local and national press (Humphries 2018, Nazia 2018). The House of Commons Home Affairs Committee singled out Merseyside for comment in their report *Policing the Future* published later that year (House of Commons 2018a: para.91) but also saying this was not just a Merseyside problem:

> It is unacceptable … that forces have insufficient resources to manage the risks posed to children by registered sex offenders, constantly playing 'catch-up' with a backlog of visits. We welcome efforts by the College of Policing to prioritise this issue.
>
> (ibid: para.94)

The response from the Home Office was somewhat vague. It did repeat the mantra that 'the UK has some of the toughest powers in the world to manage sex offenders in the community' (Home Office 2019a: para.57) but never directly mentioned offender managers. It did vaguely say that in 2019/20 funding would increase for the 'police system' up to £970 million (ibid: para.44) with the assumption that it would be left to local forces to allocate funding to sex offender management

MAPPA accountability

The accountability of MAPPA has always remained rather blurred. MAPPA is not a legal body and therefore not answerable as such. MAPPA activities are not always as transparent as official guidance would have us believe. A case study in Leeds shines some light on MAPPA accountability when things go wrong.

Zuzanna Zommer was a 14-year-old girl who was sexually assaulted and then murdered in Leeds on 1 October 2007 by a man on the sex offender register. The man, Michael Clark, was arrested within a few days and later convicted and sentenced to life imprisonment.

Case study 7.1

Zuzanna Zommer was aged 14 when she was sexually assaulted and murdered in her own home in Harehills, Leeds on 1 October 2007. Her parents had been out for the day and returned to find her body in a state of undress and with her throat cut ('Teenager murdered: a piercing scream and grim discovery' *Yorkshire Evening Post* 2 October 2007). The parents called the West Yorkshire Police who promptly arrested them both on suspicion of having committed the crime and took them into police custody. Within eight hours the parents had been released and a new suspect had been arrested ('Quiz goes on over stab girl' *Yorkshire Evening Post* 3 October 2007).

The new suspect was 39-year-old Michael Clark who lived in the same street as the Zommer family. Clark had a long history of sexual offending and consequent custodial sentences and was a registered sex offender. He had left HM Prison Hull on 17 November 2006 after serving a prison sentence; throughout the final months of his sentence Clark had stated his intention to live in Leeds (his home address was Scunthorpe) because of the better employment opportunities. He was sentenced to life imprisonment for the murder of Zuzanna Zommer at Sheffield Crown Court on 8 May 2008 and ordered to serve 35 years before he could apply for parole.

The Zommer family had only been in England a matter of months having come here from Poland in search of work; Mr Zommer was an IT software engineer and his wife a physiotherapist. Zuzanna was aged 14 and had a nine-year-old brother. The family returned to Poland within days of the murder.

Four reports were written on what had happened in the Zommer case but only one of them was ever made public. Two Serious Case Review (SCR) reports were written under the auspices of the West Yorkshire MAPPA and the Leeds LSCB (Local Safeguarding Children Board); both of these reports were accompanied by summary reports. The LSCB Executive Summary is the only insight we have into what happened with the MAPPA Offender Management in this case.

The MAPPA Serious Case Review

The MAPPA Serious Case Review for Zuzanna Zommer produced two reports:

- the full SCR Report
- the Overview Report which is a summary of the full Report.

Neither report has ever been made public.

In 2009 guidance was given to MAPPAs that Serious Case Reviews should be carried out when an offender managed by MAPPA at levels two or three commits a serious further offence. The guidance stated that it is 'essential' that the 'activities of the agencies involved is scrutinised and this *must be a transparent process*' (NOMS 2009: para.28.1 emphasis added); at the same time, it also stated that 'the [SCR] report must not be widely distributed or published' (ibid: para.28.14). A summary of the report, known as the Overview Report, should be shared with the victim/family but not with the public; it should be marked 'Restricted' (ibid: para.28.15). This guidance was updated in 2012.

The 2012 Guidance still says the SCR is 'in the public interest' (NOMS 2012: para.20.5) but at the same time it should remain 'Restricted' (ibid: para.20.18) and 'must not be widely distributed or published' (ibid: 20.21). On completion, the 2012 Guidance still states that the family should only be given verbal feedback on its contents and 'a copy of the MAPPA SCR *should not be provided*' to them (ibid: para.20.24, emphasis added).

The MAPPA SCR in the Zommer case has therefore not been published. It is unclear whether the Zommer family now in Poland have had the findings shared with them. In reply to a parliamentary question the Secretary of State for Justice confirmed that 'no summary has been prepared for publication, but the SMB [Strategic Management Board of the MAPPA] is prepared and has offered to share the findings of the review with the family of Zuzanna Zommer' (*Hansard House of Commons Debates 21 July 2009 col. 1401W*).

The Leeds Local Safeguarding Children Boards (LSCB): Serious Case Review

The Leeds LSCB refused to publish the full Overview Report despite changes implemented from 10 June 2010 requiring overview reports to be published in full. Their argument was simply that this SCR began, and was carried out, under the earlier guidance and therefore full publication was not required.

The Leeds Executive Summary published in March 2012 is a 24-page document that refers to Zuzzana only as *Child K*. The Report came five years after the murder. A first attempt at the Report was sent back to Leeds by Ofsted because it 'did not comply with the statutory guidance governing the conduct of Serious Case Reviews' (LSCB 2012: 2).

The Executive Summary gives a brief outline of what happened and what agencies did to try to prevent Clark committing more offences. The inadequate planning for Clark's move from Humberside to West Yorkshire is covered, including the decision by the Humberside authorities to only tell West Yorkshire that a registered sex offender was moving into their area the day before he arrived, even though they had known of his intended move for months.

The Report concluded that Zuzanna's murder 'may have been prevented had the agencies (according to their role and level of responsibility) charged with protecting the public from high-risk offenders worked more effectively within the mechanisms available' (ibid: 17).

The Executive Summary is less than clear on the police activities. It fails to explain the reasons the police gave for initially arresting the parents but whatever those reasons were it 'raised questions' for the report writer (ibid: para.4.18). It is also unclear who exactly arrested the parents – the West Yorkshire Police local officers in Leeds or officers of the 'Homicide and Major Enquiry Team' or officers of the CPPU (Child and Public Protection Unit). All three were involved in the case at one time and we are told that communications between them were not good (ibid: para.3.7; Findings 9, 10 and 11).

Clark had lived in Leeds for 11 months before the crime and during that time been 'charged with threatening behaviour and criminal damage' (ibid: para.3.7). Throughout this time, he had been on the sex offender register, but this 'charge' was not reported to the police officers acting as offender managers and responsible for his registration. There is also no indication in the Executive Summary as to whether the Crown Prosecution Service was consulted on this charge or any explanation as to why the case did not go to court where the full picture would possibly have been revealed. A MAPPA 'emergency' meeting took a month to organise but the Executive Summary fails to say why (ibid: para.4.15).

Serious Case Reviews – the future

Serious Case Reviews on child deaths had originally been informally known as 'Part 8 Reviews' when introduced by the Children Act 1989; 'Part 8' being that section of the relevant guidance at the time (Home Office et al. 1991). The overt aim of these Reviews was to learn lessons when a child's death was non-accidental and possibly preventable had the child protection agencies provided a more effective service. The unspoken aim of the Part 8 Reviews was to avoid the numerous public enquiries that had been entered into on child deaths over the 1970s and 1980s and to keep the reviews 'in house'. Parton notes 45 public inquiries between 1973 and 1989 but only 14 between 1990 and 1999:

> That is not to say that the problems in the 1980s had gone away, as a reading of Part 8 reviews indicates, the same problems were evident concerning the failure to 'spot the signs' and the inadequacies of communication and coordination. It did mean, however, that *the issues were much less in the public domain*
>
> (Parton 2006: 40 emphasis added)

A study into Part 8 reviews carried out at Liverpool John Moores University stated that 'it has become the norm to keep Part Eight reviews unpublished' (Corby et al. 2001: 73). Where reports had been made public, it had been the result of considerable pressure from relatives, the community, media and presiding judges (ibid: 185). Part 8 Reviews were renamed as Serious Case Reviews by the Children Act 2004 which also created Local Safeguarding Children Boards (LSCBs).

A National Panel of Independent Experts on Serious Case Reviews was instituted in 2013 to look at all SCR reports and advise on their writing and publication, and to produce an overall annual report on them. The Panel were quite critical of the reports stating that the 'quality is disturbingly variable, with good reports being outnumbered by the number of reports still failing on key points' (DfE 2014: para.24). Changes were proposed by the Wood Report that had found 'the recommendations of Reviews tend to be predictable and or banal, unfocussed and not addressed to specific individuals or organisations' (Wood Report 2016: para.161); not only that but some LSCBs were avoiding writing them altogether (ibid: 88 FN31).

The Children and Social Work Act 2017 introduced the idea of Child Safeguarding Practice Reviews and a national Child Safety Practice Review Panel that would expect all serious incidents to be reported to them (2017 Act: chapter 2); it spelt the end of the Local Safeguarding Children's Boards.

In June 2018, the government announced that LSCBs were to be replaced in September 2019 by teams of safeguarding partners who would in essence be the local authority, a clinical commissioning group for an area any part of which falls within the local authority area, and the local police (see Children Act 2004 as amended by the Children and Social Work Act, 2017s16). Reviews in future were to be published in full unless 'the safeguarding partners … consider it inappropriate to do so' (Children and Social Work Act 2017 s16F (4) amending Children Act 2004).

No changes have been announced for the MAPPA SCRs and their complete lack of publication. The police do still have their own Police Internal Management Review (PIMR) report covering further serious offending by any registered sex offender and others managed by the MAPPA (NOMS 2009: Section 29). These reports are marked 'Restricted' and are exempt from the Freedom of Information Act (ibid: para.29.5). The most recent 2012 version of the MAPPA Guidance omits any reference to PIMRs (NOMS 2012).

Risk assessment and management

Risk assessment tools

Risk Matrix 2000 predicts the likelihood of reconviction for a sexual or violent offence and helps to predict which offenders are most likely to be reconvicted and who, therefore, require greater resources to manage their risk. Offenders are categorised into levels rated Low, Medium, High or Very High dependent on the statistical likelihood of reconviction.

OASYS (Offender Assessment System) is the risk assessment tool used by the Prison Service and the National Probation Service to assess the likelihood of the risk of reoffending and the risk of causing serious harm. It is a comprehensive assessment tool that applies to all offenders aged 18 and over. It enables the practitioner to examine the likelihood of reoffending by systematically examining a number of offending-related factors, including offending history; education, training and employability; relationships; drug misuse; alcohol misuse; emotional well-being; thinking and behaviour; and accommodation, lifestyle, and associated thinking, behaviour and attitudes. Risk assessment will help to prioritise public protection concerns and establish the basis for risk management plans.

The year 2010 was the year of the Coalition government beginning its era of 'austerity' that included the reduction of police numbers by some 20,000 officers (Home Office 2016: Chapter 3). Most of the headlines at this time were about unsafe streets and a need for more officers on the beat. What was missing was any analysis of how less visible teams like offender managers were affected by the austerity cuts.

In Chapter Six we looked at the way in which risk assessment was used to guide offender managers in the number of home visits that should be made to registered sex offenders and how that number could be reduced whilst still ensuring defensible public protection levels (see Whitehead 2009 and 2010). As journalists had spotted the reduction in the number of home visits being related to changes in different risk assessment levels for people on the register (see previous chapter), so too academics had now turned their attention to variations in risk levels across the 42 MAPPA areas in England and Wales and their accompanying level of management. Hudson and colleagues looked at the geographical differences across the country. Why, for example, was the percentage of registered sex offenders managed at Level 2 or Level 3 set at 29.64% in London but only 4.66% in neighbouring Essex? (Hudson and Henley 2015).

The concern was that there was no consistency in practice across the different MAPPA areas. There also appeared to be variations in the level of risk assessment over time periods and not just between geographical areas. Hudson and Henley found variations over the nine-year time period from 2004/5 to 2010/11. Other variations included differences in the applications for civil orders and differences in the use of sanctions for non-compliance with requirements by those on the register. The underlying theme appeared to be concerns about the fairness of MAPPA practice policies based on so-called 'precautionary logic' (Hebenton and Seddon 2009) which failed to take into account the basic rights of those on the register (see also Hudson et al. 2015).

The Active Risk Management System (ARMS)

The Active Risk Management System (ARMS) was introduced into policing in 2014 as a pilot scheme. It enabled the police making risk assessments to look beyond static historical factors, such as the original crime and subsequent criminal history, to dynamic risk factors about the 'here and now' that were subject to change. This meant that the former risk management approaches were more 'reactive' and the new ARMS approach was more 'active'. For the police, an ARMS assessment would usefully become the new way to inform decisions about 'level of management' of registered sexual offenders.

The original pilot scheme received favourable reports in its evaluation but it was recommended that another wider evaluation should precede any national roll-out:

> The size of the pilot and subsequent evaluation was too limited in scope to draw conclusions on several key questions, which remain to be explored. ARMS should be comprehensively piloted to encompass greater diversity of geographical areas, shared assessments between agencies, offender types and officer experience/working practice … This would lay a strong foundation for potential national roll out, and ensure that ARMS is valid, reliable and fully integrated into existing sexual offender management processes.
>
> (NOMS 2014a: para.6.6)

In fact, there was to be no further evaluations and ARMS was rolled out nationally on 25 January 2017. The police announced that their risk assessment work with registered sex offenders was changing and they introduced ARMS as what they called a new 'personalised risk management plan'. This meant that each person on the register would get 'a tailored approach rather than following a one-size-fits-all model' (NPCC 2017). The national ARMS roll-out would be evaluated by academic research, but that would not be completed until March 2020.

Following the introduction of an active risk management system and individual risk management plans, police are making three further changes:

- Officers will now determine the frequency of home visits as part of a holistic plan instead of all offenders receiving a set number of visits based on their risk category.
- Success will no longer be measured solely by the completion of home visits. Instead, supervisors will now assess performance by reviewing the

quality of the risk management plan, progress in completing actions and re-evaluation of an individual's risk.

- Those who have not reoffended and are consistently assessed as low risk for at least three years will be considered for reactive management where they do not receive home visits. They will continue to be monitored and will be subject to annual notification requirements at a local police station. Any intelligence or changes to their circumstances will trigger a review of the risk assessment with the potential for their level of risk to be increased or for home visits to be reintroduced.

(NPCC 2017)

In the same press release David Tucker, head of crime and criminal justice at the College of Policing, said:

> The College supports forces taking a risk-based approach *to target police resources* to manage those registered sex offenders assessed as posing the greatest risk to the public.
>
> (ibid: emphasis added)

'Targeting police resources' reaffirms that the underlying reason for the introduction of ARMS is lack of resources. Later the Home Office stated that the changeover was 'to address the increasing rise in the number of sexual offenders' and that 'reactive management' meant:

> a bespoke visit regime based upon the individual risk management plan for every offender, introducing reactive management for only those offenders who have been assessed as a low risk consistently for at least three years and have not reoffended ... If at any point there are any concerns about an offender in reactive management, they will be reverted back to active management. The police estimate that of the 52,000 Registered Sex Offenders in England and Wales [in 2017], those subject to the reactive management regime will, at this moment in time, be in the low hundreds.
>
> (*Hansard House of Commons Debates 6 July 2017 PQ 2391*; see also *PQ 2388 and PQ 2390*)

The press was still not quite sure what was happening although senior police officers were said to acknowledge the policy change was 'an emotive issue' (BBC News 2017; see also Hamilton 2017). Some police officers had their own misgivings about the ARMS approach:

> Participants also appeared disengaged with the new type of interview style or approach needed because they felt it to be 'more a touchy, feely kind of thing really isn't it' (FG2. p.30). They feel a drift

> towards probation practice, but 'we're not probation officers and we're not trained to that level … I hate using the word touchy feely, that's what, you know, we're asking to be trained people and we're not' (FG3. p.91).
>
> (Kewley 2017: 11)

In January 2019, the opposition spokesperson on policing, Louise Haig, asked the Home Secretary whether he thought the number of home visits to registered sex offenders had been adequate over the last 12 months. Minister of State at the Home Office Nick Hurd answered with the familiar preamble:

> The UK has some of the toughest powers in the world to deal with sex offenders and we are committed to ensuring that the system is as robust as it can be …
>
> In 2017, the police made key changes to their management regime. Officers can now determine the frequency of home visits as part of a personalised risk management plan, instead of visiting all offenders a set number of times based on their risk category.
>
> (*Hansard House of Commons Debates 21 January 2019 WA 207585*)

A further evaluation of the ARMS approach did eventually take place after the national roll-out in 2017 and its report published in 2020. Ironically the report found that the completion of an ARMS interview and assessment took up more time than the previous risk assessments:

> ARMS is well embedded in police practice across England and Wales, however, the majority of police practitioners felt that its implementation had created additional work and an added strain on resources. The theoretical effectiveness of ARMS stems directly from the detailed nature of the assessment, which reportedly takes between 6 and 8 hours to complete.
>
> (Mann and Lundrigan 2020: para.3.4.2)

Probation officers had similar misgivings:

> Current workloads were also concerning for NPS practitioners who reported that increases in staff shortages and impractical expectations by managers (i.e. the allocation of 3 hours to complete an ARMS interview and assessment) were creating additional pressures. Practitioners felt that the completion of ARMS in addition to the OASys assessment was the proverbial 'straw', which created additional workload but little benefit to offender supervision.
>
> (ibid)

Case study 7.2

In July 2006, a man living in the south of England, who was on the register for life, visited a friend in North Yorkshire. He had met this friend through a dating agency and this was to be their first meeting. When he reached Selby in North Yorkshire, he went to a police station to inform the police that he was staying in the area. He showed officers a document with the name Robert Williams and an incorrect address for his friend's house. He also claimed his placement on the sex offenders register had expired.

The police became suspicious and tracked him to the correct address he was staying at in Selby where he was arrested for giving false details and failing to have registered his new address within the three-day time notification limit. The man later told police that he had got his friend's address wrong because he had never met her before and his visit to the police had been out of courtesy. He was held in custody for 110 days.

When he eventually came to court the case was dropped and he was later awarded £3,075 compensation after a judge at Leeds County Court found he had been wrongfully arrested and imprisoned by North Yorkshire Police. The police were also ordered to pay more than £20,000 in legal fees.

(BBC News 2009)

Case study 7.3

During the early hours of 26 June 2016, a registered sex offender sexually assaulted two women in Harrogate town centre. The two separate incidents were witnessed by CCTV operators who reported them to North Yorkshire Police and named the suspect.

Following the first report, an officer attended at the scene, spoke with the suspect but did not arrest him. Following the second incident, two other officers attended at the scene, and made attempts to locate the suspect and arrest him. They did not locate him but spoke with the victim.

Neither of the offences were effectively investigated by North Yorkshire Police and the offender was not arrested. Two weeks later, he committed a further serious but unconnected sex offence against a woman. At that point, the earlier incidents were referred to us so that the force's involvement could be investigated. The actions of the police public protection officer who had responsibility for risk managing the suspect was also examined.

During this independent investigation, we examined CCTV evidence, radio communications and police records made in respect of the offences, and interviewed four subject officers under misconduct caution.

The investigation concluded that there was sufficient evidence to recommend a case of misconduct against two officers who were responsible for investigating the offences of sexual assault.

A misconduct meeting was held in relation to the officer who attended the first incident. The case of misconduct was proven and the officer received recordable management action.

IOPC (2018)

Case study 7.4

A high-risk registered sex offender in Cleveland was convicted in August 2015 for sexually assaulting a 26-year-old woman while her children were in the house. He was convicted and received a suspended sentence. The following month he underwent an ARMS assessment. At the time of inspection, the last visit made by the force to him was in July 2016 – a pre-arranged visit. Before that he had been visited by the force only twice – in August 2015 and February 2016 – both of which were pre-arranged (as opposed to unannounced) visits. This meant that a high-risk offender (who, at the time, should have been visited every three months) had not been visited for ten months and had never received an unannounced visit. In August 2016, the man returned to the attention of the force after he was the victim of an assault. He subsequently moved away from the Cleveland area, apparently fearing for his safety. Records show that he may have breached his notification requirements when he moved. However, there is no evidence that this was investigated or that any further action was taken.

(HMICFRS 2017: 40)

The Davies Review

The Association of Chief Constables (ACPO) (now the National Police Chiefs' Council (NPCC)) commissioned a review of the civil prevention orders made under the Sexual Offences Act 2003 in early 2013; in general terms the police were getting a good deal of criticism for their handling of sexual offences and especially the lack of civil orders being applied for. The report was completed by May 2013 and was referred to as the Davies Review after the chair of the working party Hugh Davies QC; its full title was *Civil Prevention Orders Sexual Offences Act 2003: ACPO commissioned review of the existing statutory scheme and recommendations for reform* (Davies Review 2013).

The Davies Review concluded that the existing statutory regime 'presents unnecessary and unreasonable obstruction to the objective of preventing sexual abuse of children' (para.2.1) and should therefore 'be simplified so as (i) to create a single, and straightforward, evidence-led test justifying a prevention order without other pre-conditions, and (ii) that the range of applicants should be extended' (ibid: para.2.4).

The Review also recommended removal of the word 'serious' from the law; they argued that the word 'serious' was not necessary: 'We resist the term "serious", borrowed from existing legislation, since it pre-supposes that there is some category of sexual harm that may be caused to a child that is not intrinsically serious or that is not worthy of prevention' (Davies Review 2013: para.2.6).

The Review recommended a new single order given the name of a 'Child Sexual Offences Prevention Order' in the following terms:

> On the application of a qualifying person [Chief Officer of Police or other qualified person (CEOP/SOCA/NCA/CPS, etc.)], or on conviction for a qualifying offence, a court may make a child sexual offences prevention order in respect of any person if it is satisfied that it is necessary to make such an order for the purpose of protecting a person of under 18 years' from [serious] sexual harm from the defendant/respondent
>
> (ibid: para.2.5)

The Review working party has been referred to as 'independent'. In the House of Commons one MP described the Review as '*written independently* by Hugh Davies QC and a team of experts' (*Hansard House of Commons 14 October 2013 col.482* emphasis added). In a later interview Davies himself called the Review 'a well-researched *(multi-agency) independent report*' (Davies 2015: emphasis added).

The question might reasonably be asked as to who the Review was 'independent' of, when the committee members writing it were either serving police officers or people with links to the police. They included a Detective Constable from the Metropolitan Police, a Detective Chief Inspector from Hampshire Police, an Operations Manager at the Child Exploitation and Online Protection Centre (CEOP) now part of the National Crime Agency, a former Team Leader of CEOP's Offender Management Team, dealing with both UK nationals suspected of travelling overseas to target and abuse children and now working for the Border Force National Intelligence. The two non-police officers on the committee were the then Director of ECPAT and Hugh Davies the chairperson, a barrister who was a member of the ACPO child protection executive board who had 'extensive associated experience advising and representing police officers at public inquiries; IPCC supervised investigations, and internal disciplinary proceedings' (see Davies Review 2013: Appendix 1).

The description of the Review as 'multi-agency' might also be questioned, when most of the working party had policing backgrounds and there were no magistrates, probation officers, social workers, psychologists, doctors or health visitors amongst the members. The impression that this was anything other than a fully-fledged police report was further confirmed by the wording 'Not Protectively Marked' at the top of each page, in red, which was the marking adopted by the police using the then Government Protective Marking Scheme; a marking rarely used at this level by non-police agencies.

The Davies Review itself is written with an emphasis on everything being 'common sense' and 'self-evident'; in the following quotes from the *Review* the emphasis has been added by the authors:

> preventable sexual abuse of children is occurring on *a significant (if unquantifiable) scale.*
>
> (ibid: para.2.1)

> *No informed party would dispute* either (i) that the sexual exploitation of children is an endemic problem internationally; or (ii) that there is a combination of factors that is promoting an expansion, rather than reduction, in such abuse being conducted extra-territorially by UK (and other) Nationals.
>
> (ibid: para.3.1)

> It is, and remains, a well-documented problem. *The scale of it is intrinsically difficult to quantify but on any view the figures are both staggering and appalling*
>
> (ibid: para.3.10)

None of this documentation is actually cited. Elsewhere statistics (or the lack of them) are treated in cavalier fashion:

> It begs the obvious question: what proportion of this offending could have been prevented by a different prevention order regime? *The fact the data is so intrinsically unsatisfactory does not avoid the inevitable conclusions* (i) that it is a high proportion (in any event, in this context, any proportion is a significant proportion); and (ii) that the figures outlined are likely to represent a very small fraction of the whole.
>
> (ibid: para.4.43)

> The numbers – inadequate as they are in terms of data collection – do not lie.
>
> (ibid: para.8.3.1)

Statements such as 'the fact the data is so intrinsically unsatisfactory' and 'the numbers – inadequate as they are in terms of data collection' hardly bears witness to a report that Davies described as 'well researched'.

We do know that if forces disagreed with a response, the writers of the Review were quite capable of simply dismissing it rather than discussing it:

> a significant number of local forces were resistant to a national, and nationally resourced, police unit directed at international offending against children on the purported basis that it would 'remove developmental opportunities' from local forces. *We reject this approach as insular and myopic.*
>
> (ibid: para.10.2.5)

The proposed 'Child Sexual Offences Prevention Order' would take its place as a new form of pre-emptive policing to prevent criminal behaviour. Such policing it might be argued demands more preliminary safeguards rather than less as the Davies Review argues. And although they argue that simplifying the law will make for easier applications for orders, they also admit that sometimes in the past the low numbers of applications have just been a result of de-motivated police officers (ibid: para.10.2.1) and chief officers with limited resources (ibid: para.7.6.2).

The law was duly changed on the basis of the Davies Review.

The Anti-Social Behaviour, Crime and Policing Act 2014

In Parliament two new Orders were proposed to be known as the Sexual Risk Orders and Sexual Harm Prevention Orders. In the Commons debate the Davies Review was directly attributed as the source of these innovations (see *Hansard House of Commons 14 October 2013 cols 478 and 482*). Both proposed Orders went further than the Davies Review recommendations for a Child Sexual Offences Prevention Order which had focused on children as potential victims; the new orders were applicable to any age of victim.

There were arguably serious human rights and civil liberties implications in these amendments to the Anti-Social Behaviour, Crime and Policing Bill. Questions of 'liberty' 'freedom of movement' and degrees of 'privacy' were present. In the parliamentary debate however, none of these questions were discussed. Even the House of Lords/House of Commons Joint Committee on Human Rights was not given the opportunity to consider the relevant parts of the Bill. The Committee reported that 'the number of significant Government amendments to the Bill with potentially significant human rights implications has made our scrutiny of the Bill's human rights compatibility more difficult' and:

> On 8 October … the eve of our agreeing this Report, the Government tabled amendments to the Bill to reform the civil orders under the Sexual Offences Act 2003. We were … given no warning in advance that the Government intended to introduce such amendments which clearly have human rights implications. *We are pursuing with the Leader of the House of Commons our concerns about the recurring inadequacy of the time available to scrutinise the human rights compatibility of significant Government amendments to Bills.*
>
> (House of Lords/House of Commons 2013: para.9 emphasis in original)

Whether this avoidance of human rights scrutiny by the government was accidental or deliberate is hard to fathom. Policing and Criminal Justice Minister Damian Green said:

> The UK has some of the toughest powers in the world to deal with sex offenders. Today, we are going even further by giving police and National Crime Agency officers the power to place greater restrictions on any person they judge to be a risk.
>
> (Home Office 2013a)

The Home Office regarded the amendments as being compatible with the ECHR (Home Office 2013b). The new law became the Anti-Social Behaviour, Crime and Policing Act 2014 which amended the Sexual Offences Act 2003 by reducing the existing four civil orders down to two: the Sexual Harm Prevention Orders and Sexual Risk Orders.

The Sexual Harm Prevention Orders (SHPO)

The Sexual Harm Prevention Orders now read:

1 (b)the court is satisfied that it is necessary to make a sexual harm prevention order, for the purpose of—
2 protecting the public or any particular members of the public from sexual harm from the defendant, or
3 protecting children or vulnerable adults generally, or any particular children or vulnerable adults, from sexual harm from the defendant outside the United Kingdom.(Sexual Offences Act 2003 s103A)

The word 'serious' or 'seriousness' has been quietly withdrawn as recommended by the Davies Review and from 8 March 2015 that became the new law. Inclusion on the sex offender register was automatic for anyone made subject to a SHPO (2003 Act s103G).

Case study 7.5

Police received seven separate reports about a registered sex offender exhibiting worrying behaviour, such as talking to children or being seen in parks where children were present.

They missed opportunities to make an application for a Sexual Harm Prevention Order (which can be used to impose wide-ranging prohibitions on individuals previously convicted of certain sexual offences, and thought to pose current risk of sexual harm to the public), or to work actively on the case (for instance, by arresting the offender for failing to comply with notification requirements).

(HMICFRS 2016: 85)

The Sexual Risk Order (SRO)

The Sexual Risk Order enables the court to impose prohibitions on individuals if there is reasonable cause to believe that the individual poses a risk of harm to others, even if they have never been convicted or cautioned for a sexual or violent offence under Schedule 3 or Schedule 5 of the 2003 Act. The SRO has a minimum duration of two years and a maximum duration of five years. Inclusion on the sex offender register was automatic for anyone made subject to an SRO (2003 Act s122F).

The Orders, issued by courts, would place restrictions on the movements and activities of anyone convicted or cautioned of a sexual or violent offence including individuals who have committed offences overseas or who pose a risk of sexual harm to children and vulnerable adults in the UK and abroad. Restrictions can include limiting their internet use, preventing them from being alone with a child under 16, home-tutoring children or preventing travel abroad.

The SRO gathered some notoriety when the North Yorkshire Police successfully applied for one on a local resident. The Order placed prohibitions on him that he should not engage in sexual activity with anyone without first informing the police 24 hours in advance, giving the woman's name, her address and date of birth. At one point even the District Judge that made the Order said it was 'unpoliceable' (BBC News 2016a; Evans 2016).

Non-compliance

The general consensus is that people on the register are very compliant with all the conditions and requirements imposed on them. Early figures suggested the compliance rate was as high as 94% in 2000 (Plotnikoff and Woolfson 2000: 6) and 97% in 2001 (Home Office/Scottish Executive 2001: 12).

Politicians have pointed to this high compliance rate as a sign of success in itself. Charles Clarke, junior Home Office minister at the time, for example, stated in 2000 that:

> The Sex Offenders Act 1997 plays an important part in protecting the public, especially children, from the pernicious activities of sex offenders ... The Register has been enormously successful and has achieved an extremely high rate of compliance.
>
> (Home Office 2000b)

Politicians have similarly made play of the fact that having no community notification policies in the UK has given us far higher levels of compliance than the USA where such policies exist, and which drive offenders away from compliance because of fear of vigilantism.

Non-compliance is still an offence in itself and the Sexual Offences Act 2003 makes a point of listing the offences that can be committed (2003 Act s91; see also Chapter Five). These offences are going to be more akin to administrative offences involving the register itself and its bureaucratic nature and are not going to be sexual offences. The offence is committed on the first day on which the offender fails to comply with the relevant notification requirements, and continues for as long as the failure to comply persists. The offender cannot be prosecuted more than once for the same breach, however long it continues.

There are many reasons why people breach their notification requirements ranging from a malicious intent not to comply through to not understanding the requirements or simply forgetting about them. People on the register include people with forms of learning disabilities and even dementia. Whatever the reason is, it does not stop the tabloid press from painting them all as the same 'dangerous' and 'animal-like' predatory offenders, who through their noncompliance are liable to 'escape', be 'on the loose' and liable to 'prowl':

- 'Offenders may escape paedophile register' (*Independent on Sunday* 26 January 1997)
- 'Loophole allows paedophiles to escape register' (*Daily Telegraph* 25 June 2000)
- 'Yorkshire sex offenders among 300 on the loose in Britain' (*Yorkshire Post* 27 April 2010)
- 'Paedo free to *prowl*' (*The Sun* 10 March 2013, emphasis added)

The police make efforts to find the non-compliant and missing sex offenders dependent on the risk they are assessed as posing. One means of doing this has been the use of a 'Most Wanted' list which displays photographs of the missing persons. This list was posted on the NCA's Child Exploitation and Online Protection (CEOP) centre website's where it is run by the CEOP 'Tracker Team'.

A report in 2010 said that since its launch in November 2006, CEOP has helped track down 79 high-risk missing child sex offenders; some of these were found in places as far afield as South America and South East Asia (Home Office 2010f: 9). CEOP has also improved the rate of locating missing high-risk sex offenders from just over 7% in 2005 to 77% in 2009 (ibid: 14).

The College of Policing states the CEOP criteria for referral to the 'Tracker Team' are that the offender:

- is a UK RSO (registered sex offender)
- has committed a sexual offence against a child/children, i.e., the offender has been convicted of a contact offence(s) with a person(s) less than 16 years of age, or has been convicted of a non-contact offence(s) with a person(s) less than 18 years of age
- is assessed as very high or high risk
- is wanted for breach of Sexual Offences Act notification requirements.

(College of Policing 2020)

The punishment that a court can impose for non-compliance ranges from a fine to a maximum six months imprisonment (on summary conviction) through to up to five years imprisonment (on indictment) (Sexual Offences Act 2003 s.91(2)). A man who appealed against an eight-month 240 custodial sentence for offences of non-compliance argued that the sentence should have been a maximum of three months citing a further three cases where only three months had been imposed. The appeal was lost (*R v Grosvenor [2010] 2 Cr App Rep (S) 100*).

The number of cautions or convictions for breach of notification requirements has increased annually in the last three years (see Figure 7.1), driven by increases among those managed at Level 1 who usually account for 95% of these cautions or convictions. The number of cautions or convictions among those managed at Level 2 has been decreasing, partly due to decreasing number of Category 1 offenders managed at Level 2. Relatively few Category 1 14 offenders get cautioned or convicted for breach of notification requirements (3% for Level 2 and 1% for Level 3 in 2018/19.)

Reoffending

Compliance rates are not the same as no further reoffending and it is quite possible for offenders to be in full compliance with all the administrative requirements of the register, have the minimal requisite contact with their offender managers and still have reasonable amounts of uncontained free time in which to reoffend.

The critical test of the value of the register is whether or not it actually reduces further sexual harm or, more importantly, more sexual offending by those on it, and subject to offender management. In the early days the Home Office itself had recognised that the media and public were still somewhat ill-informed about

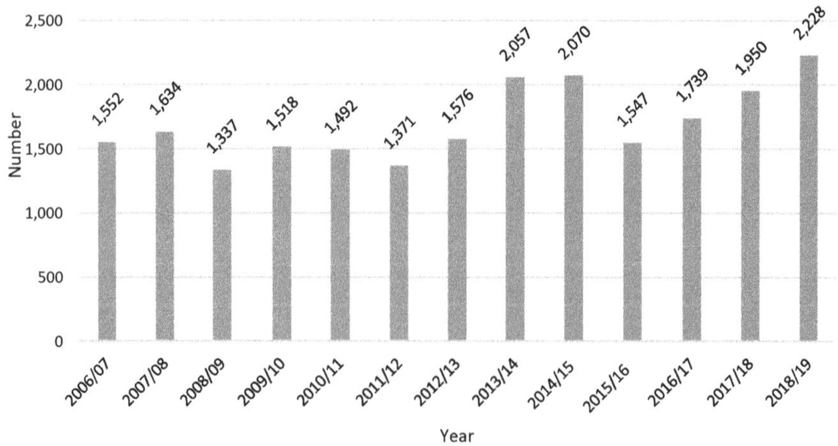

Figure 7.1 Number of Category 1 offenders (Registered Sexual Offenders) cautioned or convicted for breaches of the notification requirements

Table 7.1 MAPPA offenders supervised by probation in England and Wales, charged with a Serious Further Offence

Year	*Level 1*	*Level 2*	*Level 3*	*Total*
2009/10	162	31	3	196
2010/11	108	23	3	134
2011/12	116	24	7	147
2012/13	125	18	6	149
2013/14	143	28	3	174
2014/15	185	36	1	222
2015/16	164	28	1	193
2016/17	200	16	1	217
2017/18	220	19	3	242
2018/19	165	13	1	179
2019/20	173	17	2	192

the powers of the register and that 'Too often, the impression is given that the provisions of the Sex Offenders Act provide the ability to restrict offender's actions and movements, whereas they are principally about notification of an address' (Home Office/Scottish Executive 2001: 12).

In 2015/16, 0.13 per cent of registered sex offenders were charged with a serious further offence, and 'consistently less than 0.6% of those managed at Level 2 and Level 3 are charged with an SFO each year' (MoJ 2020a: 20).

Costs of sex offender registration

The authors used the Freedom of Information Act (FOIA) to find out how much it cost to run the sex offender register each year. The request for this information was sent to the Home Office, and a sample of police forces. No one could tell us.

The Home Office said they did not have this information:

> The Home Office does not hold the information which you have requested. We believe that this information is owned by individual police forces in England and Wales. You may wish to approach police forces for a response to your request.
>
> (personal communication dated 23 October 2019)

Thames Valley Police told us the costs incurred to find this information would be too great:

> This request is being refused under Section 12(1) of the FOIA. Section 12 of the FOIA allows that public authorities do not have to comply with

> section 1(1) of the Act if the cost of complying would exceed the appropriate limit. In accordance with the Freedom of Information Act, this letter represents a Refusal Notice for this request. This information is not held in an easily retrievable format. To retrieve the information, you are requesting will require a review of each person's salary within the team, the costs of vehicles used, IT equipment, other consumables as well as other allowances. To review all of this and try to obtain an accurate amount of cost will exceed the appropriate 18-hour time and £450 cost limit.
>
> (personal communication dated 15 November 2019)

West Yorkshire Police were unable to tell us and said they could not disclose information on staffing costs:

> The cost of running the Violent and Sex Offender Register (ViSOR) is not held. There are 5 Public Protection Units at Districts which are staffed with Public Protection Officers (police officers) who visit and manage RSOs. Public Protection Review Officers (police staff) and Clerks also access and update the ViSOR. Each district has a different structure and officers and staff may have more than one portfolio. In addition, there is a ViSOR Registrar, two ViSOR / PDP co-ordinators and 3.68 ViSOR assistants. A calculation of the cost of the above staff is not a requirement under the Freedom of Information Act 2000.
>
> (personal communication 19 December 2019)

Summary

Changes in the law to strengthen the register were made during this period. More details had to be given to the police about credit cards, foreign travel and whether or not a child was living at the same address as the person who had to register. New criminal laws were introduced to counter adults engaging in sexual communication with a child and so-called up-skirting offences. The chapter also examines the offender management process and in particular the formal inspections of this work, the accountability of the officers carrying out offender management and the changing nature of the risk assessment carried out by these officers.

Other changes made during this time period included a review of the Civil Orders available for imposition on sex offenders. The Davies Review led ultimately to the repeal of the Sexual Offences Prevention Order, the Foreign Travel Order and the Risk of Sexual Harm Order and their replacement by the Sexual Harm Prevention Order and the Risk of Sexual Harm Order.

8 Life on the register

Introduction

Having a criminal record for sexual offences can have a negative impact on a person's life in more ways than one, and negative impact may last for years past the original conviction and sentence. The impact may be formal, affecting employment or opportunities in public life, and informal, affecting, for example, contact in the local community. This may not be a direct consequence of the register, as such, but the impact of having convictions for sexual offences against your name cannot be underestimated.

Little academic attention has been paid to the actual life experiences of the person with convictions for sexual offences. Such research is difficult to conduct and much UK research has preferred to look more at the experiences of people in prison (see e.g. Hudson 2005) or those who are available and working online (Goode 2010). Court judgements have sometimes provided insights into these life experiences and some convicted sexual offenders have written-up their own stories; campaign group websites have carried insightful blogs. Other useful studies have been carried out in the USA (see below).

The purpose of this chapter is to try to gain a closer understanding of the experiences and perspectives of those people convicted of sexual offences who are living in the community. The aim is to give a voice to people who have experienced life on the register and to develop a better understanding of that experience.

Studies from America

Sex offenders have been interviewed about their lives as convicted sex offenders living in the community in studies from America. The work of Richard Tewksbury at the University of Louisville has pioneered much of this work and confirmed the general vulnerability of the sex offender in trying to resettle in the community (Tewksbury and Lees 2006); this includes neighbour harassment toward the family and threats and school problems for children of the offender (Levenson and Tewksbury 2009).

This vulnerability is enhanced by policies in the USA that have not been pursued in the UK, including community notification so that everyone can know where sex offenders reside (Logan 2009: 74–83; Levenson and Cotter 2005a, Thomas 2003). Residency restrictions are also imposed by many States to keep sex offenders at a given distance from schools and playgrounds (Levenson and Cotter 2005b) and making accommodation itself vulnerable for the offender and his or her family. Residency restrictions in Florida caused some notoriety a few years ago when offenders formed their own tent community under a highway overpass called the *Julia Tuttle Causeway* (Cave 2009). Residency restrictions are not practised in the UK, although UK prisons have in recent years been criticised for giving offenders leaving prison tents to live in because of the lack of available accommodation (BBC News 2016b).

Keri Burchfield of Northern Illinois University has linked the vulnerability of the ex-offender with the concept of social capital and the need for people to tie into community networks as well as having support from immediate friends and family. The convicted sex offender is beset by barriers and restrictions to his or her life – both formal and informal – that pose problems for him accessing the social capital that others take for granted:

> Honestly it turns my stomach if I really sit and think about it. It makes my stomach hurt, because as far as I'm concerned, I'd rather have been convicted of first-degree murder. And have society look and say 'Kill the Guy', than have society look and say 'He's a pedophile'.

and

> I'll have to go to the school and tell [my daughter's] principal, look I'm a sex offender. It's not so much how they gonna look at me – it's my kids, my grandkids. So I'm not worried about me, it's my family that I be concerned about … it's my family.
>
> (both quoted in Burchfield and Mingus 2008: 365)

The campaign group Human Rights Watch has produced a full and critical report on the position of children and young people who find themselves on the register in the USA (HRW 2013).

Life on the register in the UK

This section looks at the impact made by having convictions for sex offences against your name; these may be stand-alone convictions but most of them will carry the shadow of the sex offender register around the offender's shoulders. In here we have divided it into the impact on:

a the individual and his or her family activities
b employment activities

c other activities
d relationships with police offender managers.

The individual and his or her family activities

Being on the sex offender register can have a direct impact on a person's health. Thompson's statement in *Thompson and F* gives us an insight:

> Registration has had a huge impact on my health … caused in part by constant stress and worry … heart attacks caused by that stress … I am not able to be an active part of my community as I have to keep myself to myself … I am on permanent sick …
>
> (*R (F and Thompson) v Secretary of State for the Home Department [2008] EWHC 3170 (QB)*)

Isolation and a lack of friends was considered as one of the pervasive features of life as a convicted sex offender. Immediate family might withdraw contact depending on the circumstances of the offence. Research on people with convictions for sexual offences participating in Circles of Support and Accountability (COSA) has revealed how they feel about their lives post-conviction and sentence. COSA is a voluntary initiative that offers friendship and 'social capital' to people on the register to help build up their confidence and social skills (Hanvey et al. 2011). The following examples all come from Thompson and Thomas's research on Circles (2017):

> Well I didn't have any family to have any relationships with. Cos my family actually dumped me and told me to have no contact with them again. Even though a lot of the guys I was in prison for had done far worse and still were having their family in on visits and in touch, my family didn't want anything.
>
> (Christopher)

> Since he found out I was in jail and what it was for, he [son] called my brother and in so many words told my brother 'I never want to speak to him again' and er … I've never been in touch with anyone since. I've wrote to him three times but he doesn't want to know … I'm good at talking to people but writing letters they can just screw 'em up you know it just doesn't work … but [Probation Officer] says it takes time you know.
>
> (Matthew)

Social networks beyond the immediate family could also be adversely affected resulting in a withdrawal from the community where the person has lived all their lives and where they were well known; their criminal conviction giving them a negative label to be seen by all:

> A lot of the friends I had before I went into prison don't want to know me now.
>
> (Joe)

> I was just walking through town and somebody on the other side of the road was pointing at me and asking if it was me and one of them actually came over but they didn't do anything but I was ready if they wanted to.
>
> (Kyle)

> I was in a second-hand shop looking at video games and I was just merrily looking at DVDs and games and I hear somebody say quite clearly 'I am sure that's him'.
>
> (Pete)

The response was to literally keep your head down:

> It's like walking from one house to another it would be straight there, you know don't look around, just look at the pavement and ignore anything that might be happening.
>
> (Bill)

Wherever the person lived there was a common experience reported of withdrawal from the community and increasing personal isolation. Research interviewees put it in their own words:

> Nah I don't really have much friends, the only friends I've got are on this course I've just started on.
>
> (Jack)

> I mean at the start I'd just got my own place but I was literally spending pretty much seven days a week inside my flat staring at the TV or playing on my X-Box. You know I didn't have the confidence to meet other people or to go out and go into a situation where I hadn't been to before but they [Circles] have helped me.
>
> (James)

> And then it got to the point that I couldn't be arsed to do anything and I literally blank everyone and locked myself in my flat for two weeks. Only going out to get my dole money, sign on, get my shopping and blank every call even from my mum … On a night time I am bored shitless watching TV or playing [computer] games all the time.
>
> (Richard)

This lack of involvement and engagement in the community was driven by a number of other wider factors such as employment and accommodation.

Apart from being personally known in a small community the offence or offences had often been reported by the local newspapers and broadcast media, sometimes the national media:

> And everyone knows cos when I got sentenced it was in the paper, on the radio and everywhere, yes there wasn't any hiding it!
>
> (Bill)

> After you've done your offence you do go through that stage where you think that everyone is going to recognise you from the paper and … make judgements about you.
>
> (Gordon)

Offenders felt not only uncomfortable in their local communities but could also become fearful for their own personal safety:

> Afraid of walking down the street and someone having a go, verbally, physically – you know if Joe Public knew about me would they … you know you always have that fear of a vigilante lynch-mob wanting to put you on the nearest lamppost as a decoration for Christmas … that was a big part of the paranoia that I had after release.
>
> (Bill)

> I've got me own safety as well. My brother says my place is like Fort Knox, and I said yea too right! Like me back gate, it must have six bolts and locks and what not, and where the door is, I've heightened it so they can't climb over it, and I've got a steel door at the back of the door, plus the door, plus security deadlocks, plus I have got CCTV, plus I have this [shows home-help cord] which is for inside the home and it goes 24 hours a day and it calls if I need help, the ambulance, doctor, police … and with me having that around me neck I am safe.
>
> (Brian)

One option to manage hostile reactions in a locality was to move to a place where the offender was not known:

> I moved cos I was afraid that if it got in the paper then the town is so small that any hint of it would make me public enemy number one and bring out the lynch mob for the dirty bastard!
>
> (Phil)

> I come from a small town and everybody knows me but I come up here and people barely know me.
>
> (Norman)

Sometimes it was the family as a whole that had to move:

> Cos of my offence my family had to move. It was quite bad to be honest. So, I'm not allowed to be in [City] cos of my offence and because of my victims and also my safety. So, it was pretty much life-or-death. They were either gonna get me or my family so we've all had to move. But me and my parents were quite well known there and so they were gonna be targets that's why we had to move.
>
> (Anthony)

Case study 8.1

My client's parents are of the view that my client's self-esteem and confidence is very low. Although it is clear that he is desperate to make a fresh start, it is also clear that being subject to notification requirements makes him feel that this is almost impossible. He has complained that he feels as though people are watching him and talking about him all the time. The knowledge that this will never be subject to change or review, regardless of the risk he may pose is extremely distressing for my client. In particular, in October of last year, my client's consultant forensic clinical psychologist – who originally assessed him prior to sentence in July 2005 and who had continued to work with my client on release from custody – wrote to me confirming that my client was making significant progress in addressing the underlying issues behind his offending behaviour. However, regardless of the progress my client makes, at the moment there is no mechanism for this to be reflected in any change to the notification requirements para.41.

(*Thompson EWCA/Civ/2009/792*)

Case study 8.2

My partner Stephen is a convicted sex offender. I'm divorced and until I met him, neither I, nor anyone close to me, had ever met a person with a criminal record. Stephen and I met through an online dating agency. He was out of prison and on licence.

Little did I know that the consequences of getting involved with a sex offender are huge. The deceit you are forced into daily with everyone you meet, the decisions about who to tell and who not to tell, the horror of what those who you do tell subsequently discover on the internet, the change in your relationships with them, the difficult place you put them in when they, in turn, are forced to keep the secret, the ongoing terror of the truth eventually coming out ...

A few weeks after we'd started dating, Stephen's probation officer told him that she needed to inform the Multi-Agency Safeguarding Hub (MASH) about our relationship – apparently this was 'just a formality'. It took two months for the relevant paperwork to be processed and, when I was contacted by a woman from Social Services, it was whilst I was attending a lunch party with friends. She insisted that I repeat to her there and then on the phone the precise details of what Stephen had told me about his offence. Repeating the details aloud was a horrible experience not least because it came out of the blue.

Two days later after this telephone call I was contacted by Social Services again and told that they wanted to come along with a police officer to meet me – they gave me three hours' notice!

During this meeting Stephen was made to wait in the garden and the police officer who'd never met either of us before spent 4 hours carrying out a character assassination. Her opinion of Stephen appeared to be based only on what she'd read and, in my view, demonstrated a stereotypical judgement of all sex offenders. It included straight untruths, exaggeration and general inaccuracies.

At the end of the meeting, the police officer insisted on driving directly to my daughter's school to inform her of Stephen's convictions. I was refused any contact with her or her father and so couldn't be with her when she was spoken to. When the uniformed police officer and social worker arrived at the school, they disclosed details of Stephen's conviction in the presence of her housemistress and four other members of school staff. As my daughter had become aware of Stephen's background, I thought it was only right that I should tell my son and the children's father.

At this point, my daughter told the police officer that she didn't want Stephen to stay in our house anymore and this was added to one of Stephen's licence conditions. My son refused ever to meet him and the fragile relationship I'd built up over a decade with the children's father was destroyed. The trust and respect my two children had for me was devastated and their faith in my judgement trashed resulting in a total loss of all sense of security and stability.

I made a complaint to the police which took them four months to respond to. My complaint was not upheld and I was advised that the police officer had 'acted in good faith'.

Three months later and having got over the shock of the disclosure, my daughter told me that she had no problem with Stephen visiting our home when she wasn't there. My ex-husband and the children drew up a statement confirming this. However, the police and probation still continued to prevent him from visiting me and Social Services told me they could do nothing all the time the police and probation were denying him access.

This situation went on for 9 months and it was only when I began to threaten to expose the catalogue of mistakes made by all three agencies that they finally started to listen to me. A meeting was arranged with myself,

Stephen, police, probation and social services where it was acknowledged that mistakes had been made. We received an apology from social services and Stephen's licence conditions were immediately relaxed.

Discovering that the police and probation were so judgemental, negatively stereotyping their clients rather than treating them as unique individuals came as a real shock to me. If this is the attitude of professionals is it any wonder that employers and members of the public find it so difficult to give those with a sexual offence a chance.

(The Record 2019)

Employment activities

Many employment positions may be unavailable to people with a criminal record containing sexual offences. Employers do not have an automatic right to consult the sex offender register when recruiting and selecting staff but they may be entitled to a disclosure of a criminal record from the Disclosure and Barring Service (DBS). Employers are particularly entitled to disclosure of criminal records if the employment is going to involve work in positions with children or vulnerable adults. Any sexual offences disclosed would imply registration; recruitment decisions remain at the discretion of the employer (DBS 2020).

The recruitment and selection decisions are meant to be based on an assessment of the offence, the likelihood of reoffending and the requirements of the job; in practice they may be made for less worthy reasons, as some researchers have reported: 'Those committing offences such as rape and other sex offences, for example, are most unlikely to be recruited. This reflects the recruiter's anger about these sorts of crime rather than concerns about the risk of re-offending' (Fletcher et al. 2001: 23). Some employers are more tolerant – or less rigorous – and this has led to some offenders being employed whilst still on the sex offender register.

Journalists at the *Daily Mail* used the Freedom of Information Act to discover how many doctors on the register are still working as doctors. In 2007 there were an estimated 11 doctors in such positions all registered as competent to practice by the General Medical Council (GMC). Between 2002 and 2007 52 doctors were known to have been convicted for sexual offences, of which 38 were struck off, two were suspended and one voluntarily resigned from GMC registration (Martin 2007).

The GMC said decisions were made about doctors' competence to practice through their Medical Practitioners Tribunal Service while local employers such as the NHS decided on their employability; it was possible for a doctor to be employed in a laboratory position without contact with patients. Conservative MP David Davis was quoted as saying 'Yet again we see another massive loophole in the government's sex offender legislation' (ibid).

In 2012 another *Daily Mail* journalist found that 'at least 31 male GPs, consultants and surgeons were still practicing despite having assaulted women, been in possession of child pornography or solicited prostitutes':

> An investigation by the *Daily Mail* found that of 31 licensed doctors with convictions for sex offences, four have records of sexual assaults, four have been convicted of child pornography offences, two committed voyeurism or exposure offences and 21 solicited prostitutes or were caught kerb-crawling.
>
> (Bentley 2012)

Not all of these offences would have necessarily led to inclusion on the sex offender register but one doctor found guilty of sexually assaulting two colleagues at a hospital in Leicestershire, was given a suspended prison sentence and put on the register for seven years; he was not struck off and was reportedly free to work again within a year (ibid). The GMC has said that it inquired about an automatic ban on doctors who are on the sex offenders register but 'advice was obtained from a leading QC who concluded that an automatic bar, without exceptions, would not be compatible with human rights legislation' (ibid).

More recently a further use of Freedom of Information requests found 73 doctors convicted of sexual offences between the years 2013 to 2018 but only 60 of them struck off; the other 13 had been left free to practice (Gallagher 2018).

In January 2006 it came to light that another person on the sex offender register had been allowed to continue working in a school. The man in question had been cautioned by the police for viewing child pornography and was still working as a PE teacher at a school in Norwich. A hostile press rounded on Ruth Kelly the Education Secretary with questions as to how this might have happened. It might have happened because a risk assessment had been made and his continued employment agreed but such nuances are not acceptable to a hostile press:

> Ms Kelly told reporters she 'would not hesitate' to change the law regarding security checks. She was looking at immediate steps to ensure that everyone who was placed on the sex offenders' register was automatically barred from working in schools
>
> (Curtis and White 2006; see also *Hansard House of Commons Ministerial Statement 11 January 2006* and discussions *12 January 2006*)

Further probing revealed about another ten people on the register working in schools.

The person wishing to become an Approved Driving Instructor (ADI) may be blocked from registering as such, if they are 'not a fit and proper' person. This includes people with convictions for sexual offences (DVSA 2020: para.2.5) and people on the sex offender register (ibid: para.5.5).

Another consequence for a family could be that a family member, not involved with the alleged offending, might lose their employment. This could seem unduly harsh when the person in question had proved a perfectly good employee over many years and had demonstrated no behaviour to cause them to be dismissed. In effect this was a policy of 'disqualification by association'.

Disqualification by association was a policy first made manifest in the Childcare Act 2006 s75 (4) and Childcare (Disqualification) Regulations 2009 no.1547 where Regulation 9 stated that:

> Subject to regulation 10, a person who lives—
>
> a in the same household as another person who is disqualified from registration; or
> b in a household in which any such person is employed, is disqualified from registration.

Regulation 10 provided for a waiver if the person living in the same household had helped to identify the offender.

The campaign group UNLOCK for ex-offenders called the arrangements 'ridiculous':

> The regulations have clearly come as a surprise to thousands of people working in primary schools. Schools themselves seem unclear of how the regulations work, with many asking existing staff and new employees to make very broad declarations about not only their criminal record, but also of those that they live with. This has led to hundreds of people making declarations and being suspended as a result, where they have otherwise been working for many years with no problems
>
> (UNLOCK 2015)

Concerns were raised with the Department for Education (DfE) about the fairness and proportionality of the arrangements on childcare workers in schools and other non-domestic registered settings, in relation to the arrangement's for 'disqualification by association'. The DfE launched a consultation exercise (DfE 2016) and received overwhelming criticism of the policy that made them withdraw it at the end of August 2018 (DfE 2018a and 2018b)

Case study 8.3

Left prison in 2016 after 4 years. Nearly immediately struck lucky with an agency who were so keen to get me into a position that they even told me not to worry about finishing the application form. Two years later, fed up with being exploited on minimum wage in a 'senior' titled role, I interviewed for a higher paid role with an international company who don't ask about criminal convictions.

I got the job, and after 4 weeks I was dismissed as one of my colleagues pointed out to management that I had previously been in the newspaper. Never dismissed from any job for poor performance, but now can say I've been dismissed for a question they didn't ask at interview. I have now been unemployed for the last 4 months, in a house I now can't afford, with all the usual harassment from council tax and universal credit forcing me to apply for hundreds of jobs I'm not suitable for and don't hear back from, even before getting to the bit where I tell them I have unspent sexual convictions.

Really starting to think that this society has no place for me, that there is no hope; quite dangerous when I feel there is little left to lose.

(Inside Time 2017)

Other activities

Political posts may also be debarred to people with criminal records. The most clear cut of these is the criteria for becoming a Police and Crime Commissioner where the law states unequivocally that a person 'convicted in the United Kingdom, the Channel Islands, or the Isle of Man, of any imprisonable offence (whether or not sentenced to a term of imprisonment in respect of the offence)' is not allowed to stand (Police Reform and Social Responsibility Act 2011 s66 (3)(c)). There is no discretion to be exercised and no decisions to be made.

At the time of writing (August 2020) plans are in process to exclude anyone from a position of being a local councillor or an elected mayor if they are on the sex offender register or were subject to a Sexual Risk Order. A consultation exercise was carried out in 2017 to sound out opinions on this (Department for Communities and Local Government 2017: 11–12). Some 83% of respondents thought exclusion was a necessary step for people on the register, but opinion was more divided on the subject of the SRO; a person can be made subject to an SRO without having committed an offence and without being on the register. Responses to the SRO proposal were 39% in favour of a ban and 45% against a ban (Ministry of Housing, Communities and Local Government 2018: 7–9). Despite these figures and the fact that exclusion could be potentially harmful to the democratic process to disqualify people from standing for election, or holding office, who had not committed any crime, the government decided a ban was more appropriate:

> Having considered the responses received, the Government believes that where an individual is subject to a Sexual Risk Order, they should be prohibited from standing for election, as a member of a local authority, mayor of a combined authority, member of the London Assembly or London Mayor.
> (ibid: 9)

Presumably some sort of administrative arrangement would be needed to verify these new criteria. Meanwhile new laws were still awaited, when a suitable legislative opportunity arose (*Hansard House of Commons Debates 6 March 2019 PQ 227382*).

Charities now automatically disqualify anyone on the sex offender register from charity trusteeship and senior management positions in a charity. This followed changes to the law made in 2016 through the Charities (Protection and Social Investment) Act 2016. When first published as a Bill there were no such conditions attached; they were added later as an amendment in the House of Lords where it was argued that:

> Our policy rationale is that [registered sex offenders] are unfit to be in a position of trust, controlling funds held and activities carried out for the public benefit, and should be disqualified from being a charity trustee or being in a senior management role within a charity unless and until they are no longer subject to notification requirements or are granted a waiver from the disqualification by the Charity Commission; for instance, the commission might consider it appropriate to grant a waiver to enable someone to take up a position in a charity that works with ex-offenders.
>
> (*Hansard House of Lords Debates 20 July 2015 cols.925–6*)

The 2016 Act amended the Charities Act 2011 to read:

> A person ('P') is disqualified from being a charity trustee or trustee for a charity in the following cases—
>
> *Case K* – P is subject to the notification requirements of Part 2 of the Sexual Offences Act 2003 (2011 Act s178 (1)).

In the field of social media Facebook does not allow convicted sex offenders to use its internet services. Their 'Terms of Services' explicitly exclude convicted sex offenders although no mention is made of those who have been cautioned or are on the register:

> We try to make Facebook broadly available to everyone, but you cannot use Facebook if:
>
> - You are under 13 years old.
> - You are a convicted sex offender.
> - We've previously disabled your account for breaches of our Terms or Policies.
> - You are prohibited from receiving our products, services, or software under applicable laws.(Facebook 2020)

How exactly Facebook police such breaches of their 'Terms of Services' is not clear. Some police officers acting as offender managers have taken it upon themselves to point this out to people on the register should they find out about it but there appears to have been no direct communication between the police and Facebook on the matter.

The matter of convicted sex offenders who are subject to civil orders made under the Sexual Offences Act 2003 do allow some leeway in the use of the internet as a whole. Early attempts to ban people subject to civil orders from complete access to the internet were overturned in 2011 when the Court of Appeal made it clear that a total ban on internet use would always be disproportionate. It considered four cases in which the terms of the Sexual Offences Prevention Order (SOPO) were challenged by the Appellants, none of whom had been charged with offences involving physical sexual contact (*R v Smith & Others [2011] EWCA Crim 1772*).

Home insurance may cost more for someone with any criminal record let alone a sexual offence. Companies have to depend on the honest declaration of the person wishing to purchase insurance because they have no direct way of verifying a declaration. The problem will, however, arise later if the declaration is dishonest and thereby possibly making any claim void and making it harder to get insurance in the future. Convictions considered 'spent' under the Rehabilitation of Offenders Act 1974 do not have to be declared.

Relationships between offenders and offender managers

The main way of knowing that a person on the register is on the register is through the relationships with the police as offender managers. The requirement to notify to a prescribed police station and to allow offender managers into the home is in the name of public protection. These are low visibility activities carried out by the police and the person on the register away from the activities that take place in more visible public domains. Such low visibility activities may raise questions of professionalism and accountability.

Some people on the register complain that the offender manager police officer making home visits has little idea what to talk about. In the absence of a clear thread to pick up on some offender managers revert to talking about the details of the original offence which could have taken place 20 years ago but it becomes the only thread that some offender managers seem to be able to start from.

Case study 8.4

We do not have to stand in the dock this time as the SOR [sex offender register] is a fixed penalty under which you live and die. There is no need to wait for a hearing or for verdicts. I signed the SOR at the police station 24 hours after my release from prison on [...]. Since that day I have no feeling of being a free man in this green and pleasant land. The impact of the SOR creates a dark place where I have to stand in all weathers and at times on the slippery edge of a dark and filthy pond with a weighted belt (compulsory dress) ready at the bell to take the plunge.

In general terms it would be useful to have been given more written information about the register and the consequences of being on it. When visiting police stations to notify details and changes it would be nice to have some privacy. Making declarations of personal business to police officers in waiting areas often full of people waiting to be seen is not a pleasant experience. Often, we are not met by our offender managers but by civilian officers who do not know us. They ask in loud voices the purpose of the visit and everyone else in reception overhears. However personable the officer in attendance, one is always aware of being criminalised and judged negatively – being addressed by your first name is demeaning.

When we moved home it entailed a new police force taking over; we were told the new force would contact us. They didn't and we got blamed for not reporting. A woman police officer reminded us by a barrage of shouting that we were at fault – not the police.

On home visits by police offender managers – in my experience – they just continue in the role of 'investigating officer'. The OM we now have tells us he has a duty of care towards me but seems incapable of showing any empathy. He never has anything to discuss and shows little interest in us as people so he writes notes on my health. The only time he smiled throughout a home visit was when he told us the police had intelligence that vigilantes were going to mount a protest outside our home. They didn't.

Home visits are definitely aimed at both my wife and I. In our experience the requirements punish not only the person concerned but the whole family. We both keep diaries of our every movement so that we can answer any questions.

Any attempt to obtain house insurance makes it clear that cover is not provided for those with unspent convictions. Why is this? Is a person subject to notification requirements automatically unfit to have house insurance? Is the family also unfit? Why? What has the SOR got to do with house insurance? Are people subject to requirements expected to have a house? A tent?

We feel we are suspects for life. Does it improve levels of 'public protection'? No – because the same brush is applied to all despite assessments of risk. The SOR is simply a list of people set apart from society by a label. How do offenders rehabilitate into a society which places them on a list?

Testimony of a man currently on the register (personal communication July 2020)

Summary

In general terms we might see a particular punishment, whether custodial or in the community, as lasting for a given length of time. At the end of that time the punishment comes to an end and the offender is theoretically enabled to re-join the community he was marked out from on an equal footing with everyone else. In fact, we know that not to be the case because the criminal records or the existence of the sex offender register continue to 'label' those people and thereby constantly blocking any real hope of an equal footing with everyone else. The impact of registration also falls on other family members, on employment opportunities and various positions of public office.

9 The management of information held on the register

Introduction

One of the debates on the original Sex Offenders Bill was about what the police would actually do with all the information they were going to be able to collate on registered sex offenders. As we eventually found out the information was going to be used largely by the police to help them make risk assessments that in turn would assist their offender management work. In the meantime, what would be the rules on sharing this information with other agencies such as the probation service, Social Services/Children's Departments or health care professionals?

Or could this information even be disclosed to members of the public? The frequently heard question from the public has always been 'why can't we know when a sex offender moves into our street?' It seems such a simple request and one that would be relatively easy to meet. The model from the USA of blanket community notification – or Megan's Law – whereby any member of the public could find out where any sex offender lived was held out as the universal model. The UK instead opted for the more cautious selective model whereby information would only be disclosed on certain offenders and to certain recipients.

This chapter looks at the movement of sex offender register information between agencies and its disclosure from agencies to the general public.

Exchanging information between agencies

Prior to any computerisation personal information exchange between the police and other agencies was a pedestrian matter of paper files, card indexes and telephone calls. Police information was also considered very confidential. As one Home Secretary had put it, 'The supply of police information will continue to be governed by the general principle that no information is given to anyone, however responsible, unless there are weighty considerations of public interest which justify departure from the general rule' (*Hansard House of Commons Debates 14 June 1973 col. 1681*).

The pressure for more multi-agency work and exchange of information came from child abuse and child protection work. As early as 1976 a Home Office circular had advised the police on their role in multi-agency child abuse conferences alongside social workers, health visitors and others; they were to input 'any relevant previous convictions' and any 'other relevant information' to these conferences (Home Office 1976: paras.8–9 and 15).

The 1991 *Working Together* guide further outlined the position:

> In investigating an allegation of child abuse the police will normally collect a considerable amount of information. Irrespective of their decision whether or not to institute criminal proceedings, the information they hold may be highly relevant to a decision about a child who may need protection from abuse, and should, where appropriate, be shared with other agencies
>
> (Home Office et al. 1991: para.4.14)

The Home Office circular on setting up the register gave advice on the exchange of personal information in the interests of child protection (Home Office 1997d: Appendix A paras.16, 19 and 26). This advice was in turn criticised by the National Association of Head Teachers for being vague on how they were able to use such information the police gave them, especially when it also implied that the information, they were given had to be kept confidential. Tony Butler the ACPO lead on the register counter-argued that 'Disclosure of information to head teachers must be part of an overall risk management strategy. But I can't say they won't be stuck with moral dilemmas because I face them every day. That is the reality of this area' (quoted in Steele 1997).

The Crime and Disorder Act 1998 s115 had given a 'power' to any agency to exchange information with another if it was compatible with the aims of that Act i.e. the prevention of crime and the investigation of crime. In the past, some agencies had worked in an insular fashion or 'in silos' as the expression of the times was. Local offices had also started to use a variety of local computerised systems with information that could not easily be shared by partner agencies. This made it difficult to risk assess and keep track of offenders as they moved across police and probation service boundaries.

The Criminal Justice and Court Services Act 2000 s67 required the police and probation service to become the two 'responsible authorities' for creating a 'working together' framework which, as we have seen, became known as the Multi-Agency Public Protection Arrangements (MAPPA) specifically working with sex offenders and the register. Exchanging information was central to their joint activities; the prison service later became the third 'responsible authority' alongside the police and probation service (Criminal Justice Act 2003 s325(1))

More guidance to the police on how to manage their information came in the form of the statutory *Code of Practice on the Management of Police*

Information (Home Office 2005c) and its accompanying *Guidance* (ACPO 2006; this was updated in 2010 and is now to be found on the College of Policing (2020a) website). The police were, also, bound by the Data Protection Acts of 1984, 1998 and 2018.

Following the revelations of the Rotherham child sexual exploitation scandal (Jay Report 2014) further attempts were made to ensure professionals exchanged information between agencies in an appropriate way (see e.g. Home Office 2014, HMG 2015; the latter was updated in HMG 2018a). Five Secretaries of State wrote a joint letter to all local authorities, Police and Crime Commissioners, Local Safeguarding Children's Boards, Health and Wellbeing Boards and GPs setting out when personal information should be shared and the interests of the child put first, and for the recipients to be 'dealing robustly with staff who block, hinder or fail to share' (DoH et al. 2015: 2).

It is worth noting the 2018 version of this same document and its comparable comments:

> The police will hold important information about children who may be suffering, or likely to suffer, significant harm, as well as those who cause such harm. They should always share this information with other organisations and agencies where this is necessary to protect children. Similarly, they can expect other organisations and agencies to share information to enable the police to carry out their duties. All police forces should have officers trained in child abuse investigation.
>
> (HMG 2018b: 63 para.27)

Exchanging information between criminal justice agencies using electronic links remained slow. Only the police had their Police National Computer from 1974 with criminal records added to it in 1995.

The various Inspectorates of criminal justice services collectively produced a report on the needs of each agency entitled *Casework Information Needs within the Criminal Justice System* (CPSI et al. 2000). The MAPPA arrangements now became the focus of attention for an IT system to join the 'responsible authority' participants – the police and probation – together. The result was to be the joint database known as ViSOR.

ViSOR

The 2002 White Paper on *Protecting the Public* made one of the earliest public references to ViSOR and outlined the way forward:

> We are currently funding the development of a new database, which will give the police and probation services better access to the full range of information held on dangerous offenders nationally, including all sex offenders on the register. The database will include a wide range of information on the offender in addition to the details required for

> registration and this will enable targeted searches (by, for instance, age or occupation) to be made on offenders. We intend to pilot the new database, which will be known as ViSOR (violent and sex offender register), early next year with full implementation by the end of 2003.
>
> (Home Office 2002a: para.18)

Full implementation by 'the end of 2003' proved a bit optimistic and criticisms were made on its slow progress: 'We are concerned that this key recommendation – of high importance to public protection management – will not be in place until at best four years after the recommendation' (HMIP 2003: para.12). ViSOR was formally unveiled to the public in 2005 (Home Office 2005d).

Attempts to link up different parts of the criminal justice system electronically can be traced back to the mid-1980s (Home Office 1986). In 1989 a joint initiative between the Home Office, the then Lord Chancellors Department and the Crown Prosecution Service held the initial meeting of a Steering Committee on the Coordination of Computerisation of the Criminal Justice System (CCCJS). In 1994 a NSPIS (National Strategy for Police Information Systems) project was established to standardise the 43 police forces onto a compatible IT infrastructure. After slow progress throughout the 1990s the CCCJS was rebranded as the Integrating Business and Information Systems (IBIS) (Waugh 1991; Thomas 2007: 76–80). The ViSOR computer was more focussed, and more readily lent itself to joining up the three responsible authorities, for the exchange of information.

ViSOR was originally an acronym for the 'Violent and Sexual Offender Register' which was where the small 'i' in ViSOR came from. Today, ViSOR is no longer an acronym, but is now the formal name of the database. This was because ViSOR now included people like non-registered sex offenders, Violent Offenders, Dangerous Offenders, Registerable Terrorist Offenders, Registerable Violent Offenders and Potentially Dangerous Persons. The College of Policing gives ViSOR the sub-title the 'Dangerous Persons Database' in recognition of this widening.

The project manager in the early days of the ViSOR team, Chief Inspector John Massey, was optimistic that using a secure electronic link, offender management would be greatly facilitated and ViSOR would also assist new crime investigation:

> Not only will ViSOR significantly improve the way both agencies monitor these offenders, it will be an important aid to investigating offences when they occur. The system offers an investigative capability and will be linked to the Police National Computer, allowing officers to check on any previous convictions.
>
> (quoted in Edwards 2003)

ViSOR started within the police service in 2005 (Travis 2005) and was extended into the Probation Service and Prison Service from 2006 onwards; the

Prison Service was added in as a 'responsible authority' by the Criminal Justice Act 2003 s325(1). The NOMS National Implementation Project was to oversee the implementation of ViSOR into all probation areas and prisons (both public and private) throughout England and Wales. Work had already started on the Scottish Prison Service. The Probation Service for England and Wales started with a period of testing out different models across the country. These so-called 'Early Adopter' sites were evaluated for March 2007 (see also *Hansard House of Commons Debates 14 November 2007 col.299W*).

By 2009 ViSOR was joined up and the 'few' agencies became more, and more, as ViSOR became available to:

- 43 Police Forces in England and Wales;
- 42 Probation Areas/Trusts in England and Wales (now all in the National Probation Service);
- All private and public sector prisons in England and Wales;
- 8 Scottish Police forces (now joined up as one);
- Scottish Criminal Justice Social Work organisations;
- Scottish Prison Service;
- Police Service of Northern Ireland;
- Serious Crime Analysis Section (SCAS) (part of the National Crime Agency);
- Child Exploitation and Online Protection (CEOP) Centre;
- Joint Border Operations Centre (JBOC);
- HM Forces Service Police Crime Bureau; and
- British Transport Police (BTP).(NOMS 2009: para.2.5)

The NOMS *Public Protection Manual* of 2016 reported that plans were in hand for ViSOR to also be made available to the Republic of Ireland police, (the Garda Siochanna), the Gibraltar Police and the Channel Island of Jersey police (NOMS 2016: 33). In Northern Ireland an Inspectorate Report was concerned that the area was getting ViSOR but only the police were using it and not the other criminal justice agencies, and that this had apparently been going on for many years. Various reasons were put forward to explain why this was, including resources for implementation and a risk of compromised confidentiality, but the Inspectorate thought 'the reasons for non-usage should be easily offset by a shared database that for example ViSOR could potentially provide, or be part of' (CJINI 2019: paras.3.18–3.20)

The collection of information on ViSOR is classified under the Government Protective Marking scheme as Official (Sensitive) and National ViSOR Standards of operating have been drawn up. The Standards are not publicly available. Police staff using ViSOR are subject to specific vetting to ensure standards of confidentiality; additional vetting was introduced after those on the register were required to input details of their banking arrangements (see Chapter Seven). Separate Guidance was produced for the prison and probation service (PSI 40/2014 and PI 56/2014).

The information on ViSOR is based around a 'nominal' or named record with a front-page summary screen of information. Other information is added including photographs. More details on how ViSOR should be used are available in the MAPPA Guidance version 4.5 2012; section 8 explains how the ViSOR database operates and supports MAPPA (NOMS 2012; updated in 2019).

Police views of ViSOR

Some research has been carried out on police attitudes to working with ViSOR. Many police officers had felt it useful but that it was predominantly a police-led tool with use by probation and prison services sporadic at best. They did think that inter-agency information sharing was improving thanks to its use (O'Sullivan et al. 2016).

Police attitudes toward ViSOR have otherwise varied. Some have described it as a useful record of everything carried out with the sex offender:

> It records absolutely everything that we do. It contains all of their information … Absolutely everything that comes out of their mouths is on there. (Participant 01)
>
> essential, absolutely essential. Until they build a new database, that is what we use … it's how you organise your workloads. (Participant 14)
>
> (McCartan et al. 2018)

But some police officers in the same study found:

> it is very, very slow, and very lumpy and you get thrown out all the time, and that causes a lot of problems. (Participant 26)

and other officers even saw it as a form of managerial control:

> Its primary purpose I would say is to document and make us accountable for how we manage sex offenders. (Participant 21)

What the police did like was the ability to store so much information on ViSOR, as long as they kept it updated with the latest information and intelligence from each contact:

> Its strengths for me are around sharing information across police area boundaries; that's the main issue you know we get a lot of offenders that come in and out of the area, and it simplifies it massively if you can just look at a ViSOR record and you know exactly what they have been up to. (Participant 11)

Others were less impressed:

> ViSOR is only as good as what you put into it. (Participant 06)
>
> They all do it [ViSOR] completely differently. When you get a transfer in from another force it's like it's come from an alien planet: it's just completely different. (Participant 05)
>
> (McCartan et al. 2018)

Inspection reports

Three inspectorate reports by Criminal Justice Joint Inspection teams in 2010 (CJJI 2010), 2011 (CJJI 2011) and 2015 (CJJI 20151) remained critical of the way ViSOR was being used. The reports found that ViSOR was still being mainly used by the police with the probation service and prison service only slowly catching up. The result was that it was hardly a shared working tool. It was, for example, possible to find different risk management plans on the same person:

> The potential for confusion was compounded by the possible existence of up to three risk management plans on each offender, one drawn up by the police on ViSOR, one by probation and one as part of the MAPPA. The need for these plans, where they co-existed, to be coordinated and aligned, was paramount. We found that the plans recorded on ViSOR tended to relate solely to police activity and it was difficult to establish whether the police knew if the offender was under supervision and, if so, the nature of probation's involvement.
>
> (CJJI 2010: 6)

The second report summed up their thoughts:

> we were disappointed in what we found in 2011. Police, prisons and probation staff did not use ViSOR as a shared working tool. Where they did use ViSOR, the quality of the information provided was rarely of a high standard. Our findings four years later are not very different.
>
> (CJJI 2015: 7)

A report on ViSOR in Scotland also found the police used it well but 'there were serious problems in the way other agencies accessed it' (Social Work Inspection Agency et al. 2009: para.4.26). Criminal justice social work practitioners, in particular, had not used ViSOR effectively to facilitate information exchange:

> Though ViSOR had the potential to enhance the recording and sharing of relevant information, the problems with its implementation across agency boundaries were so serious that, in some places, they had effectively rendered the system unusable as a collective tool for sharing information and managing risk. We considered that this problematic situation required urgent attention.
>
> (ibid: para.4.28)

Disclosing information to the public

Disclosing information to the public is a different activity to exchanging information with other agencies. Here we consider two forms of disclosure as being the universal model as used in the USA and the selective model as used in the UK.

Community notification

The universal model of information disclosure is known as community notification in the USA. Sometimes it has been referred to as 'Megan's Law' in memory of Megan Kanka, a seven-year-old from New Jersey who was sexually assaulted and murdered by a man living in the same street as her and known to the authorities. Her parents campaigned for open sex offender registers and federal law decreed that each of the 50 States should comply in their own way from 1996.

At the time of the creation of the UK register back in 1997 it was quite apparent that there was a public demand for information on sex offenders. Whether this was for child protection purposes or just prurient interest was not certain. In New Zealand a woman journalist had collated a list of known sex offenders from court reports and other public sources and published it as a book. She then did the same for Australia and hinted that she was going to produce one for the UK (Milliken and Cooper 1997); for reasons unknown the UK version never appeared.

The UK Data Protection Registrar – the forerunner of today's Information Commissioner – voiced her concern describing lists of this nature as 'look-up' services. These were services developed 'by routinely scanning newspapers to extract information' and then collating it; the danger, as far as the Registrar was concerned, was the creation of a 'register of criminal convictions outside the controls that apply to the official record' (ODPR 1998). Similar unofficial 'look-up' services online still exist today (see e.g. UK and Ireland Database 2020).

During the earliest parliamentary debates on the Sex Offenders Bill the subject of just what the police were going to be doing with the information they held on the register had been raised. In particular who were they going to share this information with, and if it was going to be shared with other professionals, then why not with local residents living near the person on the register:

> I believe that [the] register should be made publicly available because parents have a right to know when a convicted paedophile moves into their area. The rights of children – the most vulnerable group in our society – must come before those of convicted criminals.
>
> (Julian Brazier MP at *Hansard House of Commons Debates 27 January 1997 col.58*)

This information would only be on the convicted and known offenders and not on suspects. There was no elaboration on how parents should be using this information once they were in receipt of it. The counter argument was that perhaps they should be seeking to safeguard their children with or without this additional information. Even before the 1997 Sex Offenders Act had appeared ACPO had completed a survey of all police forces in England and Wales to examine current practices in the disclosure of information on sex offenders and the issues that it raised. In all, 36 police forces responded (ACPO 1997a).

As the 1997 Bill went through its parliamentary stages, outside of Westminster there were rumours that the Home Secretary Michael Howard was going to amend the Bill to allow for community notification (Travis 1997). The police, in particular, had voiced their concerns that this should *not* be allowed to happen; arguably the police had a better idea than the politicians, of the sort of public disorder that might ensue and that they would have to deal with (Ford 1997). In the end no such amendment was made and Howard later admitted that he would not have allowed the register to be open to the public:

> I was not in favour of Megan's Law. I took the view that if information on a child sex offender was going to be made public, the temptation for him to evade the law and not register would be that much greater … publishing such information would be tantamount to inviting vigilante activity.
>
> (Silverman and Wilson 2002: 162)

Within a few years Mr Huw Edwards MP for Monmouth again asked the perennial question in Parliament:

> To ask the Secretary of State for the Home Department what plans he has to introduce public notification of sex offenders being released into the community.

and had received the standard answer from the Home Office:

> We have no plans to introduce measures which would require the police automatically to inform the public of the identities and addresses of sex offenders. We do not believe that this would enhance our ability to protect children. The police already have powers to inform any individual or organisation about the presence of a dangerous person in the vicinity, if they believe it would be in the interests of the public to do so.
>
> (*Hansard House of Commons Debates 6 March 2001 cols. 129–30W*)

The argument remained that there would be less overall compliance with the notification requirements and offenders would go 'underground' and be harder to police rather than easier.

At present there is no right for any member of the public to have automatic access to the register and thereby know who might be living close to them who has convictions or cautions for sexual offences. In the USA there is such a right to look at the sex offender register through their policy of community notification (Thomas 2003; Fitch 2006).

The policies of the USA to have open access to the register have not found favour in the UK, which has resisted the idea, but it does have its own variations on just how register information should be disclosed in certain circumstances.

The 'For Sarah' campaign

The 'For Sarah' campaign, which we first came across in Chapter Four, demonstrated the limitations of open access to police files on sex offenders. The *News of the World*'s campaign started on 23 July 2000 during the police hunt for the whereabouts of eight-year-old Sarah Payne.

As we noted earlier the disruption caused for the police and probation by the 'For Sarah' campaign was considerable. There was a general feeling of relief when it stopped. The Home Office decided against any blanket community notification (Silverman and Wilson 2002: chapter 8).

Sarah Payne's parents had met with Home Secretary Jack Straw on 18 December 2001 to discuss a 'Sarah's Law' comparable to 'Megan's Law' involving community notification. At that time Straw claimed that the government had 'already implemented 7/8ths of the "Sarah's Law" campaign' requests by tightening the register with increased sanctions for non-compliance, increasing post-prison supervision and by introducing Sex Offender Orders. He had also announced the idea for what would later become the lay advisers to give a voice to local areas as part of the Multi-Agency Public Protection Arrangements (Home Office 2001a; see Chapter Five).

The four ways information on sex offenders can be selectively disclosed in the UK today are as:

- duties at common law
- general obligations under MAPPA
- specific obligations under the Criminal Justice Act 2003 s327A
- through the Child Sex Offender Disclosure scheme (CSOD).

Duties at common law

The Home Office circular 'Sex Offenders Act 1997' which had advised on the wider aspects of implementing the Act had contained a separate Appendix A entitled *Managing Information acquired under the provisions of the Sex Offenders Act 1997*. Appendix A emphasised the point that information was to be actively shared with other agencies and used to make risk assessments and management plans on those required to register: 'Ministers have made it very clear that the [register] information must not merely be recorded or filed: it is essential that risk assessment should be undertaken by the police working with other child protection agencies' (Home Office 1997d: Appendix A para.1). Appendix A was described as 'interim guidance' that fell within the parameters of the law on information disclosure and the rulings of the courts.

As for information being disclosed to members of the general public, this was seen as being 'very much the exception to the rule and will remain a matter for the professional judgement of the police' (ibid: para.15); local forces were asked to ensure that they had 'a recognised framework for securing rapid advice within the force to inform disclosure decisions' (ibid: para.34).

This 'interim guidance' was followed up two years later by a further *Draft Guidance on the Disclosure of Information about Sex Offenders.* This guidance elaborated on the 1997 version and looked at the law and relevant case law in more detail. It also examined the responsibilities of the various agencies and matters of good practice (Home Office 1999b). This draft guidance was never followed up by an agreed final version.

General obligations under MAPPA

There may be times when information held on a registered sex offender is disclosed to a third party outside the MAPPA agencies. This could be a disclosure to someone who lives with the offender and who may be equally at risk, or caring for a child who may be at risk. It could also be to an employer, voluntary group organiser or church leader or someone who has a position of responsibility over the offender and other persons who may be at serious risk from the offender.

Guidance to the MAPPA responsible authorities had stated that this is a discretionary obligation to be based on professional judgement. In other words, the information 'may' be disclosed rather than 'must' be disclosed; 'must' would have made it a mandatory duty (Home Office/NPS 2003: para.93ff).

Such disclosures were to be made in a 'selective' or 'controlled' way and the following criteria should be met before disclosing information about an offender to a third party:

i the offender presents a risk of serious harm to the person, or to those for whom the recipient of the information has responsibility (children, for example);

ii there is no other practicable, less intrusive means of protecting the individual (s), and failure to disclose would put them in danger. Also, only that information which is necessary to prevent the harm may be disclosed, which will rarely be all the information available;

iii the risk to the offender should be considered although it should not outweigh the potential risk to others were disclosure not to be made. The offender retains his rights (most importantly his [ECHR] Article 2 right to life) and consideration must be given to whether those rights are endangered as a consequence of the disclosure. It is partly in respect of such consideration that widespread disclosure of the identify and whereabouts of an offender is very, very rarely if ever justified;

iv the disclosure is to the right person and that they understand the confidential and sensitive nature of the information they have received. The right person will be the person who needs to know in order to avoid or prevent the risks;

v consider consulting the offender about the proposed disclosure. This should be done in all cases unless to do so would not be safe or appropriate. Where consultation can be done, it can help strengthen the risk management plan. If it is possible and appropriate to obtain the offender's consent then a number of potential objections to the disclosure are overcome. Equally, the offender may wish to leave the placement rather than have any disclosure made, and if this is appropriate, this would also avoid the need for any disclosure;

vi ensure that whoever has been given the information knows what to do with it. Again, where this is a specific person, this may be less problematic but in the case of an employer, for example, you may need to provide advice and support; and

vii before actually disclosing the information, particularly to an employer or someone in a similar position, first ask them whether they have any information about the offender. If they have the information then no disclosure is necessary. If they have some but possibly incorrect information your disclosure can helpfully correct it.(ibid: para.95)

Disclosures of this nature were considered to require more sensitivity and to be more exceptional than the exchanges of information with MAPPA agencies (ibid: para.94). Subsequent editions of this Guidance elaborated on how this disclosure work should take place (MoJ et al. 2007: section 4.2).

In 2007 the Home Office published research into how the police were managing these discretionary disclosures in practice. The research took place over a limited time period between January and June 2006 and therefore represented a snapshot survey of practice, rather than a definitive assessment of the extent of disclosure. It looked at the circumstances in which disclosure had taken place, what information had been disclosed, who received it and the consequences of disclosure (Cann 2007).

The most common reason for disclosure were following changes in an offender's circumstances and/or more offence related behaviour, and this disclosure was usually done by police officers as offender managers. Offenders were given the opportunity to make the disclosure themselves, if it was safe to do so. The most common type of disclosure was of information about the offence an individual had been convicted for, or about the correction of something that may have been misunderstood. An offender's photograph might be distributed to enable a head teacher or staff working in leisure facilities to ensure an individual was not loitering or visiting premises unchecked. Information was mostly disclosed to school and college staff and child protection officers. For individual members of the public new spouses or partners were common recipients of a disclosure, both those with children and those without.

Overall, there were positive consequences in terms of improved child protection. Risky situations were more controlled and following a disclosure third parties were more inclined to report further incidents to the police which previously they may have overlooked or not recognised as significant. Some areas did report negative consequences of disclosure, such as destabilising a family or employment. In the long run this could lead to reoffending; one partner had felt 'deceived' as the offender had not disclosed information earlier. Some problems had occurred when disclosure had led to the information becoming public knowledge.

The research recommended the formal Guidance be revised, and re-written to include advice on undertaking disclosure through child protection procedures. Better recording of disclosures was also recommended. This was included into the third version of the MAPPA Guidance (NOMS 2009: section 6).

Specific obligations under Criminal Justice Act 2003 s327A-B

In June 2006, the Home Secretary had commissioned a comprehensive review of the arrangements for protecting children from sex offenders. The resulting *Review of the Protection of Children from Sex Offenders* identified three parties that need to be addressed in order to achieve greater child protection. First the public who work with and care for children and need to be vigilant to protect children. Secondly the offenders themselves who need to understand their behaviour and accept the legal controls over their future behaviour where necessary and finally the authorities charged with the management of known offenders through ensuring the provision of effective monitoring (Home Office 2007a).

As we saw in Chapter Six the review came up with 20 recommendations, or Actions as they were known. Two of them had particular significance for the disclosure of information from the sex offender register:

> ACTION 3 Introduce a legal duty for MAPPA authorities to consider the disclosure of information about convicted child sex offenders to members of the public in all cases. *The presumption will be that the authorities will disclose information* if they consider that an offender presents a risk of serious harm to a member of the public's children.

> ACTION 4 Pilot a process where members of the public can register their child protection interest in a named individual. Where this individual has convictions for child sex offences and is considered a risk, *there will be a presumption that this information will be disclosed* to the relevant member of the public.
>
> (ibid: Annex 3, emphasis added)

The use of the word 'presumption' made these disclosures stronger than the general obligations discussed above. Action 3 placed a duty on the MAPPA 'responsible authority' to consider disclosing specific information on child sex offenders and Action 4 enabled a member of the public to request information; Action 4 became 'Sarah's Law' (see below).

Action 3 required a change to the law to build upon the existing discretionary general powers and obligations under MAPPA held by the police. The result was the new s140 and Schedule 24 of the Criminal Justice and Immigration Act 2008 which in turn created the new s327A, and B and Schedule 34A of the Criminal Justice Act 2003. In future there was to be a presumption that convictions will be disclosed to members of the public, if a child is at risk of suffering harm through the offender's committing another child sex offence, and the disclosure is necessary to protect the child. Nobody needs to have requested this disclosure (2003 Act s327A (2)–(4)).

The Home Office has described these disclosures as being a two-way process:

> The police will continue to proactively disclose information where appropriate and members of the public will [in turn] share information with them … This model would offer the advantage of bringing to light intelligence about risk that would not otherwise have been available to the authorities.
>
> (Home Office 2007a: 11)

The implication is that anyone in a close relationship – personal or professional – with the registered sex offender could become a source of future intelligence to the police.

There has always been a fear that information about a registered sex offender disclosed in confidence to a member of the public might be passed on to others. To prevent a disclosure going more widely into the community, the responsible authority was further advised that it 'may impose conditions for preventing the member of the public concerned from disclosing the information to any other person' (Criminal Justice Act s327A(5)(b)).

Disclosure leaflets were produced for the police to give out to recipients of information. The leaflets explain what use can and cannot be made of the information and should be signed by the person to whom the disclosure is made, to verify they understand their confidentiality obligations (NOMS 2009: para.6.6). Elsewhere the Home Office had said that anyone 'misusing information disclosed, for example by engaging in vigilantism or the harassment of sex offenders, would be subject to police action' (Home Office 2007a:11).

What this 'police action' would be remains vague. The campaign group Liberty expressed their concerns that conditions of non-disclosure should be placed upon those who are given information:

> There is no indication of what these conditions will be or how they will be enforced. Would, for example, breaching them involve some sort of civil liability? If so, we do not see how civil liability can be enforced on somebody who has been given information, whether or not they wanted it, and is then told that they cannot pass it on. If there is no liability then the 'conditions' are simply requests.
>
> (Liberty 2008: para.77)

The new sections 327A and 327B into the 2003 Act came into force on 14 July 2008 (see also MoJ 2008: paras.71–81 and *Hansard House of Commons Debates 21 April 2008 col.1525W*).

The Child Sex Offender Disclosure scheme (CSOD)

Ever since the summer of 2000 when the 'For Sarah' campaign had started with its demands to open the sex offender register to the public, the Home Office had been trying to work out a way to meet these demands and get more information to the community. The problem was how to do this without causing the demonstrations, street protests and vigilante attacks that had been seen in the summer of 2000 (see Chapter Four). At that time the idea of an open access policy comparable to the community notification policies of the USA had been ruled out (Bennetto 2000). Home Secretary Jack Straw said: 'The arguments against a general right of access are well rehearsed. Such an arrangement would not in our judgement assist the protection of children or public safety. Controlled disclosure is I believe the better and safer route' (Home Office 2000a)

Since 2000 the matter of a universal community notification policy or Megan's Law had continued to raise its head. In 2006 Home Secretary John Reid had sent his junior Minister Gerry Sutcliffe to the USA to have another look at how community notification worked, but the policy was still not thought suitable for the UK (Harnden 2006; see also Chapter Six and Fitch 2006).

What was suitable for the UK was the scheme recommended in the *Review of the Protection of Children from Sex Offenders* (Home Office 2007a: Action 4) and followed up in the government response *Saving Lives. Reducing Harm. Protecting the Public. An Action Plan for Tackling Violence 2008–11*:

> we will pilot a new scheme in four police force areas, under which parents or legal guardians of children under the age of 18 will be able to register a

> child-protection interest in a named individual and apply for information about any child sex offence convictions that person may have.
>
> (HMG 2008: 26–27)

The name given to this new scheme was the Child Sex Offender Disclosure scheme (CSOD); informally it would be known as 'Sarah's Law' even though it was not a law at all but an administrative arrangement. The pilots started on 14 September 2008 on four sites in Cleveland (Stockton area), Cambridgeshire (Northern Division around Peterborough), Hampshire (Southampton area) and Warwickshire (force-wide) (Home Office 2009a).

During the pilot schemes questions were again asked about how information disclosed might still be kept confidential by the recipients and not passed around amongst the immediate neighbours or even wider. In Parliament it was said:

> In deciding whether to disclose details of convictions for child sex offences to a member of the public under the pilot scheme, MAPPA meetings will consider the risk of the recipient disclosing this information to others. Before a disclosure is made, the intended recipient will be required to sign a declaration that they will not share this information with others.
>
> (*Hansard House of Commons Debates 21 April 2008: Col.1525W*; see also Home Office 2010a: para.5.6.19)

The occasional case has come to light of people in receipt of disclosed information, who have gone on to disseminate it more widely, and there still appears to be no definitive way of dealing with it. The West Yorkshire Police gave information to a woman in Leeds who passed it on to her neighbours. She found herself being charged under the Data Protection Act and pleading not guilty to recklessly disclosing personal data. The case was discontinued and never prosecuted due to a lack of evidence (Carter 2019).

The early results of Sarah's Law were otherwise generally perceived as positive and the pilots duly expanded to all parts of these four police force areas (Home Office 2009b). There were still some critics. Marcel Berlins in *The Guardian* felt that the scheme could only increase the obsession in the country 'about the alleged though in reality much exaggerated, threat to our children from paedophiles' and pointed out how men walking alone in parks had recently been stopped by park officials and asked what they were doing there because they had no children with them; 'they must, according to the warped philosophy of our times, be suspected of being there for a more sinister reason'. All in all, it was a bad start to a new relationship if it had to begin with a visit to the police and 'Yes darling I love you and I trust you, but will you just wait a while, I've got to do a bit of checking' (Berlins 2008).

Case study 9.1

Will Self, the writer and journalist, says he was stopped and questioned when out with his 11-year-old son after a security guard called the police. The 51-year-old, who also regularly appears on television, was enjoying a long walk with his 11-year-old when a squad car and a police van stopped him on a Yorkshire roadside.

To shave some time off their walk while in Bishop Burton near Beverley, East Yorkshire, Self asked a security guard at an agricultural college if they could cut through the establishment's grounds. The answer was a firm no. Self said: 'The insinuation that I might pose some sort of threat to young people – in a word, that I might be a paedophile – was underscored by his eyes then sliding to my drooping son. He was being absurd and offensive.'

The security guard at Bishop Burton college went on to report him to the police, who drafted in a specialist female officer from 30 miles away 'since there was a presumption that a child might have to be taken into custody', according to Self.

'Far from acting as some sort of local hero, the guard had abused a child himself, in particular by exposing my son to the spectacle of his father – who was guilty of nothing – being grilled by the police on the roadside as if he were engaged in a perverse activity.'

He added: 'Can there be a more disturbing parable of the Britain we have become?'

(Self 2013)

Case study 9.2

A school will be built with obscured ground-floor windows to prevent paedophiles from looking at the children, plans have revealed.

Concerns have been raised over the opening of a large school next door to a probation centre frequented by convicted paedophiles. The new Livingstone Academy will take over a closed magistrates' court building in Bournemouth, Dorset.

But the site is just a short walk from a probation office that is used by 'people known to offend with children'.

The Department for Education (DoE), which is behind the 1,500-pupil school, insists it has incorporated 'all necessary safety features' into its plans. They include an 8ft-high fence with gates that will only open for an hour in the morning and 45 minutes in the evenings to allow children to come and go. The main entrance will be overseen by reception staff who will keep a watchful eye through glazed windows.

The school will also have CCTV cameras at all perimeter entrances and at the exits of the academy buildings. Playgrounds will be built within the perimeter of the school, hidden by the building, making it impossible for outsiders to view children while they play.

In a bid to further obscure the activities of children, planting and landscaping will act as a physical barrier. The school will also have no ground-floor classrooms and windows will be obscured up to a height of 2m (6.5ft).

The plans emerged as local residents and the police expressed their concerns about having convicted child sex offenders so close to children. Terry Fry, a neighbour, said he was worried about its 'proximity to ... convicted paedophiles having to pass the school to sign the sex register'.

(Carpani 2019)

Evaluation of the pilots

A formal evaluation of the four pilot schemes was published in March 2010. Amongst its findings were:

- the total number of enquiries and disclosures being smaller than were anticipated; 585 enquiries had led to 315 proceeded with as applications and only 21 (4% of applications) leading to disclosure as part of the scheme
- applicants were satisfied with their contact with the scheme; some were anxious because they had been left to cope with difficult situations
- applicants appear to have respected the confidentiality of the information disclosed to them
- the scheme offered greater clarity to police and offender managers although in practice they were largely operating as they had before the CSOD under MAPPA procedures
- MAPPA and CSOD seemed to run in parallel with each other
- the registered sex offenders subject to CSOD expressed some anxieties about community reactions, but it was also accepted as a part of existing controls on them (Kemshall et al. 2010).

The conclusion was that the pilots had 'worked well in some respects though it is too early to assess the longer-term impact of the scheme' (ibid: 20).

On the same day as the evaluation was published the national roll-out of CSOD was announced. It was to start with a further 18 new police force areas providing the scheme in England and Wales from August 2010 and then to all forces by the end of March 2011. Alan Johnson, the latest new Home Secretary, said 'the UK already has one of the most robust systems in the world for the management of sex offenders, the new scheme will build on this ensuring more children are kept safe' (Home Office 2010b).

More detailed guidance for the practitioners who would be implementing the scheme was now published. This confirmed that other relevant information apart from criminal records information could be disclosed to applicants

(Home Office 2010a: paras.2.4–2.5) and that information from the applicant back to the police was part of the deal (ibid: para.3.4).

The Home Office Guidance is also clear that everyone on the register should be forewarned about the introduction of the CSOD scheme:

> Prior to implementation, it is vital that the remit of the Scheme is effectively communicated to [registered sex offenders] residing in the area and those being released from prison into the area. The provision of information and reassurance about the Scheme's remit is vital to minimising the risk of their going 'underground' and not complying with their supervision requirements. [Registered sex offenders] should be regularly updated about the Scheme to ensure that key messages are continually embedded
>
> (ibid: para.3.8)

In Scotland a similar pilot scheme had been carried out in Tayside (Weaver 2009) and then nationwide in October 2010. An evaluation report found similar results to those in England and Wales and, as regards the registered sex offenders, there was no evidence to suggest the scheme had a negative impact on their behaviour, and no reports of vigilante attacks or other negative outcomes were noted (The Scottish Government 2010a and 2010b).

The change of government in May 2010 did not change anything with CSOD. The incoming Home Secretary Theresa May said she would be continuing with the roll-out that had been started (Home Office 2010c). The critics could still be heard in the background with the NSPCC predicting the scheme might lead to vigilantism and sex offenders going underground; ACPO's response was that: 'People say people will go underground – frankly, people go underground anyway' (Morris 2010).

At the end of the first 12 months of the CSOD scheme the Home Office claimed that 200 children had been protected (Home Office 2012c). What exactly the details of this protection were and what protection actually meant in practice, was left unsaid. The police had made 160 disclosures relating to child sex offences, this from a total of more than 1,600 enquiries and over 900 formal applications (ibid). Home Secretary Theresa May said:

> Thanks to Sarah's Law, we know that more than 200 children have been protected from potential harm over the last year. We are doing everything we can to protect the public, and especially children, from predatory sex offenders by tightening the law and closing loopholes
>
> (ibid)

Research on the CSOD scheme looking at the views of those on the register found a general acceptance of why such a scheme was thought to be needed. Some expressed an anxiety that their whereabouts might leak out and increase the potential for hostility from the community if not vigilante activity. One registered sex offender knew nothing about the scheme until the researcher explained; he was so distressed that the interview was terminated (Kemshall et al. 2012). Other offenders were under the misunderstanding that information would only be disclosed with their consent. Acceptance was more likely when the offender manager advised the offender about it in a helpful way:

> I was a little bit worried but after talking to [police officer] he calmed me down. [He] was very helpful in every way, very pleasant, he put you at ease, no need to worry unless you had anything to worry about. But no, he has been brilliant.
>
> (ibid)

No vigilante activity was reported but the researchers felt there might have been some hindrance to an offender moving towards a more positive definition of self and the 'good life', which has been advocated by some researchers (e.g. Ward and Gannon 2006). In those circumstances CSOD might just reaffirm an offender's personal narrative of self-condemnation and fatalism and take him or her backwards and away from more maturation and the 'good life'.

One surprising factor about the scheme was the continued low take-up in terms of applicants actually receiving disclosed information. Kemshall and colleagues reported:

> the volume of enquiries and subsequent applications made under the pilot was less than half of the expected volume … [and this] in contrast to the perceived media clamour for a 'Sarah's Law' and the presumed public appetite for public disclosure
>
> (Kemshall et al. 2012)

This could, of course, mean there was no real demand for such information in the first place, or it could mean poor marketing and targeting of the scheme (Kemshall and Weaver 2012). This supports findings from the scheme's pilot evaluation:

> I still think that there will be a large proportion of the community that probably don't know. (Participant 21)
>
> Could it be used more often? Potentially, but I think that it is very borderline whether it is a fishing trip or a genuine concern … that is why we have the follow-up interview, which I think should hopefully weed that out. (Participant 25)
>
> (O'Sullivan et al. 2016)

Despite limited CSODS applications, police officers complained that applications were time-consuming and impacted on core business and should their volume increase, this would overburden already limited resources:

> You know when you're allocated a CSODS there is a lot of work involved; it takes a lot of time away from the day job. (Participant 13)
>
> I think at the moment, as it stands, we are coping with the enquiries. I think if it was on a billboard somewhere and it was pushed, I think we would go under. We are already dealing with our own case load, managing our 80-odd offenders per person. I think if we were then inundated with enquiries amongst other things, I think we would struggle. (Participant 04)
>
> (ibid)

Disquiet surrounding resources was not restricted to CSODS. In particular, there were growing concerns regarding the steady rise in registered offenders, conflated with diminishing public sector budgets:

> You're going to get more and more registered sex offenders as time goes on, but we don't get the increase in staff to correlate with that … because of the cuts to funding and all the rest of it, it's always going to be a struggle to put more people in the department because they haven't got the money. (Participant 23)
>
> (ibid)

A legal challenge to Sarah's Law

A man on the register for life in South Yorkshire was told about the possible implications of CSOD when it was introduced in his area in 2011. He decided to challenge the CSOD Guidance in the courts, arguing that he should be allowed the right of representation before disclosure was made to protect his right to privacy. The questions before the court were:

1 whether the CSOD Guidance misstates the legal obligations imposed on the person making the decision to disclose, and
2 whether the Guidance is unlawful as it sets out a 'presumption of disclosure', thereby failing to reflect the need for a balancing exercise to be conducted prior to any decision to disclose being taken.

The claimant succeeded on the first of these challenges, but not on the second. The court therefore granted a declaration that the Guidance be amended to incorporate a requirement that any person about whom disclosure might be made, should have the right of representation to the disclosure decision maker (*X (South Yorkshire) v Secretary of State for the Home Department and Chief Constable of South Yorkshire [2012] EWHC 2954 (Admin)*).

The CSOD scheme allows for 'other relevant information' to be disclosed alongside any criminal records. It was this sort of information that the court homed in on:

> In the case of disclosure of information other than previous convictions the decision maker will have to be satisfied as to its accuracy. It is difficult to see in most cases how he could be satisfied in such cases without ascertaining what the offender has to say about that information
>
> (para.39)

Case study 9.3

A charity received an anonymous call reporting a concern for the safety of three children. [Police] Officers attended, saw the children and found the house to be clean, warm and well stocked with food. The mother of the children was at the address, along with a female registered sex offender who stated she only stayed at the address once a week. The attending officer recorded that they believed the call to be malicious. However, the records do not show whether the officer knew the visitor was a registered sex offender. A vulnerable person referral form was completed with a recommendation of no further action. The registered sex offender's index offence was not against young children, but did involve a level of manipulation of younger people. The SOU (Sex Offender Unit) supervisor reviewing the incident identified that the original call may not have been malicious. The registered sex offender was later visited by the offender manager. Further intelligence indicated that the registered sex offender may have been supplying drugs to children, encouraging them into a 'den' in a park and exploiting them. This intelligence was dealt with by neighbourhood officers who executed a warrant at the home of the registered sex offender. It should have been part of a wider risk management plan involving communication between the SOU and local officers to manage the risks. Although the drug dealing may not relate to sexual offending, it brings the registered sex offender into contact with children who are put at risk of potential harm. This should be considered as part of the continuing assessment of risk. In this case the risk management plan was not updated as additional information became known.

(HMICFRS 2018b: 34)

Scotland

The MacLean Report, in Scotland, felt that local protocols on the exchange of information between agencies were well enough developed to suit immediate purposes and did not wish to venture into any US type community notification schemes at present (MacLean Report 2000: paras.9.25–9.29).

In Scotland a multi-agency Information Sharing Steering Group (ISSG) was established in 2003 to take forward recommendations of the Cosgrove Report (2001 recs. 60–70).

The remit of the ISSG was:

> to ensure the efficient and effective flow of information between the key agencies involved in the management of sex offenders by developing protocols, guidance and strategies. These will address where necessary, issues of confidentiality and data protection in a way which underpins the improved multi-agency arrangements endorsed by the report of the Expert Panel on Sex-Offending 'Reducing the Risk'
>
> (cited in The Scottish Government 2007: 118)

The Group included representation from key agencies working in this area, including local authorities representing social work; education and housing; the police; the Health Service; the Scottish Prison Service; the Crown Office and Procurator Fiscal Service; the Scottish Courts Service; the Voluntary Sector; and the Scottish Executive. The Group developed a national Concordat for sharing information on sex offenders.

Summary

The movement of information held on known sex offenders takes two forms. The first is that information held by differing agencies who share that information and exchange it between themselves to assist one of the agencies to make valid interventions to ensure 'public protection'. This exchange of information on sex offenders is now carried out using the ViSOR computerised communications system introduced in 2005. The second form of movement is the disclosure of information on sex offenders that is made directly to members of the public by the agencies who hold it; mostly these are disclosures made by the police on common law grounds, MAPPA obligations both discretionary and statutory and information made available through the Child Sexual Offender Disclosure scheme. One problem with disclosures is that it could harden the public's view that the threat to their children's safety only comes from convicted child sex offenders.

10 The registration of children and young people who commit sexual offences

Introduction

There has always seemed a certain irony that a register devised to improve the level of protection for children and young people from 'paedophiles' and child sex offenders has ended up having those same children and young people on the register itself. It was always the intention that children and young people who committed sexual offences should be included on the register, the main concession being that they would be on for half the time period that adults would be on. As the register developed and took shape this inclusion of children and young people has continued to cause concern.

The low minimum age of criminal responsibility in the UK – 10 in England and Wales and Northern Ireland and 12 in Scotland – raises the question of how we should deal with sex offenders aged between 10 and 18. Should they even need to be included on the sex offender register?

The age of consent to heterosexual activity has remained at 16 since 1885 when it was raised from 13 to help prevent child prostitution. A report in 1981 recommended the age remain at 16 (PAC 1981). The age of consent for gay men in England and Wales was reduced from 18 to 16 in 2001, bringing it in to line with heterosexuals; lesbians, who until then had faced no statutory age of consent, were included in that legislation.

Some context

The idea that children and young people commit sexual offences is not a new one. One of the leading reports suggesting this was a problem in the UK first appeared in *The Report of the Committee of Enquiry into Children and Young People who Sexually Abuse Other Children* (NCH 1992). At the time this report constituted the most significant attempt to summarise the state of the field in the UK. In 1993 the law on the prosecution of rape as an offence had been changed to allow those over 10 to be so prosecuted; prior to this the offence could only be committed by young people over the age of 14 (Sexual Offences Act 1993s1).

The *Setting the Boundaries* report of 2000 made a number of recommendations affecting children and young people:

> Recommendation 17: As a matter of public policy, the age of legal consent should remain at sixteen.
>
> (Home Office 2000c: para.3.5.7)

> Recommendation 27 There should be an offence of sexual activity between minors to replace the existing offences of unlawful sexual intercourse, buggery, indecency with children and sexual activity prohibited for children. It should apply to children under the age of 18 with those under the age of consent.
>
> (ibid: para.3.9.13)

> Recommendation 28: We recommend that further consideration be given to appropriate non-criminal interventions for young people under 16 engaging in mutually agreed under-age sex who are not now, and should not in future, normally be subject to prosecution.
>
> (ibid: para.3.9.19)

> Recommendation 29: The criminal law needs to have measures in place which can be used to deal with children who sexually abuse other children. Sentencing decisions should reflect specialist assessment of risk and potential for longer term offending and include treatment options.
>
> (ibid: para.3.10.7)

Why Recommendation 17 was needed is unclear because the review's original terms of reference had specifically said the 'Review will not be considering … further revision of the age of consent' (Home Office 1999c).

The Youth Justice Board produced a 'background source document' to inform the debate on young people who sexually abuse; they had little to say on the register. Part of their conclusion was that:

> The needs of young people who sexually abuse are complex and often ongoing. Young people have typically suffered abuse, which can have important mental health consequences and may affect the impact of future intervention for their sexually abusive behaviour. They show poor social skills and a tendency to impulsiveness, and are coping with disrupted and neglecting family backgrounds.
>
> (YJB 2008: 51)

Other academic work on young sex offenders was produced by Hackett and colleagues (see e.g. Hackett 2014; Smith et al. 2014). In the USA a major report on the specific damage caused to children and young people who were on the register was produced by Human Rights Watch (HRW 2013).

A 2016 report supported by Barnardo's has more recently looked at the wider issues surrounding children and young people displaying 'harmful sexual behaviour' and committing sexual offences. This report looked at causes, cultural changes, the advances of technology and the complex links between child sexual exploitation (CSE) and trafficking for sexual exploitation. The aim of the report was to provide Parliament, government and other local and national decision makers with a better understanding of the issue. They summarised their own brief as:

> Harmful sexual behaviour covers a wide spectrum, and whilst at the extreme end only a small number of children will be at risk, we now live in an age where children sharing sexual images online and through 'sexting' has become ubiquitous. Technology also means that children are being exposed to ever more extreme pornography at an ever earlier age, which can distort the way they come to understand relationships. It is hardly surprising that more children are at risk not only of becoming a victim of sexual abuse, but also inadvertently finding themselves labelled a 'perpetrator'.
>
> (Barnardo's 2016: 2)

Sexting was defined as sending, receiving or forwarding sexually explicit messages, photographs or images, primarily between mobile phones, of oneself to others. Barnardo's decided that 'harmful sexual behaviour' consisted of a wide spectrum of behaviours:

> but the key unifying factor is the notion that, with the right support, the children involved can overcome the causes underlying their behaviour and be prevented from causing further, potentially more serious, harm as they move towards adulthood.
>
> (ibid: 10)

The Barnardo's report had little to say on the register as such but concluded that 'being on the sex offenders register has negative implications for the ability to take part in education, find a job and the level of confidence and self-esteem' (ibid: 38).

The Sex Offenders Act 1997

Even before the Act introducing the register became law the critics of registering children and young people were making themselves heard. The Howard League for Penal Reform responding to the 1996 *Sentencing and Supervision of Sex Offenders* consultation document had said that: 'We do not think the proposals are appropriate for juveniles. Treatment for juveniles is the prime concern and can be otherwise arranged through probation and supervision orders' (Howard League 1996: para.13).

While the Sex Offenders Act 1997 was still a parliamentary Bill an amendment had been moved by Peter Thurnham MP that would have left children and young people off the register completely and thereby making it just for adults. Thurnham argued that this was a complex issue but there were more appropriate ways to deal with child sex offenders. In essence his arguments were that:

- children and young people were more amenable to change and therefore the register was less applicable
- children and young people may well be victims of sexual abuse themselves and even to still be living in the same house as their abuser
- the stigma of registration should be avoided
- whatever change could be made they might still be on the register for life.

Thurnham said he was supported by a number of organisations wanting to leave children off the register; these included the NSPCC, Barnardo's, Save the Children and the Association of Chief Officers of Probation. The government refused to accept the amendment arguing that registration was not a punishment, but simply a device to secure public protection from those who have committed sexual offences (for the full debate see *Hansard House of Commons Debates 25 February 1997 cols.235–239*).

With no amendments to the Act having been made, children and young people below the age of 18 – or 16 in Scotland – who committed sexual offences were required to register in the same way as adults. The time periods for adults were simply halved for young offenders (Sex Offenders Act 1997 s4 (2)) and there was no custodial sentence imposed for non-compliance with notification requirements (s4(4)).

The other compromise was that those under the age of 20 committing offences under sections 6,12 and 13 of the Sexual Offences Act 1956 would not be required to register; this included intercourse with a girl aged 13 to 16, and buggery and indecency between men (Sex Offenders Act 1997 Schedule 1 para.2a)

The inclusion of young sex offenders on the register has continued to raise concern. Within a month of the register starting, the NSPCC put out a press release suggesting that separate arrangements should be put in place:

> we are concerned that juveniles under 16 are being required to register their names and addresses with the police and that the Register can apply to children as young as ten. We believe separate arrangements should be made for the monitoring and supervision of offenders aged under 16.
>
> (NSPCC 1997)

This separation would enable social workers, therapists and others to work on young people on the understanding that young people were more amenable to treatment and change than adults were. This also raised questions about the length of time children and young people should be on the register. If there was a welfare role to be administered then perhaps it could be argued that they should have twice as long on the register rather than just half the time of the adults. As one critic put it, 'Registration does not provide the level of public protection that adequate child welfare resources would provide. It only provides surveillance without any resources for meaningful intervention' (Myers 2001).

In these early days of registration, press coverage of children or young people going on the register otherwise seemed to content itself with reporting on the youngest child they could find; this included a 13-year-old (Elliott 1997), two 12-year-olds (Burton 1998, Bunyan 1998) and an 11-year-old ('Boy put on adult list', *Community Care* 1999). Nobody in the media seemed willing to write about the register turning from a means of protecting children into a repository of children's names or that the register would become a means of further affecting their future life chances, through the requirement that children be subject to mandatory notification requirements.

The position of parents

A court sentencing a child under 18, or under 16 in Scotland, for a sexual offence, may, at the same time, make a Parental Direction which places the responsibilities regarding registration on the parent rather than the child; a parent's consent to a Parental Direction is not required although their views may be heard by the court. It is the parent who must ensure that the young offender attends at the police station with him or her, when a notification is being given. Parents who fail in their responsibilities, despite their best efforts to ensure that the juvenile offender complies, will not have committed an offence. Breach of notification requirements by a parent subject to a Parental Direction is an offence and carries the same penalties as breach of the notification requirements by the sex offender themselves (Sex Offenders Act 1997 s4(3); now the Sexual Offences Act 2003 ss89–90). For some reason the 1997 version of the Parental Direction order in the Sex Offenders Act 1997 did not apply to children and young people getting cautions for their offending; this was corrected by the follow-up version of the law in the 2003 Sexual Offences Act 2003 s.89.

Parenting Orders could also be made on parents by the courts following a child's offence or the imposition of a Sex Offender Order on a child. Parenting Orders were made under the Crime and Disorder Act 1998 ss8–10 and were designed to help parents fulfil their parenting role; the core of this 'help' was a course of counselling or guidance completed in sessions spread over three months within a twelve month period. The idea was that sanctions on the child were aimed at their *past* criminal behaviour but a Parenting Order was aimed at the parent and child's *future* behaviour.

The Act states that the Parenting Order 'would be desirable' in the interests of preventing any repetition of the kind of behaviour which had led to the

Order being made or the injunction granted; or the commission of any further offence by the child or young person (1998 Act s8(6)). The Home Office had to agree to any courses of counselling and guidance being provided in a given area (1998 Act s8(3)) and courses were to be provided by social workers, probation officers, someone nominated by the local Chief Education Officer or a member of a Youth Offending Team (1998 Act s8(8) as amended). The courts had to explain to the parent in 'ordinary language' what was required (1998 Act s9(3)) but once an Order was made the parent was expected to comply; failure to comply could lead to a conviction (1998 Act s9(7)). Research on how useful Parenting Orders have been, is limited and not least in relation to children on the sex offender register (but see Burney and Gelsthorpe 2008, and Holt 2010).

Consultation Paper on the Review of Part 1 of the Sex Offenders Act 1997

The Home Office first gave notice of their intention to review the workings of the register jointly with the Scottish Executive in June 2000 (see Chapter Four). The review was to look at all aspects of the notification requirements including the position of children and young people who had committed sexual offences (Home Office/Scottish Executive 2001). The *Setting the Boundaries* review of all the laws on sexual offending hardly examined the matter of the registration of children and young people, and referred that subject to the Home Office/Scottish Executive review, suggesting that 'this is a question that merits careful in-depth consideration, and is a task for the separate review of the Sex Offenders Act' (Home Office 2000c: para.9.5.6).

The proposals

The Home Office and Scottish Executive published the Review's Consultation Paper in July 2001. The Consultation Paper focussed on four main areas; one of these areas was that of children and young people who sexually abuse others. As we outlined in Chapter Four, the Home Office said they were actively seeking views from the public about the best way forward with respect to whether and how the Act should apply to children and young people who sexually abuse and that views were specifically sought on the following possible (a) to (e) alternatives:

a continuing the present registration regime for those aged under 18.
b continuing to register those over 16 as at present whilst removing the registration requirement from those under this age unless they had been sentenced to a custodial sentence of any length or admitted to hospital subject to a restriction order.
c registering children and young people who sexually abuse with an agency other than the police which had a remit to address both their abusive behaviour and their wider needs.

d judicial discretion to require registration only in those cases where this was considered necessary after hearing the circumstances of the case.
e continuing registration as at present but introducing provision for de-registration when the young person reached 18 if they were assessed as no longer presenting a risk.(Home Office/Scottish Executive 2001: 27)

These stated alternatives were quite wide ranging in their possibilities. The sex offender register could disappear totally for those under 18 or even under 16 or a different agency than the police could administer the register for these age groups. The Consultation Paper recognised that children and young people who commit acts of sexual abuse were less likely to be entrenched in patterns of deviant behaviour than is the case with older sex offenders. Effective intervention to stop their abusive behaviour ought, therefore, to be comparatively easy and registration would therefore be less necessary for the protection of the community.

Other suggestions were that sanctions for breach of the notification requirements by children and young people should be toughened up and include a two-year custodial sentence; up until now only non-custodial sanctions were available. The courts should also be able to continue to make Parenting Orders to ensure that advice and support can be made available to those with parental responsibility for children and young people failing to meet the requirements of the register. And finally, sexual activity between minors should only lead to registration if the victim was under 13 years of age and if the offender had received a Detention and Training Order of any length, or community supervision of 12 months or more had been admitted to hospital subject to a restriction order.

The responses

A total of 46 responses were received and most were in agreement with the proposals before them; these were made up of 24 respondents from England and Wales, 7 from Scotland and 15 from Northern Ireland. Taking the (a) to (e) list of possible alternatives above:

a had only six respondents agreeing wholly with it
b had 11 agreeing wholly with it
c had 13 agreeing wholly with it; but no one from Scotland
d 18 were in agreement
e 15 were in agreement (Home Office 2002c: 12–13).

Only 26 responses were made about toughening the sanctions for young people not in compliance with registration requirements; 12 from England and Wales, 4 from Scotland and 10 from Northern Ireland. Twenty-four agreed with toughening the sanctions.

This focus on non-compliance was somewhat surprising because the 2001 Consultation Paper had put the compliance rate as high as 97% and 'steadily improving'. Most people would be quite happy with a new criminal justice project reporting a 97% successful completion rate on at least one part of its operations. It was therefore difficult to see why these additional sanctions were needed (see also Thomas 2009).

At the same time the Consultation Paper admitted that 'it is not currently possible to interrogate the [register] data … to produce collated statistical information about particular groups of offenders, for example, the number of them below the age of 18 years' (Home Office/Scottish Executive 2001: 11) and that 'aggregated statistical information on the number of registered offenders under 18 when convicted or cautioned [was] not currently available from the information held on the PNC' (ibid: 25). These statements seemed to contradict an earlier report commissioned by the Home Office that had used ACPO statistics to break down the ages of people on the register into three categories – under 18s; between 18 and 21; and over 21. These figures demonstrated that most people on the register were over 21 but there were otherwise variations between forces amongst the younger groups (Plotnikoff and Woolfson 2000: 6 Table 1).

There was a general agreement with Parenting Orders and that sexual activity between minors should only lead to registration if one of them was under 13 years of age or there was a serious offence involved (Home Office 2002c: 14).

The Home Office proposals were, therefore, quite clear:

> Registration will continue to apply to offenders above the age of criminal responsibility (10). We are introducing sentence and age thresholds for some of the offences which will mean that a young offender is only required to register where the seriousness of the offence warrants it.
>
> (ibid: 13)

> The courts will be able to use the full range of penalties available for juveniles in cases where they are convicted of a failure to comply with the Acts requirements. The maximum penalty available will be two years in custody (Detention and Training Order) and community sentences or a fine will also be available as will parenting orders.
>
> (ibid: 14)

The resulting 2002 White Paper contained changes but made hardly a mention of the young sex offender except to increase the sanctions for non-compliance by them (Home Office 2002a).

Case study 10.1

The only point that hindered me moving on was the Sexual Offenders Register. Having completed 2 years at Glebe House and then doing A-levels and heading off to uni, having to sign the register at the start of every term and when moving house was just a constant reminder of 'yeah you've screwed up' which really does knock your self-esteem and confidence. Additionally, as part of this, having two police officers randomly turning up at your uni flat where your mates are and then having to explain that one is a bit of a tough one! Personally, in my opinion, I felt that the whole process was over the top and unnecessary but then, from my dealings with the police during the whole time from court case to close that doesn't really surprise me.

I guess having the Sex Offenders Register over you can feel quite self-critical. It reminds you that you have done something really bad which can knock your self-esteem, confidence etc.

At the time I felt angry, scared, embarrassed, and shocked. I guess at the time I was young which felt overwhelming with the Police there and going to Court was an experience I won't forget. It was strange, and I didn't understand what was going on. It was very daunting.

(Barnardo's 2016: 89)

The Sexual Offences Act 2003

The 2003 Act maintained the halving of notification periods for children and young people on the register and introduced more 'thresholds' before registration became necessary. These 'thresholds' included registration if the child or young person had received a custodial sentence of 12 months or longer for a sexual assault (2003 Act Schedule 3 para.18), production, distribution or possession of indecent photographs of children (2003 Act Schedule 3 paras.13 and 15) and other specific offences (see NACRO 2004: Appendix). Registration for two years following reprimands or final warnings for juveniles was now lowered to one year.

The reprimand cases in Durham and London

One area likely to impact on children more than adults was that of the police caution. The caution avoided the need to go to court although it could still be part of a future offender's antecedents should they be back in court later. The caution was for minor offences that were seen as 'out of character' and were considered as 'diversionary' from the criminal justice system. The police caution did lead to sex offender registration under the Sex Offender Act 1997 s1(c) and now under the Sexual Offences Act 2003 s.80 (1)(d). For children and young people these cautions were replaced in 1998 by the Reprimand and Final Warning scheme introduced by the Crime and Disorder Act 1998 ss65–66. They were changed back to police cautions in 2012.

Two fifteen-year-old schoolboys had both separately received reprimands for their behaviour that amounted to a sexual assault; their names were added to the sex offender register. In Durham, 'R' was alleged to have committed sexual assaults at school on girls roughly the same age as he was, and in London 'U' engaged in similar activity on a railway station. The two appealed against their caution and the inclusion of their names on the register.

The judges ruled that their reprimands were incompatible with Article 6 of the European Convention on Human Rights – the right to a fair hearing (Alleyne 2002). The argument was made that the police administering the reprimands never said anything to the boys about them going on the register (*R(U) v Commissioner of Police of the Metropolis; R (R) v Chief Constable of Durham Constabulary, The Times, 10 December 2002*; see also Gillespie 2005).

Later guidance affirmed the need to ensure the police tell the young person about registration following a caution:

> The police officer must explain to a young offender and their parent/guardian/appropriate adult that on receiving a Youth Caution for such an offence they will be subject to the notification requirements of the Sexual Offences Act 2003. Where the YOT has carried out a prior assessment of a young person who has been reported for a sex offence, this is an opportunity for them to explain about the notification requirements to the young person and his or her parents.
>
> (MoJ and YJB 2013: para.11.10)

F and Thompson

The case of *F and Thompson* will be discussed in more detail in Chapter Twelve concerning reviews to have a name taken off the register. *Thompson* was a man in his sixties but *F* was a young person. When he was 11 years old *F* committed a number of serious sexual offences, including two offences of rape, on a six-year-old boy. On 17 October 2005, having been convicted of these offences, he was sentenced to 30 months' imprisonment on each count concurrent. This sentence automatically brought into effect the indefinite notification requirements.

F and Thompson was a judicial review made by the two people on the register and who were required to notify the police of their circumstances for the rest of their lives. Both claimed they were no longer a risk to anyone but having no right of a review of their 'indefinite' status, breached the European Convention on Human Rights. In the High Court it was said:

> The courts have consistently approached consideration of measures which are to be applied to children on the basis that the immaturity of a child offender must be taken into consideration as being of prime importance. This recognises the fact that a child may well change as he or she matures so that any problems or dangers which may have been apparent at the time of the commission of the offence may ultimately no longer be present.
>
> (*High Court R (F and Thompson) v Secretary of State for the Home Department [2008] EWHC 3170 (QB)*: para.19)

F and *Thompson* won their case but the Home Office appealed.

In the Court of Appeal, a Mr Johnson for the Home Office argued that being a young person on the sex offender register held no great hardship because:

i there is no justification for treating young offenders differently from adult offenders, since it is inevitable that young offenders will be adults before any realistic possibility of a review will arise;

ii the policy underlying the regime is for the benefit of victims of sexual offending, many of whom are children and it is necessary to have regard to their interests; and

iii in so far as different treatment is justified for young offenders, Parliament had regard to this by providing for the determinate notification periods to be halved in the case of offenders under the age of 18.

(*R (TF and Thompson) v Secretary of State for the Home Department [2009] EWCA Civ 792* para.51)

Comments (i) and (ii) appeared to contradict each other. The Court of Appeal responded by saying:

> We conclude, therefore, that the case for holding that the absence of a right of review of indefinite notification requirements renders section 82 (1) of the 2003 Act incompatible with article 8 is even stronger in the case of young offenders than it is in the case of adult offenders
>
> (ibid: para.54)

The Home Office appealed again to the Supreme Court and again lost. The Court held that:

> In the meantime, it must be open to Parliament to take the view that, as a precaution against the risk of them committing serious sexual offences in future, even such young offenders should be required to comply with the notification régime indefinitely. But that makes it all the more important for the legislation to include some provision for reviewing the position and ending the requirement if the time comes when that is appropriate.
>
> (*R (on the application of F (by his litigation friend F)) and another (Respondents) v Secretary of State for the Home Department (Appellant) [2010] UKSC 17* para.66)

This Supreme Court case is returned to in Chapter Twelve when we look at reviews to come off the register.

Summary

The position of children and young people on the register is very similar to that of adults except that they are registered for half the time of that of adults. The low age of criminal responsibility in the UK does mean that we have the anomaly of a public protection policy to protect children, having many children caught up in its arrangements as perpetrators of sexual crime. Where interventions are possible there is the belief that children and young people are more amenable to change during their adolescent years and therefore more time should be spent with them rather than less.

11 The travelling sex offender

Introduction

Registered sex offenders may, like anybody else, wish to travel abroad. This could be for business purposes or for holidays. It could also be to avoid the restrictions of being on the sex offender register or for purposes of continuing their offending career in countries where policing is less rigorous and the country is free of public protection arrangements. People on the sex offender register may have additional restrictions placed on their international travel arrangements.

One of the early concerns about people going from the UK to areas of the world where poverty drove young people in to sex work was often referred to as 'sex tourism'. The term 'sex tourism' has, in turn, been criticised for being too narrow and overlooking the fact that some visits may start out as business visits but may change in nature during those visits. Some people may move to countries for employment purposes that then leads on to sexual offending.

This chapter considers the position of both the outgoing traveller from the UK and the incoming traveller to the UK. Registered sex offenders may have restrictions placed on them for both forms of travel.

The 'outgoing' sex offender – leaving the UK

Restrictions on international travel for registered sex offenders will depend on the risk they are thought to pose, in particular to children in other countries. These travel restrictions were not in the original Sex Offenders Act 1997 but have been built up incrementally over the years mostly in response to campaign groups who have identified the dangers. In these early days of the register, before restrictions came in, some offenders, in breach of register requirements or when found to have been missing from their registered address, were able to claim that they were abroad at the time and thus were not in breach of any registration requirements of the Act.

Registered sex offenders are not the only group of people liable to face travel restrictions. Football supporters thought likely to cause trouble in terms of street fights and vandalism may be made the subject of Restriction Orders and Banning Orders that prevent them travelling (Football Spectators Act 1989, Football (Disorder) Act 2000), and people subject to a conviction for a 'drug trafficking offence' may also be made subject to a Travel Restriction Order (Criminal Justice and Police Act 2001 ss33–37).

Notifying travel of over eight days

The first-time people on the register had to notify the police of their intention to travel abroad came in 2001. Amendments were made to the Sex Offenders Act 1997 by the Criminal Justice and Court Services Act 2000 and new Regulations made the restrictions.

The Regulations required notification to the police of not only details of departure, destination and point of arrival for any travel lasting more than eight days, but also details of return. The period of eight days had been chosen to reflect both the large numbers of registered offenders and thus the potentially high volume of notifications and to ensure that there is time for the police to take any necessary action resulting from the notification (*Hansard House of Lords Debates 8 May 2001 cc973–7).*

The new Regulations were the Sex Offenders (Notice Requirements) (Foreign Travel) Regulations 2001 (SI 2001 no.1846) which came into force on 1 June 2001 for England, Wales and Northern Ireland and the Sex Offenders (Notice Requirements) (Foreign Travel) (Scotland) Regulations 2001 (SSI 2001 no.188) which was implemented on the same day. Regulation 5 wanted the following information on an 'outgoing traveller' who was on the register:

> a where he intends to travel to more than one country outside the United Kingdom, his intended point of arrival in each such additional country,
> b the identity of any carrier or carriers he intends to use for the purposes of his departure from and return to the United Kingdom, and of travelling to any other point of arrival,
> c details of his accommodation arrangements for his first night outside the United Kingdom,
> d in a case in which he intends to return to the United Kingdom on a particular date, that date, and
> e in a case in which he intends to return to the United Kingdom at a particular point of arrival, that point of arrival.
>
> (The Sex Offenders (Notice Requirements) (Foreign Travel) Regulations 2001 (SI 2001 no.1846) Regulation 5)

The Regulations also specified that the person in question must attend a police station in person to give the required information (Regulations 8 and 9). This was apparently intended to assist the offender who may not remember from one trip to the next precisely what information is required of them and the only way of ensuring that they provide what is required is by attendance in person. It was also considered important that the required information was conveyed within the timescales specified and requiring attendance in person was thought to be the best way of achieving this. A notification made by post may not arrive in time or there may be disputes about whether or not faxes had been sent (*Hansard House of Lords Debates 8 May 2001 cc973–7).*

These initial Regulations did not actually *stop* anyone from travelling. On receipt of notification of the intention to travel the UK police had to make a decision as to whether or not to notify their colleagues in the country of destination that the person in question was on his or her way. This would be based on whatever risk had been assessed. What the overseas police or immigration authorities in receipt of this information did with it was up to them.

After the Regulations had been in place for nine months further parliamentary questions were asked about what recent co-ordination of efforts had been made between countries to reduce the incidence of child sex abuse by 'tourists'. Specific questions were asked about whether the government would introduce legislation to require sex offenders to notify the authorities if they were travelling abroad for less than eight days. The Home Office answered that:

> The qualifying period for notification of travel abroad was the subject of discussion during the review of the Sex Offenders Act 1997. The Review included representatives of the police, probation and social services, and children's charities. The conclusion reached was that a qualifying period shorter than eight days would result in an unwieldy, unresponsive and consequently less effective, system for the police to administer.
>
> (*Hansard House of Commons Debates 12 February 2002 col.306–7*)

The Review in question was the 2001 Review (Home Office/Scottish Office 2001; see Chapter Five). Beverley Hughes for the Home Office concluded that 'we have no plans to change this aspect of the system at this stage' (ibid).

In the House of Lords, during debate on the Sexual Offences Bill, Lord Hylton again raised the question of, what he called, the 'eight-day loophole':

> My first concern is with the so-called eight-day loophole, which allows convicted British sex offenders to travel abroad for less than eight days without notifying the United Kingdom authorities or the foreign authorities. It therefore allows registered offenders to travel to the Continent and even as far as south-east Asia to commit further offences and return here with impunity. It encourages sex tourism at its worst, because the offences often involve children. I am glad that the Home Secretary has reportedly undertaken to reduce that loophole …
>
> (Lord Hylton cited at *Hansard House of Lords Debates 13 February 2003 col.842*)

For the government Lord Falconer of Thoroton later outlined the proceedings in place for further consultation:

> In addition to introducing the proposed foreign travel banning order, we will be consulting with interested parties on the arrangements for the notification of foreign travel by registered sex offenders. We are aware that this issue has generated considerable interest. We will consult quickly on the issue with a view to making the Government's intentions clear by the end of March. This will enable our intentions to be considered and debated fully during the passage of the Sexual Offences Bill through Parliament.
>
> (*Hansard House of Lords Debates 6 March 2003 col.123WA*)

In March 2003 the government issued a consultation paper setting out its proposals for amendments to the Sexual Offences Bill, on people with convictions for sexual offences who wished to travel. The paper, entitled the *Sexual Offences Bill: Government Proposals on the Issue of Sex Offenders who Travel Abroad*, can be found as an Annex to the Home Office press release 'Government action on Sex Tourism' (Home Office 2003d).

There were four main proposals:

- a complete re-enactment of Part 2 of the Sex Offenders Act 1997 i.e. enabling the courts in England, Wales and Northern Ireland to deal with British citizens committing sexual offences against children abroad;
- a new Order requiring people who have committed offences overseas arriving back in the UK to be added to the register whether UK citizens or foreign nationals;
- a new Foreign Travel Banning Order that could prevent people on the register from leaving the country;
- a complete re-enactment of the Regulations requiring people on the sex offender register to notify the police of their travel intentions (Home Office 2003d).

The consultation period on these proposals was quite short. The proposals were published on 5 March 2003 and comments requested by 21 March 2003. The large majority supported all the proposals. The Regulations that had followed the Criminal Justice and Court Services Act 2000 required that notification of travel should be made at least 48 hours in advance of the travel; the recommendation now was to extend this to seven days in advance. The Foreign Travel Banning Order now became simplified as the Foreign Travel Order (FTO). FTOs would become applicable for any travel for over three days abroad (Home Office 2003d).

As noted under the 2001 Regulations if the UK police did not apply for an FTO to stop the travel – or had applied and failed to get one – they could still notify their law enforcement colleagues in the country of destination that the person in question was on his or her way. What the police receiving this information did with it was again up to them. If the UK police were aware that some overseas police forces were unlikely to do anything, that could be the cue to apply for a Foreign Travel Order:

> the police may have tried … with a particular country in the recent past and found that the information was not acted upon by the local authorities. If this is the case, the court may be satisfied that, in this case, only a Foreign Travel Order is the only effective means available to prevent serious sexual harm against children in that country.
>
> (*Hansard House of Lords 19 May 2003 col. 660*)

Notifying travel of over three days

The Sexual Offences Act 2003 s.86 enabled new Regulations to be made requiring registered sex offenders to notify the police of their intention to travel abroad and of their return. Section 86 specified that the notification must disclose the date of departure from the United Kingdom, the country to which the sex offender will travel (or, if there is more than one, the first country) and the point of arrival in that country.

The new Regulations stipulated that the length of travel was now reduced from eight days to anything over three days (Sexual Offences Act (Travel Notification Requirements) Regulations 2004 no.1220 Regulation 5). The problems cited just two years earlier that 'a qualifying period shorter than eight days would result in an unwieldy, unresponsive and consequently less effective, system for the police to administer' (see above) seemed to have been overcome. The Regulations applied to England, Wales and Northern Ireland. Separate regulations applied in Scotland with the Sexual Offences Act 2003 (Travel Notification Requirements) (Scotland) Regulations 2004 no. 205.

The Foreign Travel Order (FTO)

The Sexual Offences Act 2003 introduced the Foreign Travel Order (FTO) (ss.114–22). This was an Order applied for by the police, and authorised by a magistrate, to prevent known child sex offenders, and, in particular, those on the sex offender register, from travelling abroad, where there was evidence that they intend to cause 'serious sexual harm' to children in a foreign country. The person concerned must already have a conviction for a sexual offence against a child and his or her behaviour must have given concern and reasonable cause to believe that it is necessary for such an Order to be made. Children were defined as anyone under 16 years of age (2003 Act s.116(2)) and if granted, the FTO lasted for six months (2003 Act s.117(1)); during this six months the subject of the Order was unable to leave the UK for either a specified country or, indeed, anywhere in the world depending on the wording of the Order (2003 Act s117(2)).

The Policing and Crime Act 2009 ss22–25 later amended the 2003 Act and the provisions relating to FTOs. Children were redefined as anyone under the age of 18 rather than 16 (2009 Act s23) and the time period length of an FTO was lengthened from six months to five years in England, Wales and Northern Ireland (2009 Act s24). In the case of generic prohibitions on travel to anywhere in the world, the 2009 Act required that passports be surrendered, with failure to comply becoming a criminal offence (2009 Act s.25; see also Home Office 2010d).

Notifying travel of any length

Having reduced the 'eight-day period' of travel to 'three days', pressure started to build up to reduce the time period to cover *any* length of time. One of the most vociferous critics of the Home Office's efforts to restrict the international movements of registered sex offenders was the organisation ECPAT. ECPAT had been founded in 1994 and stood for various titles over the years ranging from 'End Child Prostitution, Child Pornography and Trafficking of Children for Sexual Purposes UK' to 'Every Child Protected against Trafficking'. In August 2006 ECPAT UK had published *The End of the Line for Child Exploitation* written by their then director Christine Beddoe.

The End of the Line for Child Exploitation offered a disclaimer that it did not set out to be a comprehensive study of sex offenders, was based on 'open sources' and had no data on the numbers of sex offenders travelling abroad because such data was not available. Nonetheless ECPAT believed that a major review was required of the use, application and effect of FTOs. It described the FTO application process as 'cumbersome and not being used' and, by its estimate, only one FTO had been issued by magistrates in 2004 (ECPAT UK 2006: 16).

The report also wanted to remove what it called 'the three-day loophole':

> with the increase of cheap air travel to many locations in Europe and particularly vulnerable communities in Central and Eastern Europe, British sex offenders can easily access these destinations in under three days. Indeed, there are confirmed cases of child sexual abuse involving British nationals in the Czech Republic, Romania, Bulgaria, Spain and France. All these countries can be accessed in under three days. ECPAT UK believes that *notification of all travel abroad should be obligatory, regardless of the length of stay.*
>
> (ibid: 16, emphasis added)

No other evidence of these 'confirmed cases' from Europe were included in the report with the illustrative case studies that were used coming from the Dominican Republic, The Gambia, Thailand, Sri Lanka and Kenya (ibid: section 5). No statistical evidence was provided on just how prevalent these trips lasting less than three days were.

ECPAT's later report *Return to Sender* was published in August 2008 to coincide with the return of 'Gary Glitter' to the UK from a custodial sentence for sexual offences in Vietnam (see below). Amongst other recommendations the report said there should be 'an immediate review of the use and effectiveness of Foreign Travel Orders (FTOs)'. ECPAT recommended this because they saw it as 'the only tool the UK currently has available to prevent travel of high-risk offenders and it is not being used by British law enforcement' (ECPAT UK 2008a: 17). One reason it was not being used was that:

> ECPAT UK has been told by police on many occasions that [an FTO] requires too much paperwork and it is unwieldy … If the administration or evidence requirements for the FTOs are a blockage for police then it must be immediately reviewed in light of the robust risk assessment and management measures within the MAPPA framework.
>
> (ibid: 17–18)

A Home Office spokesperson told *The Guardian* in August 2008 that they did intend to make such a change and make it mandatory for *any* overseas travel by registered sex offenders to become notifiable (cited in Lewis 2008); but nothing else happened on this stated intention for another four years.

ECPATs report *Off the Radar – Protecting Children from British Sex Offenders who Travel,* published in February 2011 was still advocating closure of the '3-day loophole'. This report's recommendation included the exhortation that:

> The Home Secretary should act immediately to close the 'three-day loophole' – referring to Section 86 of the Sexual Offences Act requiring registered sex offenders to notify of travel abroad. ECPAT UK recommends that *all* international travel must be notified, irrespective of the duration of the trip.
>
> (ECPAT UK 2011: Recommendation 2, emphasis added)

The week after ECPAT UK launched the *Off the Radar* report Prime Minister David Cameron announced that the government would take action to close the '3-day loophole' in the Sex Offenders Register: 'We will … use the opportunity to close some loopholes in the sex offenders' register. For instance, we will make it compulsory for sex offenders to report to the authorities before any travel' (*Hansard House of Commons Debates 16th February 2011 col.959*).

The former Labour government having done nothing for four years about introducing travel notification for 'any' travel by registered sex offenders, the 'opportunity' had now arisen for the new government. The 'opportunity' Cameron was referring to was that provided for by the Supreme Court ruling that having no review mechanism to apply to come off the register breached the European Convention on Human Rights (see Chapter Twelve). Both the Prime Minister and the Home Secretary had declared themselves 'appalled' by the court's decision which appeared 'soft' on sex offenders, and they could now match it with some new toughening of the register's requirements that presumably appeared 'hard'. Unlike 2008, action did take place this time.

Although still no evidence had been produced to show that people were actually travelling abroad for less than three days to abuse children, Christine Beddoe Director of ECPAT UK clearly regarded it as a victory declaring 'we are … delighted that the government has finally heeded ECPAT UK's call to close the "3-day loophole"' (ECPAT 2012).

The subject of the 'outgoing' sex offender will be returned to below; here we turn to the problem of the 'incoming' offender.

The incoming sex offender

If life has become ever more restricted for the registered person wanting to leave the UK, how does the picture look for those wanting to come into the country with a conviction for a sexual offence? The arrival of a person in a given jurisdiction who has convictions for sexual offences is somewhat problematic. This is true if the person is a UK national returning home having been convicted abroad or a foreign national with convictions arriving on legitimate business for the first time. It is also true of the registered sex offender who has left their country of registration and is returning to that country, whether or not any new offences have been committed during the period away.

The question for the police is just how they would know if an arrival to the UK is such an offender or is known to have been convicted for sexual offences committed abroad. If they were allowed in, could they be monitored in some way or put on the UK sex offender register? Could they be stopped altogether from coming in?

During the debate on the original Sex Offenders Bill in 1997 David Maclean for the government was pessimistic as to what could be done about incoming sex offenders:

> It is clear that those who are convicted in the United Kingdom of offences in Schedule 1 will be required to register. Those who may be convicted of offences overseas would not be required to register. [HON. MEMBERS: 'Why not?'] That would be impossible. In most cases, we would not know whether people had been convicted overseas … People might be convicted in foreign countries of offences that are not recognised in British law and that are not compatible with our requirements. For instance, we all know that the age of consent differs between countries. It is a recipe for disaster.
>
> (*Hansard House of Commons Debates 20 March 1997 col.29*)

In 1997 the matter was left at that point.

The question arose again three years later when the professional boxer Mike Tyson, who had served a prison sentence for a sexual offence in the USA, was twice allowed into the country in 2000 to take part in professional fights. The Home Secretary Jack Straw gave him permission to fight in Manchester on 30 January and again in Glasgow on 24 June. His rationale for allowing the first fight was that he 'did not want to hurt the businesses in Manchester that were expecting a windfall from the fight or disappoint the fans who had bought tickets' (Schaefer 2000).

The Home Secretary's rationale for the second visit was that he had taken into account Tyson's satisfactory behaviour on his earlier visit to Manchester and that any risk to the public would be minimised by his high media profile, the presence of his trainers and other supporting entourage, and the limited duration of his visit; he also took into account 'that a refusal to permit entry would result in a loss of economic benefit to the United Kingdom, and in particular to the areas in which engagements took place, and would not enhance the United Kingdom's standing as a venue for major sporting events' (*Hansard House of Commons Debates 18 May 2000 Col: 212W*) and on that basis 'I have today informed Mr. Tyson that he will be granted entry clearance for a single visit of three weeks' duration strictly for the purpose of a boxing match in Scotland on 24 June 2000' (ibid).

At the time there had been considerable publicity relating to the visits. Attempts to challenge both the January and June decisions by judicial review were unsuccessful (see e.g. BBC News 2000a; *The Rape Crisis Centre and Sandy Brindley for Judicial Review of a decision of the Secretary of State for the Home Department to grant Mike Tyson leave to enter the United Kingdom, Outer House, Court of Session, Edinburgh 2 June 2000*). In Parliament two Early Day Motions criticising the decisions had gained 67 signatures on 18 January 2000 (EDM no. 290) and 37 on 27 June 2000 (EDM no. 901).

It was reported that 'Home Secretary Jack Straw has ordered a wholesale review of policy on allowing convicted criminals into the UK, following the controversy over boxer Mike Tyson's bid to fight in Britain' (BBC News 2000b).

Early legislation

The Criminal Justice and Court Services Act 2000 Schedule 4 para.5 had amended the Sex Offenders Act 1997 with new sections 6D to 6G to change the law in terms of both incoming and outgoing sex offenders. In terms of the incoming offender new Regulations required any one already on the register and returning to the UK to provide information on their return. This had to be done within eight days of his or her return to the United Kingdom (Regulation 7(2)) s2(6 F).

The UK had considered the possibility of requiring all incoming registered sex offenders to automatically report themselves to the authorities (Home Office/Scottish Executive 2001, chapter seven) but had so far not implemented any such requirement. The Republic of Ireland, for example, had required just such automatic reporting in their Sex Offenders Act 2001 s13.

In March 2002 Bob Spink MP for Castle Point in Essex asked the Home Secretary a series of questions about the problem of the incoming sex offender:

1 what plans he has to propose a change to the law so that people convicted abroad of crime with a possible sexual element or motivation can be monitored on the Sex Offenders Register on their return to the United Kingdom;
2 what plans he has to enable the (a) police and (b) Probation Service to monitor and control the activities of people who have been convicted abroad of offences including violence to children with possible sexual motivation;
3 what notice can be given to a community when a convicted child murderer returns to the UK to live in that community after serving their sentence abroad;
4 how many people who have been convicted of an offence abroad involving a sexual element have returned to live in the United Kingdom in each of the last three years for which records exist; and what mechanisms are in place to monitor and control their behaviour on their return to the United Kingdom;
5 what powers exist to protect a community when a person who has been convicted abroad of child murder, with the strong possibility of a sexual motive in that crime, returns on release from prison to that community (*Hansard House of Commons Debates 13 March 2002 cols.1103–4W*).

For the Home Office Beverley Hughes replied that:

- The Home Office does not keep records of those convicted of offences abroad, including those involving a sexual element, who have returned to the United Kingdom. We are therefore unable to supply figures for the last three years.
- Mechanisms already exist for the monitoring and controlling of dangerous offenders who come to the UK after having been convicted of an offence abroad.
- The Criminal Justice and Court Services Act 2000 imposed in relation to any area, a statutory duty on the chief officer of police and the local probation board to establish arrangements for assessing and managing the risks posed by persons who may cause serious harm to the public. This would include those convicted abroad.
- If someone falls into this category, for example if a person who has been convicted of a violent offence with a sexual element abroad returns to this country, these multi-agency public protection arrangements will come into play.
- Multi-agency public protection arrangements provide for the risk assessment of all potentially dangerous offenders. Following this a management plan is formulated according to the level and nature of risk that the

offender poses. Typically, this would have components of monitoring, interventions designed to reduce re-offending and steps necessary to protect victims or potential victims. After the risk assessment, if it is in the interest of public protection, the police may also disclose information about the offender to relevant members of the community. Social Service departments who are the lead agency for child protection are members of the multi-agency public protection panels.

- The review of the Sex Offenders Act 1997 looked at requiring those convicted of sex offences abroad to register on their arrival in the UK. The Government have asked for consultation and responses are currently being analysed to decide what appropriate action, if any, the Government should take.

(*Hansard House of Commons Debates 13 Mar 2002: Col. 1103–4W*)

Hughes appeared to be avoiding the question of knowing about these incoming offenders and being able to identify them by diverting on to the subject of MAPPA.

Case study 11.1

Poor supervision or investigation

A British citizen committed an offence abroad and was deported back to the UK. His deportation triggered a good response from the MPS (Metropolitan Police Service). The central team applied for and obtained a summons and subsequent notification order.

There was then an unacceptable delay in borough Jigsaw staff visiting the offender at his home (during this period he was resident at two addresses, one for a period of 12 days and the second for 15 days), which did not happen until nearly a month after he returned to the UK. The risk assessment was carried out at this point and the offender was classed as very high risk.

The offender contacted Jigsaw officers to state that he had received some emails that were subsequently found to contain indecent images of children. The response to this offence was not effective. There was a delay in despatching an officer once the Jigsaw team received the information, and then they decided against arresting him at the first opportunity.

We found very little evidence of supervision of this case, and at the time of the audit there was no evidence of what enquiries were being made to identify the sender of the email.

(HMIC 2016: 84)

Notification Orders

The Sexual Offences Act 2003 introduced new provisions to try and regulate the movements of the travelling sex offender. In terms of the incoming offender the main innovation was the new Notification Order (NO). Notification Orders could be made by magistrates, on application by the police, in respect of individuals who had been convicted abroad of sexual offences equivalent to the sexual offences listed in Schedule 3 of the Sexual Offences Act 2003. On return to the UK the effect of a Notification Order was to make such offenders subject to the UK registration requirements as if they had been convicted in the UK of a relevant offence (2003 Act ss97–103). The concept of dual criminality meant there had to be some equivalence between the offences committed in the different countries (2003 s99(1)).

Notification Orders are still in use today. Once granted the person concerned has three days to complete an initial notification; thereafter they must notify details to the police when changes take place and on an annual basis. In making the Orders magistrates have their own rules to follow in the Magistrates Courts (Notification Orders) Rules 2004 no.1052 (the whole process is described at *Hansard House of Commons Debates 15 July 2010 Col 824–5W*).

A perennial problem about people with convictions arriving in the UK from all over the world has still been that of actually identifying them. It was easy enough when they were famous sportsmen or other celebrities but not so easy when they were 'ordinary' people without any claims to fame. The decision to apply for a Notification Order still depended on knowledge of the offender's arrival in the country.

There was an existing system that could have helped, regarding the notification of offences committed by UK nationals in Europe. In 1959 the Council of Europe had agreed a Convention whereby criminal records were exchanged between the European Member States:

> each Contracting Party shall inform any other party of all criminal convictions and subsequent measures in respect of nationals of the latter Party, entered in the judicial records. Ministries of Justice shall communicate such information to one another at least once a year.
>
> (CoE 1959: Article 22)

In other words, anyone from the UK convicted for any offence in one of the Council's (now) 47 member countries would have details of that conviction sent to the UK; similarly, we would send details of convictions to the home country of another offender. Although a member of the Council of Europe and a signatory to the Convention the UK only got round to ratifying it in 1990 through the Criminal Justice (International Cooperation) Act 1990. That meant 30 years with no notifications coming through. From 1991 onwards these conviction records did start to arrive at the Home Office who in turn sent them on to the old National Identification Bureau (NIB) at the Metropolitan Police Service, for inclusion on the Police National Computer.

Within four years this system had broken down. In 1995 the NIB was downsized, wound up and replaced by the National Identification Service

(NIS) and criminal records could all go directly on to the PNC from forces around the country. Meanwhile, after 1995, the records coming into the Home Office from across Europe continued to come in, but only to gather dust in the Home Office. They were eventually discovered in January 2007 (Morris 2007).

The discovery was made after the UK signed the EU Council Framework Decision on taking account of convictions in the Member States of the European Union in the course of new criminal proceedings (2008/675/JHA of 24 July 2008) that effectively bypassed the Council of Europe Convention to introduce a new system of exchanging conviction information between the EU Member States. The new system required there to be a new central authority appointed to collect the records. This now became the Association of Chief Police Officers Criminal Record Office (ACRO) based in Hampshire and it was ACRO that discovered the estimated 27,500 records gathering dust (*Hansard House of Commons Debates 10 January 2007 cols.31–32WS and cols 285–299; and 16 January 2007 cols 31–32WS*). Home Secretary John Reid announced an inquiry into how this had happened. The resulting Amroliwala Report appeared in February 2007 (Amroliwala Report 2007).

Meanwhile the Home Office has continued to advise UK police forces that there are a number of possible sources that might assist them to identify the incoming sexual offender (Home Office 2004b: 33–4; Home Office 2010e: 44). The most recent version suggests:

- A British citizen is being released from custody overseas, after conviction for a sexual offence, and the authorities in the relevant country or the diplomatic service are organising return to the UK.
- A British citizen is returning to the UK after receiving a caution for a sexual offence overseas. During his dealings with the authorities in the foreign country, he was assisted by the authorities overseas or the diplomatic service.
- A British citizen is being repatriated to a UK prison to serve his sentence received overseas for a sexual offence.
- Authorities in the UK have been informed by a foreign country that one of their citizens, who has previous convictions for sexual offences, is intending to come to the UK.
- An individual comes to the attention of the police, and on investigation of his criminal history it becomes apparent that he has convictions for relevant sexual offences overseas.(Home Office 2018: 57–58)

ECPAT saw this as an area of weakness:

> A common misperception by the general public is that British sex offenders who are convicted abroad automatically go on the UK Sex Offenders Register. This is not the case. Indeed, it is possible for a British sex offender to be prosecuted abroad for a range of different offences and for

> the British authorities never to know because the system of reporting the prosecution or conviction to the UK is not mandatory between governments. It relies heavily on the role of British Embassies and missions abroad and even then; they do not necessarily have to know about the case.
> (ECPAT UK 2008a: 15)

New Regulations gave the details about reporting to the police on return from overseas in the Sexual Offences Act (Travel Notification Requirements) Regulations 2004 no.1220. Regulations 8, 9 and 10 deal with notification to be given on return to the United Kingdom.

The ECPAT report *Return to Sender* also recommended that local UK police forces and other MAPPA responsible authorities should be asked to think more widely on an international scale (ECPAT UK 2008a: 16). This is not always the easiest thing to do when you are hard-pressed with local issues but the fourth version of the MAPPA Guidance did carry a new chapter 21 called 'MAPPA and foreign travel' (NOMS 2012). When and how the police might be made aware was left unsaid. ECPAT wanted there to be a new system to return offenders to the UK with a chaperone after sentencing, 'so they are duly placed on the Sex Offenders Register to be risk assessed and managed in the UK' (ECPAT UK 2008a: 19).

The incoming pop star – 20 August 2008

The subject of the 'travelling sex offender' became a major news story during a week in August 2008. The former pop star Gary Glitter – real name Paul Gadd – had been convicted and sentenced for sexual offences against children in Vietnam in 2006. His custodial sentence having ended he was due back into London on Wednesday 20 August 2008.

Glitter knew that coming home he would be met by intense media interest. He would also be required to be on the sex offender register and face other restrictions on approaching children and further restrictions on foreign travel. He had previous convictions for downloading child pornography in the UK in 1999 along with experience of seven years on the register; he had also been deported from Cambodia in 2003 for alleged sex offences (Edwards 2008).

The Home Office and other NGOs also knew that Gary Glitter coming home would be met by intense media interest and that this could be used to their advantage. On 17 August the campaign group ECPAT published their report *Return to Sender – Child Sex Offenders Abroad – Why More Must Be Done (*ECPAT 2008a) with an accompanying press release that called for:

> an urgent shake-up in the way that the UK deals with British nationals who have been prosecuted abroad for child sex offences. ECPAT UK is calling on the government to immediately bring offenders back to the UK after sentence is served so they can be placed on the sex offenders register then risk assessed and managed, and where appropriate, that

> future foreign travel is restricted so they cannot be a threat to vulnerable children. British law enforcement has the tools to protect children abroad, they just don't use them.
>
> (ECPAT 2008b)

On 18 August a Home Office spokesperson had told *The Guardian* they were also thinking of making changes to international travel notification to the police: 'From the autumn, we also intend to make registered sex offenders notify the police of any travel abroad. Presently, sex offenders have to notify police if they will be abroad for three days or more' (cited in Lewis 2008). That would end ECPAT's 'three-day loophole'.

Home Secretary Jacqui Smith made it clear that she wanted to make an example of Glitter. 'I want Gary Glitter to be controlled whilst he's here and I don't want him to be able to go anywhere else in the world in order to abuse children' (quoted in Edwards 2008).

On 20 August the Home Secretary published a press release saying she would be introducing new laws to tighten restrictions on travel for sex offenders. The press release outlined plans for:

- requiring registered sex offenders to notify the police earlier of their intentions to travel abroad
- automatic removal of an individual's passport when they are subject to a blanket foreign travel order
- extending the duration of a Foreign Travel Order (currently six months).

The Home Secretary said she had 'spoken to child protection experts and the police and they have told me that these changes will further restrict the ability of child sex offenders to harm children both here and overseas. I will legislate for these measures as soon as possible' (Home Office 2008b). For some reason the requirement to notify the police of any travel, and not just that which lasted over three days, was missing from this list; it was to be another four years before such a requirement came into law.

On the morning of 20 August, the Home Secretary appeared on *BBC Breakfast* and was asked if she thought enough Foreign Travel Orders were being issued. Ms Smith said:

> I don't think there are enough issued at the moment – I think there is more that we can do to prevent people from travelling abroad. What police and others say to me is that one of the reasons that they don't apply for them is because they only last for six months. I think we can extend that time period.
>
> (BBC News 2008)

On 20 August 2008 a media scrum had descended on Heathrow airport London. Gary Glitter was due to be landing on a flight that afternoon. On his release in Vietnam he flew initially to Bangkok in Thailand where he was due to change planes for a flight to London. In Bangkok, however, he complained of heart problems and refused to board a plane transporting him to Britain. His reception in London was waiting in vain.

After 20 hours in Bangkok airport he boarded a plane for Hong Kong. In Hong Kong he was refused entry and promptly sent back to Bangkok.

> it now appears most likely that Glitter will leave Bangkok at around 1am and arrive at Heathrow at 7am on Friday morning [22 August 2019], to be met by around 35 British policemen. At least 19 countries have now refused to admit him, finally giving him little choice but to return to Britain where he is guaranteed a hostile reception from the press and public.
>
> (Bell and Moore 2008)

Gary Glitter duly returned to the UK where he was assessed by the police. No special protective measures were offered to him and by the weekend he was thought to have left London for Cornwall; a lawyer was reported to have been recruited 'to help him prevent his name being added to the sex offenders register indefinitely' (Osley and Philippidou 2008)

Still not working

As we saw in Chapter Seven the UK government introduced two new civil orders in the Anti-Social Behaviour, Crime and Policing Act 2014 – the Sexual Harm Prevention Orders (SHPO) and the Sexual Risk Order (SRO). These two orders replaced three previous civil orders in the Sexual Offences Act 2003 – the Risk of Sexual Harm Order (RSHO), Sexual Offences Prevention Order (SOPO) and the Foreign Travel Order (FTO). It was the FTO that would be applied to restrict overseas travel if they were on the register and it was thought the travel would lead to harm to children; it was the SHPO and the SRO that replaced the FTO (Home Office 2013a).

Between the introduction of the Sexual Harm Prevention Order in March 2015 and September 2015, 2,425 Sexual Harm Prevention Orders were issued in England and Wales but there appears to be no data on how many of those Orders contained international travel restrictions on sex offenders (*Hansard House of Commons Debates 24 April 2017*PQ 70883).

In 2019 ECPAT gave evidence to the Independent Inquiry into Child Sexual Abuse (IICSA) that the SHPOs and the SROs were still not working well. Bharti Patel, the new CEO of ECPAT UK, provided the evidence on these failures that suggested UK citizens were still able to travel abroad and sexually exploit children with impunity (ECPAT UK 2019). She highlighted a range of institutional failings:

- Widespread *lack of awareness and use* of these civil orders and extra-territorial jurisdictional measures among UK authorities and NGOs abroad;

- Between 2017 and 2018, 5,551 individuals were convicted or cautioned for sexual abuse offences in the UK, *but only 11 had foreign travel restrictions imposed*;
- Since the introduction of the new civil orders three years ago, 15,355 individuals received a Sexual Harm Prevention Order but only *27 had foreign travel restrictions imposed (less than 2 in every 1,000 convicted or cautioned*);
- Since the introduction of extra-territorial jurisdiction in respect of sexual abuse abroad in 2004, only seven child sex offenders were reported to have been extradited from the country where they offended and prosecuted in the UK;
- Between 2013 and 2017, 361 UK nationals sought consular assistance following being arrested for child sex offences abroad, *yet it is not known if these offenders were brought to justice either locally or in the UK.*

(ibid; emphasis in original)

Case study 11.2

Police in London received seven separate reports about a registered sex offender exhibiting worrying behaviour, such as talking to children or being seen in parks where children were present.

They missed opportunities to make an application for a Sexual Harm Prevention Order (which can be used to impose wide-ranging prohibitions on individuals previously convicted of certain sexual offences, and thought to pose current risk of sexual harm to the public), or to work actively on the case (for instance, by arresting the offender for failing to comply with notification requirements).

(HMIC 2016: 85)

Case study 11.3

Unacceptable delay: A British citizen was voluntarily deported from abroad. He had an extensive criminal record, including a number of child sex offences and indecent images of children offences.

The initial response by the central Jigsaw team was good: they met the offender off the flight at the airport, with a notification order obtained on that same day. Staff from the borough Jigsaw team then took responsibility for his management; but they then did not see the offender for 27 days after he had registered his details with the police.

As a result, a very high-risk registered sex offender was resident in the UK for a number of weeks without being seen at his home address for a full assessment of the risk he posed.

(HMIC 2016: 84)

Case study 11.4

Eight years after release and on the Sex Offenders Register (SOR) I continue struggling to cope with ever-increasing bureaucracy. When my sentence finished, I applied for a passport so my partner and I could have holidays in Europe. I was issued with a new electronic passport. My partner also has one. Every time we've been out of the UK, my partner's passport works on the scanners, but mine does not and I end up being questioned at passport control. This made me suspicious. I asked the police if there was a 'marker' on my passport. This was denied.

Very recently, returning from a Spanish holiday my partner went through the scanner successfully. He stood behind the passport control officer who I was redirected to. He saw what came up on the screen – it was totally different to others whose passports had failed to scan.

As a result, I challenged the Public Protection Team on my annual unannounced visit two days ago. This time it was admitted: there is an electronic marker on passports of sex offenders. I tried searching for information on this. There's plenty on the same in the USA but I can find nothing on Britain.

Having paid for my shameful past I've rebuilt a new clean living and crime-free life, but this new 'Big Brother' system prevents me and others on the SOR from travelling like anyone else. I'm obliged to tell the Public Protection Unit if I'm going abroad on holiday. They, in turn, inform Special Branch. I've therefore complied with the SOR. Arriving at holiday destinations, I get pulled aside and interrogated, and returning home, the same. Yet nobody is willing to admit this online. I'm thankful for the honesty of a Public Protection Officer for being up front with me.

So, for men and women still doing time for sexual offences, be prepared to face even tougher restrictions when you're released. After eight years, with my conviction finished, I'm still paying for wrongdoings over 20 years ago – and they are never likely to go away.

(Inside Time 2016)

The particular case of travel between Northern Ireland and the Republic of Ireland

In the early days of the UK sex offender register it was reported that offenders living in Northern Ireland were going south across the border to live in the Republic of Ireland to avoid its requirements; this was facilitated by the Common Travel Area that existed between the two countries (Sunday Times 1997); the reports of this easy international crossing were quickly denied by the politicians in Dublin (House of Oireachtas 1997). In 2001 the Republic got its own register with the passing of their Sex Offenders Act 2001.

If there was a problem with sex offenders moving between the two countries attempts were soon put in place to rectify them. A 'Protocol for the sharing of information on the management of sex offenders between the Probation Service and the Probation Board for Northern Ireland (PBNI)' was signed by the Heads of both countries' probation services in March 2006 and was subsequently up dated as required (PBNI/The Probation Service 2017).

In order to improve the policing between the North and South the police forces of the two countries – the Police Service of Northern Ireland (PSNI) and the Garda Síochána – also met together and a Memorandum of Understanding on information sharing arrangements was signed on 27 November 2006. The rationale for the Memorandum was that such information would be shared between police forces for the purposes of public protection from the risks presented by sex offenders and for investigating serious sexual offences. The Memorandum covers the transmission of any information necessary to achieve these purposes (Home Office 2006a and 2006b; Moriarty 2006). A Registered Sex Offender Advisory Group was also established at the same time made up of representatives of the Garda Síochána, the Police Service of Northern Ireland, the Department of Justice, Equality and Law Reform and the Northern Ireland Office. As part of its work, this Group was to evaluate the potential for sharing information, examining the registration criteria in both jurisdictions for sex offenders and identifying areas for further cooperation (DJE 2006).

When an offender notifies the UK police of his or her intention to travel to the Republic police forces in the UK will inform the Garda, and when an offender notifies the Garda of an intention to travel to the UK the Garda will notify the UK police. Contact will be made between the relevant police force and their corresponding office in Belfast or Dublin or through their respective National Central Bureau (NCB) for Interpol. In September 2008 the two police forces met again to sign an Agreement on the sharing of personal data for investigating sexual offences and for purposes of 'public protection' monitoring (DJELR 2008).

Summary

The problem of the travelling sex offender has been identified and pursued by NGOs such as ECPAT and measures put in place to limit the opportunities of registered sex offenders to travel freely abroad. The outgoing offender leaving the UK must advise the police of their intentions and the police may apply for civil orders to prevent that travel if they believe children, in particular, will be at risk. In the light of few of these orders being made, the process of obtaining them has been simplified by the introduction of the Sexual Harm Prevention Orders and Sexual Risk Orders in 2014 but the numbers applied for remain resolutely low.

The opposite side of the coin to the outgoing sex offender leaving the UK has been that of the incoming offender arriving here without the knowledge of the authorities. Notification Orders requiring offenders to register can be applied for if the police become aware of these arrivals.

12 Coming off the register

Introduction

When the sex offender register was first introduced there was only one way of coming off it before the scheduled applicable time period and that was to have the original conviction and sentence quashed. Just as registration was an automatic add-on to the sentence so any quashing of the sentence brought an automatic dispensing of registration.

This position changed following firstly changes in the law that meant some people were on the register for behaviour that no longer constituted a crime and secondly following a successful legal challenge that the lack of a review for indefinite – life-long – periods of registration was in breach of the European Convention on Human Rights and required new laws to remedy this breach.

Applications to come off the register

Sexual Offences Act 2003 s93 and Schedule 4

The 2003 Sexual Offences Act recognised that changes in the law meant there were some men on the register for behaviour that was no longer criminal. The Sexual Offences (Amendment) Act 2000 had lowered the age of consent for homosexual men from 18 down to 16 giving it equivalence to the age of consent for heterosexual activities. The 2003 Act had abolished the offences of consensual buggery and indecency between men. The result was that some men were on the register for activities that were no longer a criminal offence and would, in future, not lead to prosecution, conviction, sentence or registration. In the interests of justice these men were now invited to apply to the Home Secretary to come off the register.

In an ideal world the Home Office would have known who was eligible for removal without having to ask the people concerned to apply but:

> the Home Office admitted yesterday that the register does not contain enough detail to determine who should be removed. Because of this, police are to invite registered offenders to apply to have the restrictions

lifted. The official information systems are so poor they will be asked to supply details of their convictions so case files can be found.

(Travis 2003)

These applications were to be dealt with on a case by case basis starting in May 2004. The criteria for removal were set out in Schedule 4 of the Sexual Offences Act 2003. Local police forces were to write to people on the register telling them of these new arrangements. Home Office officials considering the application, known as the 'Schedule 4 Team', were to base their decisions on the application they received, the applicant's criminal record, any police investigation files, CPS files and court papers (Home Office 2004c: para.16). The Home Office estimated that there would be a maximum of 300 legitimate applications (ibid: para.14).

Protection of Freedoms Act 2012 ss. 92–100

The Protection of Freedoms Act 2012 ss92 gave powers to the Home Secretary to 'disregard' convictions and cautions made under the now repealed Sexual Offences Act 1956 ss12 and 13 for offences of buggery and gross indecency. Applications were made to the Home Secretary. The disregard only took place if there had been consent by the other person involved and that person had been over 16 at the time. The Home Office had also to issue a disregard notice on the offences in question.

Once the disregard had been approved the convictions and cautions could not be used in future court appearances as 'antecedents' or in any other disclosure such as an employment criminal records check. A removal from the sex offender register could also take place. Between October 2012 and April 2016, a total of 242 individuals had made disregard applications in respect of 317 cases. Of these 317 cases, 83 had been accepted for a disregard, 233 rejected and one was still pending resolution (*Hansard House of Lords 27 April 2016 PQ HL7758*).

Policing and Crime Act 2017 s165

The disregard process was later extended to include 'pardons' for people with criminal records convicted under old laws that no longer existed. In December 2013 the *Enigma* code-breaker Alan Turing had received a posthumous Royal Pardon for his sexual offences committed in the early 1950s. In October 2016 amendments were now added to the Policing and Crime Bill to allow more people in Turing's position to apply for pardons. This became informally known as 'Turing's Law' (Policing and Crime Act 2017 s165).

Section 164 of the Act automatically conferred a posthumous pardon on any person who died before the section comes into force and who was convicted of, or cautioned for, a specified offence, where the people involved had consented and were over 18.

The review of indefinite registration

From 1997 to 2010 those offenders who had to meet the notification requirements for life had no means of appeal against their indefinite registration. No matter how many treatment programmes they attended, how consistently they desisted from reoffending or how old and disabled they grew this was a case of 'life meant life'.

This situation had been foreseen and discussed in the parliamentary debate on the Sex Offenders Bill; for the opposition Alun Michael argued that lifetime registration was unduly inflexible and:

> creates the possibility of an individual's having to go on reporting changes of address for decades, including moves from a residential home for the elderly to a hospital or hospice. There is at present no mechanism in the Bill for ending the requirement.
>
> (*Hansard House of Commons 4 February 1997 Standing Committee D col.28*)

The government was not moved. Timothy Kirkhope, the then Under Secretary of State for the Home Office, said that he knew of 'cases of very elderly men, who have been in residential homes, who have molested children' (ibid). Alun Michael told him this could be 'an elephant sitting on the Minister's doorstep in years to come saying, "Minister I am an elephant and you did not see me coming in Committee"' (ibid).

Some MPs even wanted everyone on the register to be there for life regardless of the seriousness of the offence. David Maclean, for the Home Office, thought that was somewhat excessive:

> I am open to the suggestion that the registration periods are not right, that they could be extended or perhaps that they should be shortened, but it would be a draconian measure to impose a lifetime requirement on any person convicted of any of the sexual offences in the Bill.
>
> (*Hansard House of Commons Debates 27 January 1997 col.28*)

The position remained that a time period for registration could only be altered or ended if the courts quashed the original conviction or caution that had led to inclusion on the register.

On 7 December 1999, Rupert Massey was sentenced to a total of six years' imprisonment and made subject to the registration requirements of the Sex Offenders Act 1997 for an indefinite period. On 20 December 2001, the Court of Appeal dismissed Massey's appeal against conviction and refused an application for leave to appeal against his sentence. In 2003 Massey turned to the European Court of Human Rights. In and amongst a number of complaints the Court was asked to rule on the lack of a review system to challenge the indefinite period the applicant was to spend on the register. Massey told the

Court that 'there is no assessment or review of the necessity of registration in his particular case' (*Massey v the UK – 14399/02 [2003] ECHR 710*).

The Court accepted that Article 8 (the right to privacy) was 'engaged' in this case, but that the lack of a review did not breach the Article:

> the requirement to provide information to the police under the Sex Offenders Act 1997 did constitute an interference with the applicant's private life but that they were 'in accordance with the law' and pursued legitimate aims, namely, the prevention of crime and the protection of the rights and freedoms of others. The Court found that the requirements placed upon the applicant were proportionate to the aims pursued by the legislation in view of the gravity of harm which may be caused to victims of sexual offences.
>
> (*Massey v the UK – 14399/02 [2003] ECHR 710*: The Law para.2(iii))

The Court rejected the complaints. The Court cited *Adamson 1998* where the European Commission of Human Rights had also established that the sex offender register did 'engage' Article 8 but did not actually breach it; the sex offender register had been deemed 'necessary and proportionate' (*Adamson v UK (1999) Application 22293/98*).

The 'elephant' eventually turned up in December 2008 when an elderly man and a juvenile, both on the register for life, jointly brought a case to the High Court arguing that the lack of a review mechanism was a disproportionate interference with their Article 8 rights.

The case of Thompson and F

The High Court

Angus Aubrey Thompson had been jailed for five years in 1996 for two indecent assaults and other assault offences. Originally from Newcastle, Thompson was released on licence in 2000 and had not been in trouble since. But the 1997 Sex Offenders Act came into force while he was in prison, meaning he had to be on the register for life; the 2003 Sexual Offences Act had reaffirmed his position. Now in 2008, aged 58, Thompson had suffered a series of heart attacks and suffered from arthritis. In the High Court his barrister said the stress of being on the register was making his ill-health worse.

F was from Wigan and was just 11 years old when in 2005 he was sentenced to a 30-month youth custody sentence at Liverpool Crown Court and also placed on the sex offender register for life. He complained he was unable to go on a family holiday in 2007 due to restrictions placed on foreign travel and was unable to join his local amateur rugby league team. There were also concerns that having his name on the sex offenders register would damage his career prospects.

The Court agreed with both Thompson and F and duly granted a 'declaration of incompatibility' between section 82(1) of the 2003 Act – the notification time period – and Article 8 of the European Convention on Human Rights to the extent that indefinite notification periods are not subject to any review mechanism where the proportionality of the notification requirements can be evaluated (*R (F and Thompson) v Secretary of State for the Home Department [2008] EWHC 3170 (QB)*).

The Court of Appeal

The Home Office appealed. The Court of Appeal recognised that both sides agreed that Article 8 was 'engaged' and that the interference with a person's privacy was in accordance with law. The sex offender register itself was held to purse a legitimate aim in trying to offer 'public protection' and prevent crime. For the Court the question was whether the measures were 'proportionate' to that legitimate aim and that – the real question was 'whether an offender who can *clearly* demonstrate that he presents no risk, or no measurable risk of re-offending, should be precluded from obtaining a review of the notification requirements' (emphasis in original; *R (TF and Thompson) v Secretary of State for the Home Department [2009] EWCA Civ 792*: para.36).

The Home Office argued that 'the indefinite notification requirements without a review mechanism were proportionate' (ibid: para.37) and that the:

> interference with the claimants' Article 8 rights is very slight and amounts only to an inconvenience. So long as the offenders comply with the notification requirements, they are not prevented from doing anything. The information that is required to be provided is not highly personal. It is information of a type that any citizen may be required to provide to the State authorities or other organisations, such as banks, from time to time.
>
> (ibid. para.38)

The Court of Appeal disagreed. They thought the Home Office was underestimating the significance of the impact on offenders.

> We accept that for those who do not travel abroad and who do not travel for periods in excess of 7 days at a time in the United Kingdom, the notification requirements may be little more than an inconvenience. But for those who frequently travel, sometimes at short notice, the position may be quite different.
>
> (ibid: para.40)

The Court gave some examples of the problems in an Annex to their judgment.

The Home Office now argued that if people were excused from being on the register, the police database would be incomplete and therefore compromised in its purpose. Again, the Court was unwilling to accept this submission and argued that the Home Office's arguments were based on two false assumptions:

1 that there is a risk that those sentenced to custodial sentence of at least 30 months may commit further serious sexual offences for the rest of their lives; and
2 that the register will assist the police in preventing and detecting such offences and may deter others from further offending.

According to the Court of Appeal the two assumptions were falsified because it was clear that there was no real risk that the sexual offender would reoffend and therefore no purpose served by keeping him on the sex offender's register. To keep such a person on the police database did nothing to promote the aims of the notification requirements.

The Court would also not accept that the police database would be 'incomplete' and therefore compromised in its purpose. They turned the question around and asked what a complete database would look like?

> In our judgment, it should not include offenders who no longer present a risk of sexual offending … we do not see how the inclusion of a right of review of indefinite notification requirements would render the whole scheme unviable… but where there is no real risk of further offending, there is no benefit in keeping the police so informed. On the contrary, the lack of a system to review those who are no longer a risk may adversely affect the efficacy of the system as police forces become burdened with notifications from an ever-increasing number of offenders.
>
> (para.44)

The Home Office brought the question of resources to the attention of the Court by pointing out that a review mechanism would have significant resource implications especially as 'the vast majority of those who are subject to the indefinite notification regime would seek a review and that many would challenge any refusal'. The Court of Appeal said they were 'not impressed by the appeal to resources' (ibid: para.48).

Finally, the Home Office said that it would be difficult to operate a right of review and difficult for the offender to show that he or she no longer presented a risk of sexual offending. It would also 'be difficult for the decision-maker to make an accurate assessment of risk: there would always be the possibility of mistakes' (ibid: para.49). Such an argument from the Home Office rather dismissed the work of the police offender managers who did such risk assessments all the time, ever since the Criminal Justice and Court Services Act 2000 ss66–7 had placed the duty upon them.

The Appeal of the Secretary of State for the Home Office was dismissed.

The Supreme Court

The Home Office appealed again to the highest court – the Supreme Court. In April 2010, the Supreme Court agreed that indefinite notification requirements for sex offenders with no opportunity for review, as stipulated in section 82 of the Sexual Offences Act 2003, was incompatible with both section 4 of the Human Rights Act 1998 and Article 8 of the European Convention on Human Rights.

The Supreme Court dealt with the case in terms of proportionality and in so doing asked itself three questions:

i what is the extent of the interference with the Article 8 rights?

ii how valuable are the notification requirements in achieving the legitimate aims?

iii to what extent would that value be eroded if the notification requirements were made subject to review.

(*R (on the application of F (by his litigation friend F)) and another (Respondents) v Secretary of State for the Home Department (Appellant) [2010] UKSC 17*: para.41)

The conclusions:

> If someone subject to the notification requirements could demonstrate that they no longer posed any significant risk of committing further sexual offences, there was no point in subjecting them to the interference with their Article 8 rights, which would then merely impose an unnecessary and unproductive burden on the responsible authorities.
>
> (ibid: para.51)

> The critical issue was whether a reliable risk assessment could be carried out in the case of sex offenders. The research into reoffending rates relied on by the Secretary of State showed that 75% of the sexual offenders who were monitored over a 21-year period were not reconvicted and there was no evidence before the court that showed that it was impossible to identify some at least who posed no significant risk of reoffending.
>
> (ibid: para.56)

Accordingly the lower Courts had been correct to find that the notification requirements constituted a disproportionate interference with Article 8 rights because they made no provision for individual review of the requirements (*R (on the application of F (by his litigation friend F)) and another (Respondents) v Secretary of State for the Home Department (Appellant) [2010] UKSC 17* paras.58, 59 and 61).

The political reaction

We had to wait some ten months for any formal political reaction to the Supreme Court decision – from April 2010 to February 2011. Eventually in the House of Commons Philip Davies the Conservative MP for Shipley in West Yorkshire asked the Prime Minister:

> After votes for prisoners, we now have the potential for human rights legislation to give sex offenders the opportunity to come off the sex offenders register. Is the Prime Minister aware that my constituents are sick to the back teeth of the human rights of criminals and prisoners being put before the rights of law-abiding citizens in this country? Is it not time that we scrapped the Human Rights Act and, if necessary, withdrew from the European convention on human rights?
> (*Hansard House of Commons 16 February 2011 col. 955*)

Davies's comment about the Human Rights Act and the ECHR should be placed in a wider political discussion going on at this time on the value of human rights legislation in the UK. The specific matter of giving votes to prisoners had caused an on-going hostility ever since the European Court of Human Rights had ruled that the UK should introduce such voting rights. As the campaign group Liberty put it, this announcement of the Supreme Court's decision on the sex offender register came 'against a backdrop of poisonous and ill-informed debate about prisoner voting' (Liberty 2011: para.3).

Prime Minister David Cameron replied in equally robust fashion:

> My hon. Friend speaks for many people in saying how completely offensive it is, once again, to have a ruling by a court that flies in the face of common sense. Requiring serious sexual offenders to sign the register for life, as they now do, has broad support across this House and across the country. *I am appalled by the Supreme Court ruling. We will take the minimum possible approach to this ruling* and use the opportunity to close some loopholes in the sex offender's register. For instance, we will make it compulsory for sex offenders to report to the authorities before any travel, and will not allow them to change their name by deed poll to avoid having their name on the register.
> (*Hansard House of Commons 16 February 2011 col. 955*; emphasis added)

Cameron was giving the first indication that the government intended to 'use the opportunity to close some loopholes in the sex offender register' such as requiring sex offenders 'to report to the authorities before any travel' (see Chapter Eleven). These additional requirements coming exactly the same day as the announcement of the Supreme Court ruling could be interpreted as more political manoeuvring to blur and confuse what could otherwise be seen as a weakness imposed on the government by the Courts; for clarity these additional requirements have been treated separately here (see Chapter Seven).

On the same day as Cameron's comments, Theresa May, then Home Secretary, followed up with a Ministerial Statement declaring that she too was 'appalled' by the judgement. Using phrases that could have come from the same briefing paper as that used by the Prime Minister, the Home Secretary said:

> The Government are disappointed and *appalled by that ruling.* It places the rights of sex offenders above the right of the public to be protected from the risk of their reoffending, but there is no possibility of further appeal. The Government are determined to do everything we can to protect the public from predatory sexual offenders, so *we will make the minimum possible changes to the law in order to comply with the ruling.* I want to make it clear that the Court's ruling does not mean that paedophiles and rapists will automatically come off the sex offender's register. The Court found only that they must be given the right to seek a review.
>
> (*Hansard House of Commons Debates 16 February 2011: Col. 959* emphasis added)

She also revealed that the final decision on whether an offender should remain on the register would be down to the police and with no right of appeal:

> There will be no right of appeal against the police's decision to keep an offender on the register. That decision will be final. Sex offenders who continue to pose a risk will remain on the register, and will do so for life if necessary.
>
> (ibid: col.959)

Shadow Home Secretary Yvette Cooper was equally frustrated by the Supreme Court judgement, saying that 'the new system [will have to be] extremely tough if it is to have the support of the House' and asked the Home Secretary to 'ensure that the focus is on public protection, rather than on the convenience or rights of those who have been convicted of serious crimes?' (*Hansard House of Commons Debates 16 February 2011: Column 961*).

The Home Secretary responded that:

> it is absolutely our intention that we should make the scheme as tough as possible and make it clear that it is about an ability to seek a review of a decision. We will frame it in the toughest possible terms and ensure that the process is absolutely right, so that we reduce the opportunity for it to be subject to any sort of judicial review once the decision is taken.
>
> (*Hansard House of Commons Debates 16 February 2011: Column 964*)

The aim was to make the police decision – or 'determination' as it became known – the endpoint of any discussions (for the Home Secretary's full statement and subsequent questions from MPs see *Hansard House of Commons Debates 16 February 2011 cols. 959–969*).

Outside of Parliament the police themselves were more sanguine in their acceptance of the Supreme Court ruling. Then Assistant Chief Constable Michelle Skeer representing an ACPO management of sexual and violent offenders working group said 'protecting the public from harm is a fundamental role for the police service but we recognise that this must be balanced with the rights of individuals, as highlighted by the Supreme Court judgement'. She outlined how '[the police] have worked closely with the Home Office and other key partners to develop a robust review process that ensures a full assessment of the risks posed before an offender is removed from the notification requirements' (NPCC 2011).

Changing the law and setting up a new review system

In order to correct a human rights 'declaration of incompatibility' in the law the government had to introduce new legislation that would provide a 'remedy'. This could be done through secondary legislation in the form of a Statutory Instrument and a draft *Sexual Offences Act 2003 (Remedial) Order* was duly laid before Parliament on 21 April 2011.

The draft Order would amend the Sexual Offences Act 2003 by introducing new sections 91A to 91F. The new sections would say who was to be a 'qualifying offender for review', at what point in time they could apply for a review and how such an application could be made. The amended Act would also demonstrate how the police would make their 'determination', and what factors needed to be taken into account to assess the degree of risk the applicant might still pose; the draft Order identified 15 such factors in its proposed section 91D including seriousness of original offence, details of subsequent offending, time elapsed since last offence, views of the victim and any reports the applicant wanted to submit to support his or her case. Where the offender was over 18 years of age on the day of conviction, the application may be made 15 years after complying with the relevant notification requirement, or eight years if under 18 (see original draft at Legislation 2020).

As this was a response to a Supreme Court 'declaration of incompatibility' with the European Convention on Human Rights the draft Statutory Instrument was to be firstly examined by the House of Lords and House of Commons Joint Committee on Human Rights; the same Joint Committee that had completely missed this breach in the European Convention when they had examined the Sexual Offences Bill back in 2003. The Committee was not altogether happy with the draft Order and recommended that it should not be tabled in the terms proposed. They felt that, without 'significant amendment', the proposals in the draft Order would lead to repeat litigation and further violations of Article 8 of the ECHR. Of particular concern was the lack of any appeal from the police decision; as it stood:

> We consider that the draft Order should be amended to introduce a review by application to an independent and impartial tribunal, with a requirement that the Chief Police Officer (and other MAPPA institutions) should be notified of the application and should submit reports on their assessment of the risk posed by the applicant; or that the Order is amended to introduce a full statutory right of appeal from the decision of the Chief Officer to an independent and impartial tribunal.
>
> (House of Lords/House of Commons 2011: 3)

The campaign group Liberty had submitted evidence to the Joint Committee on Human Rights pointing out that:

> Requiring police to keep track of those who pose little risk of re-offending alongside those who do, the register imposes an impossible policing burden. It is conceivable that certain ex-offenders will no longer pose a risk, such as offenders who are no longer physically capable of offending. Punishment for the original crime will of course have been justified, but it does not make sense to divert police resources to continue monitoring, for the rest of their lives, ex-offenders who no longer pose a risk.
>
> (Liberty 2011: para.13)

If risk assessment could identify the high risk from the low risk offenders surely it could also identify those now safe enough to come off the register all together and the lack of a review mechanism was considered disproportionate.

Liberty also identified what they saw as the underlying problem:

> The flaws in this draft Order appear to stem from a declared political commitment to minimal action to comply with a Supreme Court judgment. Implementing a half-hearted policy to comply with a sound and reasonable judgment does not make for sensible policy, and nor will it promote and protect the safety of us all.
>
> (ibid: para.24)

The government response to the Joint Committee on Human Rights accepted the criticisms and adjusted the draft Remedial Order accordingly. On the matter of the need for an appeal from the police determination they stated that:

> The Government accepts the Committee's recommendation and will provide for a right of appeal to the magistrates' court from the determination by the police. This process retains the role of the police as the initial

> decision-maker and the Government believes that this should remain a police-led process.
>
> (Home Office 2012d: para.15)

In choosing local magistrates as the appeal tribunal, the government had decided against the Committee's idea that it should be a High Court or Crown Court. The appeal would also be in the public domain by being in the magistrates' court rather than the confidential setting of the police station, a fact sure to put some applicants off. Other criticisms were accepted including the need for more details on the test which the police must apply when making determinations, and the need for separate statutory guidance on the review scheme.

James Brokenshire Minister of State at the Home Office followed up with a Statement to the Commons; once again the Home Office took the opportunity to mix the changes brought about by the remedial Order with the new additional requirements they were intending to make to the notification requirements. Brokenshire's opening paragraph was about 'the tough new measures' being introduced simply because the 'opportunity' – to use the Prime Minister's word – was available, thus relegating the far more important remedial measures imposed on the government by the Supreme Court to the second paragraph (*Hansard House of Commons 5 March 2012 cols. WS143–4*).

The Joint Human Rights Committee made a second response to the changes made to the draft Order (House of Lords/House of Commons 2012) and the government duly replied again through a letter from Lynne Featherstone, Under Secretary of State at the Home Office dated 15 June 2012. There was a general acknowledgement of the revisions that had been made and an acceptance that the incompatibility with the European Convention had been removed (Featherstone 2012). The final version of the Order is considered below.

The Sexual Offences Act 2003 (Remedial) Order 2012 no. 1883

The 2012 Remedial Order for England and Wales contained the new sections 91A to 91F to be inserted into the Sexual Offences Act 2003 that gave people on the register indefinitely their right to a review. If the review and the 'determination' was successful they could come off the register and the obligation to notify the police of their circumstances would come to an end. The Order was made on 16 July 2012 and applications for review could be made after 1 September 2012.

A summary of the new sections relating to reviews are as follows.

91A Review of indefinite notification requirements: qualifying relevant offender

A qualifying relevant offender was anyone on the register for life, and they were entitled to make 'an application for review' to their local chief officer of police. They could not apply if they were also the subject of a Sexual Offences Prevention Order (SOPO) or a Sexual Harm Prevention Order (SHPO).

91B Review of indefinite notification requirements: application for review and qualifying dates

Applications for reviews must be made in writing. Adult applicants (over 18) must wait 15 years from their initial notification and under 18s have to wait eight years. This time period of 15 years was recognised in the start date of the review system (1 September 2012) which was just 15 years since the start date of the register on 1 September 1997. A police determination that an offender should not come off the register means a further eight year wait till the applicant can apply again (unless they appeal – see s91E below); sometimes they may have to wait longer than eight years if the police decide that the risk of sexual harm posed by them is sufficient to justify an extension.

91C Review of indefinite notification requirements: determination of application for review

For the purposes of the determination of an application for review under this section, a person on the register must satisfy the local chief officer of police that it is not necessary for the purpose of protecting the public or any particular members of the public from sexual harm for them to remain subject to the indefinite notification requirements. If the police determination is that the person in question should remain subject to the notification requirements, he or she must be given the reasons in writing and details of how to appeal. A successful application is also put in writing and starts from the day of receipt of that written notice.

91D Review of indefinite notification requirements: factors applying to determination under section 91C

In determining an application for review the police must consider any information given to them by the local MAPPA responsible authorities, the risk of sexual harm posed by the applicant and they must take into account the matters listed in this section. The latter are comprised of 15 items of information and are reproduced here as they appear in the Act:

a the seriousness of the offence in relation to which the qualifying relevant offender became subject to the indefinite notification requirements;
b the period of time which has elapsed since the qualifying relevant offender committed the offence (or other offences);
c where the qualifying relevant offender falls within section 81(1), whether the qualifying relevant offender committed any offence under section 3 of the Sex Offenders Act 1997 (a);
d whether the qualifying relevant offender has committed any offence under section 91;
e the age of the qualifying relevant offender at the qualifying date or further qualifying date;

f the age of the qualifying relevant offender at the time the offence referred to in paragraph (a) was committed;

g the age of any person who was a victim of any such offence (where applicable) and the difference in age between the victim and the qualifying relevant offender at the time the offence was committed;

h any assessment of the risk posed by the qualifying relevant offender which has been made by a responsible body under the arrangements for managing and assessing risk established under section 325 of the Criminal Justice Act 2003;

i any submission or evidence from a victim of the offence giving rise to the indefinite notification requirements;

j any convictions or findings made by a court (including by a court in Scotland, Northern Ireland or countries outside the United Kingdom) in respect of the qualifying relevant offender for any offence listed in Schedule 3 other than the one referred to in paragraph (a);

k any caution which the qualifying relevant offender has received for an offence (including for an offence in Northern Ireland or countries outside the United Kingdom) which is listed in Schedule 3;

l any convictions or findings made by a court in Scotland, Northern Ireland or countries outside the United Kingdom in respect of the qualifying relevant offender for any offence listed in Schedule 5 where the behaviour of the qualifying relevant offender since the date of such conviction or finding indicates a risk of sexual harm;

m any other submission or evidence of the risk of sexual harm posed by the qualifying relevant offender;

n any evidence presented by or on behalf of the qualifying relevant offender which demonstrates that the qualifying relevant offender does not pose a risk of sexual harm; and

o any other matter which the relevant chief officer of police considers to be appropriate.

(Sexual Offences Act 2003 s91D (2))

As section 91D (2) (i) above states, the police will consider information from victims as a factor when reviewing an application. The victim must register their contact details with the police to enable them to make contact in the event that an application for review is made. The police will not make contact if the victim has not registered their details on the basis that some victims and survivors prefer not to be contacted at all in the event of the offender making an application. Information from victims will not be the sole determining factor but will be considered alongside other information. Guidance has been published to help victims make their decision (Home Office/NPCC 2017).

Section 69 of the Criminal Justice and Court Services Act (2000) had imposed a statutory duty on Probation Areas to consult and notify the victims of sexual or other violent offences about the release arrangements for the offender where he or she is sentenced to one year or more in prison. Victims should be contacted within two months of the sentence being passed and offered:

- face to face contact with the probation service
- the opportunity to be kept informed about developments throughout the offender's sentence, if they wish
- an opportunity to contribute to the eventual release plans, to have their views taken into account by the Parole Board or other decision-maker, and to receive information about licence conditions which are directly relevant to them or members or their family.

91E Review of indefinite notification requirements: appeals

A registered sex offender may appeal against a police determination by applying to a magistrates' court within the local police area.

91F Review of indefinite notification requirements: guidance

The Home Office must issue guidance to relevant chief officers of police in relation to the determination of applications (see Home Office 2012e). Despite the production of guidance, the courts still made errors about registration and the law. One person applied directly to the criminal courts for the right to come off the register missing out both the police and magistrates' court whose job it was to make this decision. the criminal court effectively deregistered him despite having no authority to do so. The police in turn then had to bring a judicial review against the courts where the High Court relied upon the two principles:

- firstly, that the rule of law should be upheld; and
- secondly that there was a public interest in the proper procedure under the Sexual Offences Act 2003 being followed (*Commissioner of Police for the Metropolis v Central Criminal Court and others [2013] EWHC 179 (Admin)*).

Scotland brought in their remedy to the Sexual Offences Act 2003 before the Home Office did for England and Wales. The Scottish government, bound by the same Supreme Court decision, had published its draft Sexual Offences Act 2003 (Remedial) (Scotland) Order 2010 SI 370 on 25 October 2010 for consultation.

Scotland published its final Sexual Offences Act 2003 (Remedial) (Scotland) Order 2011 no.45 coming into force on 28 January 2011. The Order contained new sections 88A to 88H for the Sexual Offences Act 2003; many of these were directly comparable to the England and Wales version. One difference was that Scotland had automatic reviews and registered sex offenders did not have to make an application; they still had to wait for the required 15 years for adults or eight years for juveniles but then everyone was reviewed automatically. If it is assessed that the offender presents a risk which requires that they continue to be on the register, a Notification Continuation Order (NCO) will be issued. If it is assessed that they no longer require to be subject to Notification Requirements, the offender will be advised accordingly and their notification requirements will cease.

Northern Ireland also brought in legislation to allow for reviews of indefinite registration, in their Criminal Justice Act (Northern Ireland) 2013 implemented from March 2014. The Act inserted a new Schedule 3A entitled 'Review of Indefinite Notification Requirements' into the Sexual Offences Act 2003 and the Department of Justice in Northern Ireland produced formal Guidance (DoJ 2014a). The person on the register must initiate an application as in England and Wales. The arrangements are otherwise very similar to those in England, Wales and Scotland. The Northern Ireland Department of Justice has stated that all three jurisdictions 'consulted with each other to ensure that the broad principles of their respective review mechanisms were consistent' (DoJ 2014b: para.8).

Results of the new law in England and Wales

Reports of the numbers of people coming off the register through the new review system started to appear in the press in May 2013. The *Daily Mail* used the Freedom of Information Act and asked all 43 police forces in England and Wales for the number of applications they had received and the outcome of those applications. A total of 27 forces replied revealing 91 applications and 43 registered sex offenders being allowed to leave the register since 1 September 2012. The *Daily Mail* emphasised the low visibility of these applications and, what they called, the 'secrecy' in which they took place: 'Police have secretly removed dozens of convicted sex offenders … from the Sex Offenders Register … applications have been approved behind closed doors' (Doyle 2013).

One applicant had been turned down by a West Yorkshire police determination and had taken his case to appeal. In the magistrates' court his solicitor said he thought the police had denied the application because they did not want the responsibility of such a decision. He also asserted that being on the sex offenders' register did not 'serve any purpose', as he was only visited once a year for a 'general chat'. The District Judge said 'the order has now served its purpose. I cannot see any benefit in it remaining' and the applicant was allowed to come off the register ('Landmark register victory for child sex offender', *Yorkshire Post* 11 March 2013).

Philip Davies MP called the ruling 'ludicrous' and said judges appeared 'completely clueless':

> The only thing a decision like this can do is put more people at risk. It is very worrying that this sets a precedent for other cases. It opens the

floodgates. I do not see any case where people should be removed from this register.

(cited in Atkinson 2013)

A few months later *The Sun on Sunday* revealed 108 people to have been removed from the register (Wooding 2013) and the BBC using the Freedom of Information Act got replies from 40 police forces who had received a total of 1,289 applications for reviews of which 679 (53%) were approved (BBC 2016a).

The annual Ministry of Justice reports on MAPPA activities started carrying official statistics on the numbers coming off the register in their 2016–17 edition when 364 received a determination that they could leave (MoJ 2017b: 9); the 2017–18 edition reported a further total of 334 (MoJ 2018:10); and between April 2018 and March 2019, 330 Registered Sexual Offenders had their lifetime notification requirements revoked on application (MoJ 2019a: 12). None of these reports carried the numbers of those who made applications for a determination.

The *Daily Mail* using the Freedom of Information Act tried to get a figure for the percentage of applicants who were successful in being allowed to leave the register. On replies from 36 out of 43 police forces they estimated that 72% of applicants were granted leave to come off the register for the years 2016, 2017 and 2018 with only 363 of 1,288 applicants refused permission to come off. One victim told the *Daily Mail* ‘she lived in fear of bumping into her attacker after he successfully applied to have his name removed from the register’. Nobody seems to have told the victim – or the reporter – that this could have equally happened if the offender lived in the community and had not been taken off the register (Norton 2020).

Some people on the register who have had their review turned down by the police, and again on appeal by a magistrate’s court, have taken it further, and sought a judicial review. In the case of *Hamill* in 2014 the High Court referred their appeal back to another magistrates’ court for a second opinion (*R (Hamill) v Chelmsford Magistrates’ Court [2014] EWHC 2799 (Admin)*). In the case of NE and NM in 2015 the High Court held that the first claim by NE was allowed, and the appeal was sent back to be reheard by the magistrates’ court. The second claim by NM was dismissed (*R (NM & NE) v Birmingham Magistrates’ Court [2015] EWHC 688 (Admin)*).

An e-petition

Towards the end of 2016 an e-petition was started by the family of April Jones, a five-year-old child abducted and murdered in her home town of Machynlleth, Wales in October 2012. E-petitions are organised by the government and Parliament and are a way of enabling members of the public to petition the House of Commons and press for action from the government. Petitions with 10,000 or more names on them will be ‘noted’ and those with over 100,000 names will be considered for debate.

E-petition 166711, started by the Jones family, read as follows:

> We the undersigned call on the prime minister to make all sex offenders remain on the register for life no matter the crime, for service providers and search engines to be better policed regarding child abuse images and harder sentences on those caught with indecent images of children.

The petition ran for six months and got 127,296 signatures before it was closed. A debate was held on the topic of what was now called 'April's Law' on 13 March 2017. The Jones family were in Westminster Hall for the debate where MPs argued the case in the presence of Sarah Newton Under Secretary of State for the Home Office. The argument was again brought forward that all sex offenders should remain on the sex offender register for life no matter the crime, and therefore no reviews should have been introduced allowing those required to register indefinitely to come off the register even if they were assessed as low risk (*Hansard House of Commons Debates, 13 March 2017, cols.1–20 WH*).

Summary

The 2003 Sexual Offences Act recognised that changes in the law meant there were some men on the register for behaviour that was no longer criminal. The Act itself, for example, had abolished the offences of consensual buggery and indecency between men and the Sexual Offences (Amendment) Act 2000 had lowered the age of consent for homosexual men from 18 down to 16 giving it equivalence to the age of consent for heterosexual sex. The result was that some men were still on the register for offences that were no longer offences. Arrangements were made for these men to apply for their records to be 'disregarded' when it came to employment, insurance and other similar applications.

The law underpinning the register was also found in breach of the European Convention on Human Rights when it came to people required to register for life. A lifetime's registration was considered to be disproportionate and remedial measures in the form of 'a review' were called for to bring it back into line with the European Convention; this was achieved by amendments to the Sexual Offences Act 2003 which allowed for a review process to be put into place starting from 1 September 2012.

13 The register in Scotland, Northern Ireland, the Channel Islands, the Isle of Man and other British Overseas Territories

Introduction

Throughout this book we have made references to the way in which the register differs in different parts of the UK such as Scotland and Northern Ireland. The idea of the register has also extended to the Channel Islands and the Isle of Man and to other British Overseas Territories including Gibraltar and the Cayman Islands. In this chapter we take an overview of the registration arrangements in these parts of the world and the nature of this ever-extending form of offender management.

Scotland

The Scottish sex offender register was implemented from 1 September 1997 under the same Sex Offenders Act 1997 that was the basis for the arrangements for England and Wales and Northern Ireland. The Act's Schedule 1 paragraph 2 listed the 19 offences in Scotland that would lead to registration. The Scottish Executive provided guidance to the agencies who would be implementing the register (Scottish Executive 1997) and early reports were positive:

> The police and social work services have worked very effectively in ensuring the success of the sex offender's register as a monitoring tool and in developing risk assessment and management processes in order to offer greater protection to the public. These arrangements provide excellent examples of best practice that could be built upon in other inter-agency arrangements.
>
> (SWSI 2002: para.3)

Two major reports on sex offending followed on from implementation day in the form of the MacLean Report (2000) and the Cosgrove Report (2001). It was the latter report that was the more pertinent to the Scottish sex offender register.

The Cosgrove Report was the report of an Expert Panel established in 1998 to advise the Secretary of State on any relevant issues relating to sex offenders. Chapter Four of the report made recommendations about the register in Scotland and the management of sex offenders that included broadening the scope of offences leading to registration and extending registration to other offences where there had been a sexual element at the discretion of the sentencing judge (ibid: Recommendations 40–47).

Case study 13.1

The police had encountered the accused, who was very drunk and leaning back against a window in a busy public street. His trouser buttons were undone and the police initially thought he was urinating, only to realise that he was in fact masturbating. The Sheriff accepted that there was no underlying sexual deviancy in the conduct of the accused and that the catalyst for that conduct was the fact that he was very drunk; but he decided that what had happened was not something which was commonly, or indeed even occasionally, encountered in connection with intoxicated persons in city centre public streets and that accordingly the sexual aspect of the case was 'significant'. The High Court refused a bill of suspension against the Sheriff's decision.

(Stoddart 2012)

The matter of risk assessment and management was taken seriously in Scotland and made the subject of a separate government report. The MacLean Committee reported to Scottish Ministers on 26 June 2000, covering areas including the assessment of risk; a proposal for a new Risk Management Authority; a proposal for Risk Assessment Order and Risk Management Plans; a proposal for a new Order for Lifelong Restriction; high risk offenders with a mental disorder; supervision in the community and personality disorder (MacLean Report 2000). The MacLean proposals were included in the Criminal Justice (Scotland) Bill.

The Criminal Justice (Scotland) Act 2003 provided for the Risk Management Authority (RMA) to be established as a public body and the introduction of the Risk Assessment Order (RAO) and Order for Lifelong Restriction (OLR). The Act also introduced changes to Restriction of Liberty Orders to enable the transfer of these orders between courts and to make them a direct alternative to custody. The Act gives the RMA a number of statutory functions in relation to risk assessment and minimising risk.

As in England and Wales the notification requirements of the Sex Offenders Act 1997 were replaced by the Sexual Offences Act 2003 Part 2 which, with some exceptions, applies to Scotland. Changes in the 2003 Act included giving the police the power to check the fingerprints and take a photograph of a sex offender each time a notification is made, not just on his or her initial notification; a Notification Order enabling the notification requirements to be applied to offenders with convictions abroad was introduced and registered sex offenders were required to reconfirm the accuracy of the above information on an annual basis; Sex Offender Orders became Sexual Offences Prevention Orders (SOPO) and Foreign Travel Orders were introduced.

The Sexual Offences Act 2003 listed the offences that would lead to registration in Scotland in its Schedule 3 paras.38–60. Many of the Cosgrove recommendations were covered in the Act including the one major difference between Scotland and England and Wales in the form of a discretionary route on to the register rather than an automatic one. In Scotland paragraph 60 of Schedule 3 read:

> An offence in Scotland other than is mentioned in paragraphs 36 to 59 if the court, in imposing sentence or otherwise disposing of the case, determines for the purposes of this paragraph that there was a significant sexual aspect to the offender's behaviour in committing the offence.

The paragraph was later amended in 2005 and 2009 to include a total of 38 more offences from the Protection of Children and Prevention of Sexual Offences (Scotland) Act 2005, and the Sexual Offences (Scotland) Act 2009 (see below); the paragraph now reads 'mentioned in paragraphs 36 to 59ZL'.

There was, inevitably, discussion in the courts about the meaning of 'significant sexual aspects'. In the end it was agreed that it all came down to 'common sense' or what the 'reasonable person' thought was 'significant' in terms of 'public protection' (*Hay v HM Advocate 2012 SCCR 281*; see also *Thompson v Dunn 2012 SCCR 298, McGuire v Procurator Fiscal, Glasgow [2012] HCJAC 86* (11 May 2012)) and *Appeal against Sentence by Liam Joseph Allan Reid Rodgerson against the Procurator Fiscal Alloa [2016] HCJAC 12*)). The offender has a right of appeal against the order.

Management of Offenders etc (Scotland) Act 2005

A report by Professor George Irving, following the murder of an eight-year-old boy by a sex offender already on the register made 36 recommendations on the registration, assessment, monitoring and management of sex offenders in the community (Irving 2005). Many of these recommendations were realised in the Management of Offenders etc (Scotland) Act 2005 which placed a duty on the police, local authorities, prison service and health (the responsible authorities) to establish joint arrangements for the assessment and management of risk posed by certain offenders. This followed the England and Wales model of the MAPPA. Offenders were categorised as:

- Category 1: registered sexual offenders
- Category 2: offenders – violent offenders and other sexual offenders
- Category 3: other dangerous offenders

and levels of management as:

- Level 1: ordinary agency management. Carried out by a single agency (e.g. criminal justice social work). A duty to share information with other responsible authorities is required.
- Level 2: active multi-agency management. Offenders who are deemed to present a high or very high level of risk which requires a multi-agency response.
- Level 3: active enhanced multi-agency. Cases where the involvement of senior members for each responsible authority is required in the management of the offender. For example, where considerable resources are required or public and media attention is anticipated.

These MAPPA arrangements were inspected in 2015 by HM Inspectorate of Constabulary for Scotland (HMICS) and The Care Inspectorate. They noted that MAPPA was well established across Scotland and working well; the inspection still made ten further recommendations including the need for:

- Additional guidance on practice standards, including risk assessment of online offenders Recommendation 1);
- Enhanced skills and equipment required to monitor devices used by registered sex offenders (Recommendation 3); and
- Enhanced understanding of the risks associated with 'sexting', particularly in relation to children and young people (Recommendation 4) (HMICS and Care Inspectorate 2015: 10–11).

National guidance on organising MAPPA was published in 2016 (Scottish Government 2016) and a follow up report on progress published in 2017 (HMICS and Care Inspectorate 2017).

Protection of Children and Prevention of Sexual Offences (Scotland) Act 2005

The primary objective of this 2005 Act was to improve the protection given to children and young people from those who would wish to cause them sexual harm, or exploit them for sexual purposes. The Act introduced new offences including that of sexual grooming of a person under 16 and paying for the sexual services of a person under 18. It introduced Risk of Sexual Harm Orders (RSHOs) which are designed to protect children from those who display inappropriate behaviour towards them and extends the use of Sexual Offences Prevention Orders (SOPOs) enabling criminal courts to impose them on sex offenders at the point of sentence.

Police, Public Order and Criminal Justice (Scotland) Act 2006

Part 2 of this Act amended the legislation on control of sex offenders. It introduced new powers for the police to take data and samples from persons subject to notification requirements and makes failure to comply an offence. This meant DNA samples, fingerprints, palm prints and photographs of other identifying marks such as tattoos

The Sexual Offences Act 2003 (Notification Requirements) (Scotland) Regulations 2007 no.246

This Act requires offenders to notify passport and bank account and credit card details.

Sexual Offences (Scotland) Act 2009

The Sexual Offences (Scotland) Act provided a statutory framework for sexual offences in Scots law and repeals the common law offences of rape, sodomy and clandestine injury to women and a number of other statutory sexual offences. The Act creates new statutory offences of rape, sexual assault by penetration, sexual assault, sexual coercion, coercing a person to be present during sexual activity, coercing a person to look at an image of sexual activity, communicating indecently, sexual exposure, voyeurism and administering a substance for a sexual purpose. It provides a general statutory definition of consent as 'free agreement'. The Act also makes it an offence of 'abuse of position of trust' for a person in a position of trust (over a child or person with a mental disorder) to engage in sexual activity with that child or person.

Scotland amended its Sexual Offences (Scotland) Act 2009 s9 in 2010 to make voyeurism by up-skirting a specific offence. The England and Wales Bill some ten years later would adopt a similar approach to that taken in Scotland. The two new forms of voyeurism would cover the operation of equipment or recording of an image under another person's clothing with the intention of viewing their genitals or buttocks (with or without underwear), and without that person's consent. The relevant provisions are subsections 9 (4A) and (4B); anyone convicted of a section 9 offence is placed on the sex offender's register.

The Sexual Offences Act 2003 (Remedial) (Scotland) Order (S.S.I. 2011/45)

This statutory instrument extended the list of information which must be provided to the police to include passport details, details of any bank account or credit card held with a banking institution, and to provide a valid form of identification upon notification. This proposal would align England and Wales with Scotland, who through the Sexual Offences Act 2003 (Notification Requirements) (Scotland) Regulations 2007 no.246, already required offenders to notify passport and bank account and credit card details.

Table 13.1 Numbers on the register in Scotland

Division	*Registered sex offenders in the community*	*Registered sex offenders in custody/hospital*
A Div – North East	451	112
C Div – Forth Valley	224	84
D Div – Tayside	404	158
E Div – Edinburgh	357	142
G Div – Greater Glasgow	693	252
J Div – The Lothians and Scottish Borders	357	123
K Div – Renfrewshire & Inverclyde	159	59
L Div – Argyle & West Dunbartonshire	146	49
N Div – Highland & Islands	228	62
P Div – Fife	331	152
Q Div – Lanarkshire	548	160
U Div – Ayrshire	384	127
V Div – Dumfries & Galloway	131	54
National total	**4413**	**1534**

Northern Ireland

A sex offender register was started in 1997 under the UK-wide Sex Offenders Act 1997; the Northern Ireland sexual offences that the Act applied to were listed in Schedule 1 of the Act paragraph 3. The Courts in Northern Ireland were given the power to make Restraining Orders through the Sex Offenders Act 1997 (Northern Ireland) Order 2001 no. 1853.

Registered sex offenders were originally subject to a management system, which involved the police, probation and social services along with other agencies such as the Northern Ireland Housing Executive (NIHE). This system was known as MASRAM (Multi Agency Sex offender Risk Assessment and Management). MASRAM involved those agencies that met regularly in Area Sex Offender Risk Management Committees (ASORMC) to collaborate in the management of registered sex offenders; each offender is allocated a Designated Risk Manager (DRM). The ASORMC developed an Action Plan to monitor and manage the offender during his time in the MASRAM scheme. The 2003 Sexual Offences Act contained the list of Northern Ireland sexual offences leading to registration in its Schedule 3 paragraphs 61–92Y.

In October 2008, these administrative arrangements were provided for in law, which meant that specified agencies now had a legal duty to cooperate and share information to help assess and manage risk. Article 50 of the Criminal Justice (N.I.) Order 2008 specified the agencies which had a duty to cooperate to ensure effective assessment and management of the risks posed by certain sexual and violent offenders. The Public Protection Arrangements in Northern Ireland (PPANI) were also introduced in October 2008 to replace MASRAM. Like MAPPA in England and Wales, PPANI is not a statutory body in itself but a structure that enables agencies to undertake their statutory duties and coordinate their functions to enhance public protection.

The Criminal Justice Act (Northern Ireland) 2013 introduced a review mechanism for sex offenders subject to indefinite notification requirements. The change in the law was required in to comply with the UK Supreme Court ruling which held that the current policy of indefinite retention was incompatible with the European Convention on Human Rights. Sex offenders subject to indefinite notification requirements are permitted to make an application for a review after 15 years and 8 years for under 18s in line with other UK jurisdictions.

In August 2020 there were 1,667 offenders registered in Northern Ireland; this included both sexual and violent offenders who were classified as 1,402 Category 1 (low risk offenders), 239 Category 2 (middle risk) and 26 Category 3 (high risk) (PPANI 2020).

The Channel Islands

Jersey

An investigation into historic child abuse in Jersey had started in the spring of 2007. The investigation received international attention when police moved into Haut de la Garenne, a former children's home then being used as a youth hostel. Forensic teams conducted searches in the building between the end of February 2008 and July 2008. In November 2008, the Deputy Chief Officer of the States of Jersey Police, stated that there was 'no evidence' of any child murders at Haut de la Garenne.

The States of Jersey Police said that in 2008 an allegation of an indecent assault by Jimmy Savile, the TV personality, at the home in the 1970s had been investigated, but there had been insufficient evidence to proceed. After Savile's death in 2011, hundreds of people from all over the UK came forward to accuse him of past abuse. Several people from Haut de la Garenne came forward at this time.

The island of Jersey could have used provisions under the Sex Offenders Act 1997 s.9 to introduce a sex offender register. In practice they had never used the 1997 Act. In the wake of the police investigations the idea of a register now emerged (Batty 2008) and in 2010 they passed their own Sex Offenders (Jersey) Law bringing a register to fruition (Articles 3–9). Jersey requires sex offenders arriving on the Island to register with their police force.

A MAPPA system (referred to as JMAPPA) was developed following the UK model (Sex Offenders (Jersey) Law 2010 Article 28; States of Jersey 2011) and their 2018 Annual Report revealed 147 offenders to be on the Jersey register

(States of Jersey 2019: 2). Today the register is linked to police and other agencies in the UK mainland through the ViSOR communications system.

Although no murders were uncovered in Jersey, investigations continued through the Independent Jersey Care Inquiry which started in 2010 looking at other serious offending and ill-treatment of children going back to 1945; it eventually reported in 2017 (Independent Jersey Care Inquiry 2017), but focused more on child protection services than public protection registers.

Guernsey

On the island of Guernsey, a petition in 2007 was signed by more than 300 islanders asking for their own sex offender register. The policy was first given approval in 2011 and finalised in October 2013 by the passing of the Criminal Justice (Sex Offenders and Miscellaneous Provisions) (Bailiwick of Guernsey) Law. The law requires sex offenders to register with the local police force much in the same manner as in England and Wales. Any sex offender wishing to travel will have to inform the police of any travel outside of Guernsey and any sex offender travelling to Guernsey will have to register with the local police force on arrival (States of Guernsey 2020). Guernsey has its own MAPPA arrangements (see MAPPA 2015). It is worth noting that when a determinate time period ends for registration in Guernsey, the person concerned must still apply to the police for a review of whether they should be allowed to come off the register.

Isle of Man

As with the Channel Islands the Sex Offenders Act 1997 provided that Part I of the Act (the sex offender register) could have been extended to the Isle of Man by Order in Council. In fact, it was the Isle of Man's Criminal Justice Act 2001 Schedule 1 that brought a register to the Island. The notification requirements are similar to those in the UK with some 29 'scheduled offences' leading to registration following conviction or caution; 20 of these offences come directly from the Islands, Sexual Offences Act 1992.

In 2017 there were 51 people on the island's sex offenders' register - including four UK-registered sex offenders (IOM Today 2017)

British Overseas Territories

Other British Overseas Territories (BOT) that have sex offender registers or are planning future registers include Gibraltar, Bermuda, the Cayman Islands and the Pitcairn Islands

Gibraltar

Gibraltar is a British Overseas Territory (BOT) and is in the European Union, having joined the then European Economic Community (EEC) with the UK in 1973. Under the terms of the UK's membership, Gibraltar is not in the Customs Union, Common Commercial Policy, Common Agriculture Policy, Common Fisheries Policy and the VAT regime. Gibraltar created their own sex offender register with the passing of their Crimes Act 2011 Part 13.

There were a reported 33 people on the Gibraltar sex offender register in 2019 (GBC 2019a). An online petition was launched by members of the public to have open access to the sex offender register but to no avail (Change.org 2019). By July 2019 the government had not confirmed whether or not it planned to change the law regarding Gibraltar's sex offender register to make it openly accessible to the public (GBC 2019b)

The Royal Gibraltar Police took on the offender management role. A new unit named the Public Protection Unit, was formed consisting of police officers trained as dedicated risk managers. These officers completed specialist training with the Police Service of Northern Ireland who were recognised as a lead police service, known for their good practices and procedures in offender management; these officers were then tasked to manage, gather intelligence and assess persons on the sex offender register and monitor sex offenders travelling to Gibraltar. The Royal Gibraltar Police announced that they were 'pursuing admission' to ViSOR in their Annual Policing Plan (PAG 2015: 8). Subsequent Annual Policing Plans made no further mention of this ambition.

The Cayman Islands

A Sex Offender Register Bill (2009) was first presented to the Cayman Islands Legislative Assembly for a 60-day consultation period in February 2009. It did not proceed to law.

Two years later the government was presented with a petition for the creation of a sex offender register. As part of the discussion that followed, representatives of the Caymanian Bar Association drew up a report to try and answer the question 'Would the creation of a public sex offender registry be a breach of human rights - right to privacy' (CIHRC 2013).

By 2017 the islands still had no register but they had created what was known as the Multi-Agency Safeguarding Hub, where police, social workers and health professionals have joined forces to focus on the abuse of children and vulnerable adults. The goal of MASH is to keep children safe by removing them from danger when reports are made and ensure that offenders are also apprehended.

The Pitcairn Islands

In 2004 the tiny Pacific island of Pitcairn became the centre of international media interest when allegations of child abuse emerged and seven men were put on trial for sexually abusing children. The media was particularly interested in the revelations that child sexual abuse was culturally embedded as 'normal' on the island which had been originally populated by the 18th century mutineers from the ship named *The Bounty*. British officials were brought in to conduct the trials and six of the seven men were found guilty (Fickling 2004).

Arguments continued as to whether the British actually had any rights of jurisdiction over the island but one of the stranger long-term outcomes was the idea that Pitcairn Island should have its own sex offender register; strange in the sense that the Island only has about 50 residents. An independent *Child Safety Review* commissioned by the UK Foreign and Commonwealth Office and the International Development Office was completed in June 2009. The review recommended the creation of a sex offender register and this was duly developed with the 2010 Sexual Offences (Notification and Prevention) Ordinance No. 3 enacted by the Governor of the Pitcairn Island (Hansard 2010).

Further Pitcairn *Child Safety Reviews* have been carried out by independent experts with the fifth being in May 2018. It found that the needs of the children on the island were being met and that there was an atmosphere of collaboration and cooperation amongst the community and a commitment to moving forward from the abuses of the past into a more positive future.

Bermuda

The Bermuda Parliament convened a Select Committee in December 2017 to consider the idea of a sex offender register. The Committee reported in 2018 and recommended what they termed a Tiered Sexual Offenders Register (Bermuda Parliament 2018: 16). The Parliament passed its Criminal Code (Sex Offender Management) Amendment Act (2018) in December 2018 (Lagan 2018) which was implemented from February 2019. All sex offenders given a custodial sentence are entered on to the sex offender register at the point of conviction. An Offender Risk Management Team (ORMT) will monitor these offenders and have them regularly risk assessed.

The Bermuda register is maintained by the Ministry of Legal Affairs and contains offenders' names, addresses, offences and other demographics for use by the professionals. The Register will not be made public except for the highest risk offenders, where the Minister, having considered all relevant information, makes this determination. People arriving from overseas who have a sex offence record that involved imprisonment will be entered on the register if they become a resident of Bermuda. An offender may apply to the Court to reduce his time on the register on the ground that they no longer present a risk of reoffending, but they must prove their case in Court.

Ascension Island and St Helena

Both Ascension Island and St Helena are British Overseas Territories. Ascension Island is an isolated volcanic island in the middle of the Atlantic Ocean about 1,000 miles from the coast of Africa. St Helena is further south and some 1,200 miles west of the Angolan coast of Africa. Reports of sexual improprieties on both islands had been coming back to the UK since 1998.

The Foreign and Commonwealth Office commissioned the Lucy Faithful Foundation to visit the island and report back on what was going on; the Foundation reported to the FCO in May 2013 and shared the report with the St Helena government which led to plans to put safeguarding measures in place. In the UK they only produced a short summary of their work which said that:

> there were problems relating to premature sexual activity with teenage girls on both islands, some of which was clearly abusive and exploitative. The grooming of girls in their early teenage years by older men was seen as being a significant issue which needs comprehensive attention. Efforts on Ascension Island to curb this had proved counterproductive in the short term, as the police methods had been too aggressive and had alienated those they were attempting to assist and protect. Efforts on St Helena to deal with the same problem have borne fruit, to a limited extent.
>
> (Lucy Faithful Foundation 2013)

In July 2014 the UK's tabloid newspaper *Daily Mail* published a series of articles suggesting that sexual abuse was widespread amongst the people of St Helena (Eccles 2014) and demanding the Lucy Faithful report be published. A more formal government enquiry was mounted from London in 2015 and reported back a far less salacious picture. Child abuse did exist in the more poverty-stricken areas of the islands but it was not a paedophile destination for 'sex tourism'. Change and improved standards of public safeguarding could be achieved but it might take time (House of Commons 2015 and 2016).

No sex offender registers have been instituted on either island.

Summary

The original Sex Offenders Act 1997 and the subsequent Sexual Offences Act 2003 provided the legal basis for the sex offender register for the whole of the UK. Individual differences inevitably started to appear between Scotland, Northern Ireland and England and Wales based on different criminal justice laws. Administrative arrangements like MAPPA had more common features tying them together. This chapter has looked at these differing and similar arrangements and how the idea of the register has spread to the smaller islands of the British Isles and even further afield to some of the British Overseas Territories.

14 Conclusions

In trying to make sense of the contemporary UK sex offender register we have traced its history from its origins to its present-day manifestation. We have looked at the politics and public opinion that surrounds it. In so doing we have realised the difficulties of actually pinning down the boundaries of the register. We have the bare bones of the legislation in the 1997 Sex Offenders Act, the 2003 Sexual Offences Act and the Home Office guidance to Part 2 of that Act that runs to 70 pages in length (Home Office 2018) and we have the latest MAPPA guidance that runs to 153 pages (NOMS 2012 Version 4.5), a reduction in itself from the 2009 version that had 347 pages (NOMS 2009). But none of these Acts and documents give the full flavour of the register just as an Ordinance Survey map with its blue rivers and brown contour lines does not give you the fullness of the landscape it represents when you walk through it.

From the very start of this book we wrote about the sex offender register being not even a register at all but a short-hand phrase for a system built around a legal requirement for certain offenders to notify the police of their personal circumstances over a given period of time. This left the local organisations like the police, the probation service, the prison service, the courts and all the other organisations that come to work with convicted sex offenders to interpret it as they saw best fitted their interests. Early researchers noted 'the sheer variety of practice to be found across the different areas, and in some cases, within particular police force areas' (Maguire et al. 2001: 9)

Other activities grew from the register, including the police role of offender managers, and other laws grew even further outward from it all in the name of public protection. Guidance from the Home Office and NOMS have sought to impose a certain centralised framework on all of this work. From that simple beginning we have tried to take an historical line to illustrate how the register has come to be supported by the MAPPA which surrounds it. And finally, to look at how the public, politicians, academics, NGOs and the media have viewed the register and tried to bring their own sought-after changes to bear on it.

A policy in a hurry?

From the beginning, the sex offender register in the UK has always felt like a policy in a hurry. It was conceived in the year before the 1997 General Election when both the major political parties were competing with each other to see who could become the party of 'law and order'. The Conservatives believed they were the rightful owners of this title and their leader had stated that 'society needs to condemn a little more and understand a little less', while Labour wanted to be 'tough on crime and tough on the causes of crime'.

The standard conception of a 'policy cycle' depicts a policy evolving in a sequential manner, and involving:

- agenda-setting
- policy formulation
- decision making
- implementation
- evaluation.

This heuristic concept of a policy cycle has its critics and limits, but remains a useful yardstick for analysing and assessing policy processes. A policy lacking the distinct stages of a policy cycle is liable to be contrasted as a 'policy spiral'. The policy spiral is open to a degree of de-stabilisation and parts of the policy spiral may lack the internal stability which can be acquired through the process of solid agenda-setting, policy formulation and decision making, or through other supportive structures to implement the policy. Turbulence arises through the interaction of the parts of the policy; rather than mutual reinforcement, conflict then arises from its potential for de-stabilisation and uncertain borders (Risse et al. 1999).

The original *Consultation Document* (Home Office 1996b) made no mention of a need for risk assessments and risk management, and omits any reference to the different criminal laws in Scotland and Northern Ireland or any reference to research and evaluations because they did not exist. Laws were mentioned that had been repealed and the whole idea seemed somewhat off the cuff and without any real plan to it other than hurried completion before the general election.

The omission of the need for risk assessments and risk management carries over into the 1997 Sex Offenders Bill, where someone has overlooked the matter of 'conditional discharges' and their relationship to the register. The police request further amendments to the Bill as it is going through Parliament wanting higher sanctions for those who breach the notification requirements; the government agrees to their request even though there is no evidence that non-compliance is going to be a major problem.

When the Sex Offenders Act 1997 appeared, it could be argued that the rushed nature of its start lacked a clear initial purpose or subsequent direction, progression, control and reflection. A policy spiral was therefore liable to develop and be susceptible to unresolved contradictions or gaps, direction changes and uncertain outcomes.

The protests of the 'For Sarah' campaign for community notification in 2000 takes the government by surprise and leads to yet further late amendments to the Criminal Justice and Court Services Bill as it is passing through Parliament. Some of these amendments were taken from the Review on the register about to be launched (Home Office/Scottish Executive 2001) and included the requirement for more police and probation cooperation as the 'responsible authorities' and the beginning of the MAPPA structure. The Bill also introduced risk assessment and management as a 'duty'. The omission of the Prison Service from the responsible authorities has to be corrected in the 2003 Sexual Offences Act. The ruling of *R v Wiles [2004]* regarding extended sentences is only partially implemented, so that variations in registration lengths take place across the country.

In 2006 the police criticised the government for being unduly influenced by the media in setting their goals on managing sex offenders, with politicians preferring eye-catching initiatives which only added to the spiral of confusion around meaning, mission and measurement of the effectiveness of the register. The ground keeps shifting because it has proven so difficult to offer any definitive formulations. As one of the authors of this book described it in 2008:

> The sex offender register is arguably a prime example of criminal justice policy made at a political level in response to perceived populist demands, and with no real experience or research to support it. Policy is made in a vacuum, with ill-defined and hesitant aims, which is then left 'hanging in the air' to be adjusted and amended by politicians listening to the practitioners and specialist lobby groups as well as the public reactions to the latest high-profile crime against a child.
>
> (Thomas 2008b)

Professor David Garland has described governments as 'Highly attuned to public concerns, particularly to the sentiments that dangerous offenders are being insufficiently punished or individuals inadequately controlled' (Garland 2001:172).

The sex offender register has moved on the back of these pressures and has incrementally become far more onerous for those required to register. As Michael Tonry has put it, policy is based on a 'belief that [the government's] own continuation in office justifies the unnecessary human suffering and waste of public resources that its policies produce' (Tonry 2004: ix).

Human rights matters tend to go unaddressed in such a political context. It took eleven years' experience of the register before anyone realised there was a gaping human rights question at its heart that required answering. This was the matter of the lack of a right of review for any one required to register indefinitely for the rest of their life. A full review of the Sexual Offences Bill in 2003 by the House of Lords and House of Commons Joint Committee on

Human Rights had not recognised such a problem with the Bill, but a judicial review of the Act in the courts starting in 2008 and going through to the UK Supreme Court in 2010 said the omission of a right of review meant it was clearly in breach of Article 8 of the European Convention on Human Rights.

From the politician's viewpoint things could look rather different. Jack Straw, the Home Secretary who introduced the register, recalled in his memoirs that the Home Office had a history of 'incompetence' (Straw 2012: 291). His successor David Blunkett (Home Secretary 8 June 2001–15 December 2004) equally recalled that: 'Some of these Home Office officials are the worst, most obstructive, miserable, disengaged and disinterested group of people I have ever come across, which indicates a degree of demoralisation and complete lack of leadership' (Blunkett 2006: 342).

We know also that John Reid (Home Secretary 5 May 2006–28 June 2007) had declared the Home Office 'not fit for purpose' (Mulholland and Tempest 2006). It was during Reid's time as Home Secretary that the new Ministry of Justice was formed (in May 2007) to take work off the Home Office; oversight of the sex offender register remained with the Home Office.

It was also at this time that Chief Constable Terry Grange, who took the lead for ACPO on matters of sexual offending, outlined the difficulties experienced by those working for the Home Office:

> If the officials working at the Home Office were able to speak, they would tell everyone they are in a state of complete despair as to where the strategic plans, the original intent - a coherent strategy for managing sex offenders - has disappeared to. It is impossible to work consistently, coherently when every month or every six weeks there is a policy change or reaction brought about by pressure from the media.
>
> (cited in BBC News 2006d)

This was the period we described in Chapter Six when the accusations of policy being media led were made. Chief Constable Grange now summed it up as being a time when 'the only people with any intent and understanding of where they want to go … is the News of the World' (ibid).

John Reid's successor, Jacqui Smith, (Home Secretary 28 June 2007–5 June 2009) admitted difficulty coping as Home Secretary but blamed a lack of preparation for the job:

> I think we should have been better trained. I think there should have been more induction. When I became Home Secretary, I'd never run a major organisation. I hope I did a good job but if I did it was more by luck than by any kind of development of those skills … I think there should be more emphasis given to supporting ministers more generally in terms of developing the skills needed to lead big departments.
>
> (cited in Martin 2009)

Table 14.1 'Toughest powers in the world'

Date	*Event*
12 January 2006	Ruth Kelly (Secretary of State for Education and Skills) 'All those measures significantly tightened the protection available to children and ensured that we have some of the toughest sex offender laws in Europe' (*Hansard House of Commons Debates* 12 Jan 2006: col. 435).
13 June 2007	John Reid (Home Secretary) 'I am delighted to be able to say that the United Kingdom already has the strongest restrictions on child sex offenders' (*Hansard House of Commons Debates* 13 June 2007 col.761).
June 2007	'These new measures have moved us from a system where there were no formalised arrangements for managing child sex offenders when they were released from prison, to one that is regarded as among the most effective in the world' (Home Office 2007a: 7).
16 October 2007	Jim Hood (Labour MP): 'The UK has some of the strongest restrictions on child sex offenders, but as my right hon. Friend acknowledged in his statement on 13 June, we need to do more' (*Hansard House of Commons Debates* 16 October 2007 col.800).
4 April 2008	Jacqui Smith (Home Secretary): 'We have some of the strictest controls on sex offenders in the world to protect our children. We are working together with police, industry and charities to create a hostile environment for sex offenders on the internet, and are determined to make it as hard for predators to strike online as in the real world' (cited in Johnson 2008).
2010	Alan Johnson (Home Secretary): 'The UK already has one of the most robust systems in the world for the management of sex offenders, the new scheme will build on this ensuring more children are kept safe' (cited in Home Office 2010b).
June 2011	Lynne Featherstone (Parliamentary Under Secretary of State for Equalities and Criminal Information): 'The UK has one of the most robust systems for managing sexual offenders in the world' (cited in Home Office 2011a: 1).
2013	Damian Green (Policing and Criminal Justice Minister): 'The UK has some of the toughest powers in the world to deal with sex offenders. Today, we are going even further by giving police and National Crime Agency officers the power to place greater restrictions on any person they judge to be a risk' (cited in Home Office 2013a).
29 June 2017	Michelle Skeer (Deputy Chief Constable NPCC lead for Management of Sexual and Violent Offenders): 'The UK has some of the toughest powers in the world to manage registered sex offenders with low levels of reoffending' (cited in NPCC 2017).
21 January 2019	Nick Hurd (Minister of State at the Home Office): 'The UK has some of the toughest powers in the world to deal with sex offenders and we are committed to ensuring that the system is as robust as it can be …' (*Hansard House of Commons Debates* 21 January 2019 WA 207585).

More recently there have been allegations and counter allegations that Home Secretary Pritti Patel (appointed 24 July 2019) had bullied staff at the Home Office, while she in return has reportedly been wondering why everyone in the Home Office is 'so fucking useless' (Walawalkar 2020).

Meanwhile the Home Office politicians and senior police officers maintain a constant mantra that our public protection measures for sex offenders are 'the toughest in the world', as though if they say it often enough people will believe it (see Table 14.1). In fact, many practitioners and policy makers would probably agree that the US public protection arrangements are the 'toughest in the world', with their residency restrictions on where sex offenders can live, universal community notification, and civil commitment laws.

In 2012 the British High Court refused to allow the extradition of an American citizen back to the USA to face a criminal court for allegations of sexual offending because they considered it was a breach of the European Convention on Human Rights (*Sullivan v the Government of the USA and Another [2012] EWHC 1680 (Admin)*; see also the similar case of *USA v Giese [2015] EWHC 3658 (Admin)*).

Registers for other people?

Is there scope for new registers of different forms of offenders? Since its beginning the British sex offender register has widened its scope to include violent offenders, dangerous offenders, registerable terrorist offenders, registerable violent offenders and potentially dangerous persons - all as part of the MAPPA construct.

A register of people who commit offences relating to domestic abuse

Consideration has been given to the creation of a register of domestic violence offenders, along the lines of the register of sex offenders. The idea has not been followed up. The arguments for and against have been outlined:

> If offenders were required to report changes of address to the police, a register might help to prevent future violence to a victim by allowing the police to alert the partner if they had been followed to a new location by the offender. A register might also help to improve information sharing and risk assessments, for example where a registered offender's new partner repeatedly sought medical help for injuries, or where the police were called to an incident involving a registered offender.
>
> On the other hand, the element of 'stranger danger' is significantly less in domestic violence cases than in the cases covered by the sex offenders' register. Domestic violence is also subject to major under-reporting, so a register of offenders would be far from comprehensive. In addition, the combination of a pro-arrest policy by the police with the new legal protection outline in this consultation paper means that victims of domestic

> violence should receive significant extra protection from the law without establishing a register of offenders. The Government would welcome views on whether a register of domestic violence offenders should be established.
>
> (Home Office 2003e: paras.61–2)

One of the suggestions received in the responses to the *Justice for All* White Paper was to establish a register of all civil orders, so police and prosecutors could easily check a suspect or offender's history.

A 'register of stalkers'

A 'register of stalkers' has been recommended by Paladin (the National Stalking Advocacy Service) (see Paladin 2020; Change.org 2020). The House of Commons Home Affairs Committee have taken up the Paladin recommendation that a national register of serial stalkers and domestic violence perpetrators be introduced as a matter of urgency and that individuals placed on the register should, like registered sex offenders, be managed through multi-agency public protection arrangements (MAPPA) (House of Commons 2018b: para.29)

A register of people with mental health problems who may become dangerous

An example of a register with a relatively short life span was that of the UK's mental health supervision registers. These registers were devised in the early 1990s to help keep track of people discharged from mental health hospitals who might be a continuing risk to themselves or others. The health authorities called them 'psychiatric case registers' and the local authority social services departments called them 'adult at risk registers'.

One fatal attack on Jonathan Zito by former patient Christopher Clunis led to a major inquiry into what was going wrong with the policies known as 'care in the community'. The report recommended a number of measures but included the recommendation for a register of those who had been compulsorily detained before being discharged (NE Thames and SE Thames Regional Health Authorities 1994: para.45.2.3). The register was duly introduced. The register was only going to be available to the medical profession who were to be the custodians of the register – it was seen as an extension of the medical register (NHS Executive 1994).

From the outset critics of the supervision registers could see little value in them:

> it is difficult to believe they were the outcome of considered rational decisions based on empirical evidence … for the life of me I cannot understand what supervision registers were expected to achieve … (they) were never about justice, more about making political statements …

> and ... about making the rest of us believe we can do something about the problems of the violent mentally disordered offender by putting him on a register when it is clear we can't.
>
> (Bean 1997b)

The registers were quietly abolished on 1 April 2001 (NHS/SSI 1999: para.59) - a life span of seven years - and 'in practice the Supervision Register ha(d) failed to deliver its intended objective' (Kaul 2001).

Homo Sacer

Homo Sacer is a Latin phrase meaning 'Sacred Man' – a man considered at the limits of society because of his behaviour or because of who he is. Society chooses not to protect him as it does other people. Someone almost outside the law - an 'out-law' who lives the 'bare life'. He has no place in society. The Italian philosopher Giorgio Agamben's work since the 1980s can be viewed as leading up to the so-called *Homo Sacer* project, which begins with his book *Homo Sacer: Sovereign Power and Bare Life.* Since 1995 he has been best known for this ongoing work (Agamben 1995 and 2005).

Agamben's work is not specifically about sex offenders, but others who find themselves in extreme positions including those who faced the concentration camps in the last world war. More recently some writers have chosen to apply the idea to the way we currently deal with sex offenders.

In America Dale Spencer's article 'Sex offender as homo sacer' is a useful starting point (Spencer 2009). The person who commits sexual offences is not a popular person; even more so when the victim has been a child. Indeed, for many people the sex offender is synonymous with the child sex offender or paedophile. The idea of there being some 40 sexual offences that lead to registration in England and Wales still surprises people.

The tabloid press has turned them into 'monsters' and 'animals' who are no longer people. Politicians find it 'appalling' that they should have to introduce appeal systems for them to leave the register. At one time sex offenders were the only class of offender to have their own laws that seek to register them and place bans on them that include movement and travel; more recently they have been joined by violent offenders and terrorists. Vast labyrinthine policies are put in place in the interests of child protection and public protection.

Spencer in turn draws on the work of Agamben and his idea of 'states of exception'. The ban or the expulsion of the sex offender marks him or her out as the person beyond rehabilitation and suitable only for the 'camp'. Not a fixed spatial location, such as the concentration camps that have been used in the past, but a distancing of the sex offender from the community of 'normal people' and a form of abandonment: 'the camp is the space that is opened up when the state of exception begins to become the rule' (Spencer 2009).

In general terms, the aim of penal policy has been, and still is, to identify and punish those who break the criminal law. Punishment, in turn, involves a degree of censure, containment and attempts to circumscribe and reduce the activities of the offender. At one end of the spectrum is the custodial sentence and at the other the community sentence, which still tries to delimit and reduce the offenders' activities. Since the early 1970s, there has been a retreat from sentences designed to reform or rehabilitate the offender in favour of sentences commensurate with the seriousness of the crime and which deliver 'just deserts'. This retreat has been accompanied by a questioning of the value of treatment – 'what works?' – the rediscovery and renaissance of dangerousness and the rise of the 'victim movement', which prefers to see some direct redress for the victim rather than help for the offender. The 'law and order' political lobby has been able to mobilise these features to argue for longer sentences, electronic tagging, more active databases, extended supervision and indeterminate sentences. The sex offender has been a prime candidate for all these measures.

More recently, these moves to commensurate punishments have been complemented by new forms of regulation to ensure sufficient degrees of public protection and safeguards are in place to reduce the risk posed by offenders. As with punishment, regulation seeks to contain and circumscribe the activities of offenders. Registers tell us where they are and DNA databases confirm their identity. 'Paedophile enclaves' may not yet exist, but electronic tagging, preventive orders and pre-employment screening all supposedly help to reduce the risk the offender poses by circumscribing their activities.

The detection and prosecution of sex offenders and the measures of protection from them have, none the less, to accept that the offenders concerned are still entitled to the due process of law and other rights enjoyed by all citizens. However awful the crimes, and however much we give priority to the rights of the victims or potential victims – especially children – the residual rights of the sex offender remain. Freedom of movement, for example, is usually considered a fundamental right, even if not always spelt out in statutory form. Sex offenders may find their freedom of movement curtailed in the UK by conditions attached to supervisory arrangements, electronic tagging or preventive orders that require them to stay away from certain localities and not to travel outside the country.

Privacy is held to be another basic right and is outlined in Article 8 of the European Convention on Human Rights (Council of Europe 1950). From privacy has emerged the additional right to information privacy and data protection when that information – personal information – is held on computer and most industrialised countries now have data protection legislation. In turn, this legislation becomes qualified when it comes to the 'suppression of criminal offences' (ibid: Art. 8(2)), and separate recommendations may be made on law enforcement-held information (see, e.g., CoE 1988). A balance must be struck between the need to know and the individual's right to privacy.

The right to rehabilitation or to be accepted back into society after a period of punishment – custodial or non-custodial – is another 'right' that is not clearly defined. The old adage that once you have 'paid your debt to society' you are a free man or woman again has been stated more fully: 'Rehabilitation implies the action of re-establishing a 'degraded' person in a former standing with respect to rank and legal rights and to attempt to ensure that those rights are maintained over time' (McWilliams and Pease 1990).

What McWilliams and Pease are saying is that the ending of a period of punishment, whether or not the offender is reformed, should still be marked by that offender's rehabilitation back into society in terms of the restoration of all his or her civic and legal rights and duties. In this sense, rehabilitation serves as a means of limiting the extent of the punishment to that time period decreed by the court; without it the punishment continues.

The offender, having to submit to a DBS pre-employment criminal record check years after the end of his sentence, might argue that his punishment continues. The sex offender subject to regular home visits by probation officers or police officers or required to register for life might feel the same way. The argument that these community interventions are still less of an imposition than a custodial sentence, or that certain activities are for purposes of regulation rather than punishment, might not lessen the degree of grievance the former offender believes they are experiencing.

Information technology now provides us with an everlasting memory to counter possibilities of allowing details of an offence to be forgotten and fall naturally behind a veil of confidentiality about the past. It is doubtful if the Rehabilitation of Offenders Act 1974 with its ideas of spent convictions would ever have become a law if it was introduced today. As it stands it has been battered and bruised by so many regulations over the years building exceptions into it that it is hardly recognisable as the law it once was. But the man or women as sex offender and therefore outside the law is deserving of no such assistance in their rehabilitation from Spencer's spatial area of 'the camp'.

An alternative form of sex offender registration?

There have been few attempts to reconceptualise the sex offender register to make it a more inclusive form of public protection. The emphasis has been more about exclusion and a punitive marking out of sex offenders to make them more visible for a monitored existence rather than less. To that extent registration could be seen as an extreme form of labelling. The label may not be seen by the public but it is felt by the people on the register. As David Garland has told us:

> The new penal ideal is that the public be protected and its sentiments be expressed. Punitive segregation - lengthy sentence terms, and *a marked, monitored existence for those who are eventually released* - is increasingly the penal strategy of choice.
>
> (Garland 2001: 142 emphasis added)

Garland also points out how contemporary criminal justice policies are often formulated by politicians and political activists and not by researchers and civil servants and as such are under-researched, and lack the elaborate costing and statistical projections that are standard in other areas of policy (ibid: 143), something we have come across numerous times in relation to the UK sex offender register.

Sex offender registers are based on the idea that 'they will do it again' because sex offending is such an individual trait in people. On that basis we cannot be too careful and only a punitive approach will work. A more inclusive model of registration for sex offenders might involve more treatment and a welfare approach as opposed to an approach based on the rhetoric of constantly strengthening the public protection arrangements and constantly closing the loopholes as though we will reach a time when we can guarantee a perfectly 'safe' world - even though we know we cannot. Young offenders aged 10–18 years might benefit in particular; the current reduction of the registration period for young offenders to half that of adults only demonstrates that we know how harmful registration is. It might involve a reaching out to sex offenders and an engagement based on the philosophy of the voluntary group Circles of Support and Accountability (COSA) (Hanvey et al. 2011) and the 'good lives' model that focuses on a person's strengths rather than their limitations (Ward et al. 2007).

References

All references to Hansard can be accessed at: https://www.parliament.uk/business/publications/hansard/commons/by-date/

Legal cases

Adamson v UK *(1999) Application 22293198*

AG's Ref. No. 50 of *1997 (David Victor V) [1998]2 Cr.App.R.(S) 155*

Appeal against Sentence by Liam Joseph Allan Reid Rodgerson against the Procurator Fiscal Alloa [2016] HCJAC 12

Commissioner of Police for the Metropolis v Central Criminal Court and others [2013] EWHC 179 (Admin)

Corbett v The Secretary of State for Justice and the National Offender Management Service -NOMS [2009] EWHC *2671*

Hay v HM Advocate *2012 SCCR 281*

Ibbotson v United Kingdom Application No. *40146198*

Kevin Gallagher *[2003] NIQB 26, (9* April 2003*)*

McGuire v Procurator Fiscal, Glasgow *[2012] HCJAC 86 (11* May 2012*)*

Massey v UK *(2003) Application 14399102 ECHR 710*

Minter (on the application of) v Chief Constable of Hampshire and others [2011] EWHC *1610*

Rawlinson *(1999) The Times 27 October.*

R v Davison [2008] EWCA Crim 2795

R v Devon CC ex parte L [1991] 2 FLR

R (Forbes) v Secretary of State for the Home Department [2006] EWCA Civ. 962

R v Graham (S) [2001] 1 Cr App R(S) 335

R v Grosvenor [2010] 2 Cr App Rep (S) 100

R (F and Thompson) v Secretary of State for the Home Department [2008] EWHC *3170 (QB)*

R (F and Thompson) v Secretary of State for the Home Department [2009] EWCA Civ 792

R (on the application of F (by his litigation friend F)) and another (Respondents) v Secretary of State for the Home Department (Appellant) [2010] UKSC 17

R (Hamill) v Chelmsford Magistrates' Court [2014] EWHC *2799 (Admin)*

R v Hammond [2008] EWCA Crim 1358

R v Hemsley [2010] EWCA Crim 225

R v Longworth [2004] EWCA Crim *2415*

R v Longworth [2006] UKHL 1
R (M) v the Chief Constable of Hampshire Constabulary and Secretary of State for the Home Department [2014] EWCA Civ *1651*
R v Malone [2001] 2 CR App R (s) 43
R v Manchester Crown Court ex parte McCann & Others *(2002) UKHL 39*
R v North Wales Police ex p. AB and CD The Times Law Report 14 July *1997*
AB & Anor, R *(on the application of) v* North Wales Police Area *[1998]* EWCA Civ *486 (18* March 1998)
R (NM & NE) v Birmingham Magistrates' Court [2015] EWHC 688 (Admin)
R v Odam [2008] EWCA Crim *1087*
R v Oliver and Others [2002] EWCA Crim *2766; [2003] 2 Cr. App. R. (S.) 64.*
R (on the application of) Christopher Prothero v Secretary of State for the Home Department [2013] EWHC *2830 (Admin) 18 September 2013*
R (R) v Chief Constable *of* Durham Constabulary; T*he* Times, *10* December 2002
R (on the application of Richards) v Teesside Magistrates' Court [2015] EWCA Civ 7
R v Smith & Others [2011] EWCA Crim *1772*
R v Edward Thompson [2008] EWCA Crim *3258*
R (U) v Commissioner of Police of the Metropolis; The Times 10 December *2010*
R v Wiles [2004] 2 Cr App R (S) 88
Sadler v Deputy Chief Constable of West Mercia Police *2014 EWHC 1715 (Admin*)
Shaun Eugene Sullivan v the Government of the USA and Another [2012] EWHC *1680 (Admin)*
The Rape Crisis Centre *and* Sandy Brindley *for* Judicial Review *of a decision of the* Secretary *of* State *for the* Home Department *to grant* Mike Tyson *leave to enter the* United Kingdom, O*uter* House, Court *of* Session, Edinburgh *2* June 2000
Thompson v Dunn *2012 SCCR 298*
USA v Giese [2015] EWHC *3658 (Admin)*
X (South Yorkshire) v Secretary of State for the Home Department and Chief Constable of South Yorkshire [2012] EWHC *2954 (Admin)*

Bibliography

ACPO (Association of Chief Police Officers) (1997a) *Disclosure of Information – Sex Offenders: results of survey of police forces in England and Wales* (by A Butler), February, ACPO Crime Committee, London
ACPO (Association of Chief Police Officers) (1997b) *Sex Offenders Act 1997: implementation guidelines*, August, ACPO Crime Committee, London
ACPO (Association of Chief Police Officers) (2006) *Guidance on the Management of Police Information*, London
ACPO (Association of Chief Police Officers)/NPIA (National Police Improvement Agency) (2010) *Guidance on: Protecting the Public: Managing Sexual Offenders and Violent Offenders Version 2*, London
Adkins G, Huff D and Stageberg P (2000) *The Iowa Sex Offender Registry and Recidivism*, Iowa Department of Human Rights, December
Agamben G (1995) *Homo Sacer: Sovereign Power and Bare Life*, Stanford University Press, Stanford, CA
Agamben G (2005) *State of Exception*, University of Chicago Press, Chicago, IL
Alleyne R (2002) Boys, 15, win fight to get names off sex offender list, *Daily Telegraph*, 30 November, London

Allison R (2000) Doctor driven out of home by vigilantes, *The Guardian*, 30 August, London

American Psychiatric Association (2013) *Diagnostic and Statistical Manual of Mental Disorders: DSM-5*, American Psychiatric Association, Arlington, VA

Amroliwala Report (2007) *Report of the Inquiry into the Handling by Home Office Officials of Notifications, by Other European Countries, of Criminal Convictions for UK Citizens*, February, Home Office, London

APCC (Association of Police and Crime Commissioners) (2017) Budget cuts will radically change policing, 4 September (available at: https://www.apccs.police.uk/latest-news/budget-cuts-will-radically-change-policing/ accessed 2 March 2020)

Atkinson J (2013) Paedo free to prowl, *The Sun*, 10 March

Bamber D (2000) Loophole allows paedophiles to escape register, *Daily Telegraph*, 25 June, London

Barnardo's (2016) Now I know it was wrong – Report of the Parliamentary Inquiry into support and sanctions for children who display harmful sexual behaviour (available at: https://b.barnardos.org.uk/now_i_know_it_was_wrong.pdf accessed 22 December 2019)

Batty D (2008) Jersey to get first sex offender register, *Guardian*, 2 June, London

BBC News (2000a) Tyson flying into legal row, 16 January, London

BBC News (2000b) Tyson row prompts rule review, 14 January, London

BBC News (2001) Sarah's Law unworkable, 13 December, London

BBC News (2006a) Reid attacks child sex sentence, 12 June, London

BBC News (2006b) Minister examines 'Megan's Law', 18 June, London

BBC News (2006c) New offenders' law 'not necessary', 18 June, London

BBC News (2006d) Media 'dictates paedophile plans', 19 June, London

BBC News (2006e) Paedophile policy 'not media-led', 20 June, London

BBC News (2008) Laws tighten on paedophile travel, 20 August, London

BBC News (2009) Police pay £3000 to sex offender, 20 July, London

BBC News (2016a) Man ordered to tell police if he plans to have sex, 22 January.

BBC News (2016b) Released prisoners at Bronzefield 'given tents to live in', 13 April, London

BBC News (2016c) Hundreds of rapists and child abusers taken off sex offender register, 21 March, London

BBC News (2017) Police checks for 'low risk' sex offenders relaxed, 29 June.

Bean P (1997a) Paedophiles and the Proposed Register, *Justice of the Peace and Local Government Law*, March 22: 283–284

Bean P (1997b) Supervision Registers for the Mentally Disordered, *Justice of the Peace and Local Government Law*, 17 May

Bell T and Moore M (2008) Gary Glitter 'tricked' into returning to Britain, *Daily Telegraph*, 21 August.

Bennetto J (1996) Police plan register of paedophiles, *The Independent*, 23 March, London

Bennetto J (2000) Straw refuses to grant the public access to sex offenders register but proposes stricter laws, *The Independent*, 16 September, London

Bentley P (2012) The sex offender doctors allowed to keep working: Dozens can't be banned in case it breaches their human rights, *MailOnline*, 24 September (available at https://www.dailymail.co.uk/news/article-2208117/The-sex-offender-doctors-allowed-working-Dozens-banned-case-breaches-human-rights.html accessed 4 May 2020)

Berlins M (2008) Sarah's Law will spread suspicion and hurt among friends and neighbours, and children will suffer, *The Guardian*, 17 September, London

Bermuda Parliament (2018) *Report of the Parliamentary Joint Select Committee on the Necessity for a Public Sex Offender's Register and Pertinent Matters Relating to Convicted Sex Offenders*, Bermuda (available at http://parliament.bm/admin/uploads/report/ed14934b72d4e8c5acda911fba03d1e1.pdf accessed 18 March 2020)

Blackhurst C (1997) Offenders may escape paedophile register, *Independent on Sunday*, 26 January 1997.

Blunkett D (2001) We must tackle the paedophile issue. It is a priority, *News of the World*, 10 June.

Blunkett D (2002) *Fighting crime and disorder at core of social justice* (speech to Labour Party annual conference) 2 October, Blackpool

Blunkett D (2006) *The Blunkett Tapes: My Life in the Bear Pit*, Bloomsbury, London

Boerner D (1992) Confronting violence: in the act and in the word, *University of Puget Sound Law Review* 15 (1): 525–577

Bowcott O (2014) Lie detector tests begin on sex offenders, *The Guardian*, 9 August

Brady B (2008) Prisoners 'to be chipped like dogs', *Independent*, 13 January

Bryan T and Doyle P (2003) Developing Multi-Agency Public Protection Arrangements, in A Matravers (ed.) *Sex Offenders in the Community: Managing and Reducing the Risks*, Willan Publishing, Cullompton, Devon

Bryant S, Peck B and Lovbakke J (2015) *Reoffending Analysis of MAPPA Eligible Offenders Ministry of Justice Analytical Series*, London

Burchfield K B and Mingus W (2008) Not in my neighbourhood: assessing registered sex offenders experiences with local social capital and social control, *Criminal Justice and Behaviour* 35: 356–374

Burney E and Gelsthorpe L (2008) Do we need a 'naughty step'? Rethinking the Parenting Order after ten years, *Howard Journal of Criminal Justice* 47 (5): 470–485

Burrell I (1998) Paedophile panic 'harming a generation of children', *Independent*, 21 July

Burton N (1998) Boy, 12, on 'sex list of shame', *The Northern Echo, 21 February* – editorial comments

Bunyan N (1998) Boy aged 12 guilty of raping girl aged 5, *Daily Telegraph*, 30 May

Cann J (2007) *Assessing the Extent of Discretionary Disclosure under the Multi-Agency Public Protection Arrangements (MAPPA)* (Ref. No. 13/07), Home Office, London

Canton R and McFarlane A (2014) Introduction, in A McFarlane and R Canton (eds), *Policy Transfer in Criminal Justice: Crossing Cultures, Breaking Barriers*, Palgrave Macmillan, Basingstoke

Carpani J (2019) School to be built with obscured ground floor windows to prevent paedophiles looking at children, *Daily Telegraph*, 30 August

Carter H (2019) Sarah's flaw: mum was charged with 'data protection' offence after using Sarah's Law to out paedo who moved to her street, *The Sun*, 19 May

Carter Report (2003) *Managing Offenders: Reducing Crime – A New Approach*, HMG Strategy Unit, December

Carvel J (2006) Megan's Law won't work, Reid warned, *The Guardian*, 22 June

Cave D (2009) Roadside camp for Miami sex offenders leads to lawsuit, *New York Times*, 9 July

Chan V, Homes A, Murry L, *et al.* (2010) *Evaluation of the Offender Community Disclosure Pilot*, IPSOS MORI, Scotland

Change.org (2019) Gibraltar wants a PUBLIC Sex Offenders Register & paedophiles to remain on it for life, available at https://www.change.org/p/government-of-gibraltar-the-people-of-gibraltar-have-a-right-to-have-the-sex-offenders-register-published-and-made-public-ask-that-paedophiles-remain-on-the-register-for-life (accessed 6 November 2019)

Change.org (2020) Stop serial domestic violence perpetrators and stalkers abusing multiple women, available at: https://www.change.org/p/boris-johnson-prime-minister-create-a-stalker-s-register (accessed on 15 September 2020)

Chapman L (2006) Blair in panic over sentencing, *Daily Mail*, 15 June

Chief Inspector of Social Services, Director for Health Improvement, Commission for Health Improvement, Her Majesty's Chief Inspector of Constabulary, Her Majesty's Chief Inspector of the Crown Prosecution Service, Her Majesty's Chief Inspector of the Magistrates' Courts Service, Her Majesty's Chief Inspector of Schools, Her Majesty's Chief Inspector of Prisons, Her Majesty's Chief Inspector of Probation (2002) *Safeguarding Children – a Joint Chief Inspectors' Report on Arrangements to Safeguard Children*, October, London

CIHRC (Cayman Islands Human Rights Commission) (2013) Over the past few years there have been proposals for a sex offender registry in the Cayman Islands; would the creation of a public registry be a breach of human rights – right to privacy?, available at http://www.humanrightscommission.ky/upimages/publicationdoc/11292790_1468691678_1468691678.PDF (accessed 8 April 2020)

CJINI (Criminal Justice Inspection Northern Ireland) (2019) *Lawful Duty: Public Protection Inspection iii: A Thematic Inspection of the Public Protection Arrangements Northern Ireland*, October, Belfast

CJJI (Criminal Justice Joint Inspection) (2010) *Restriction and Rehabilitation: Getting the Right Mix – An Inspection of the Management of Sexual Offenders in the Community*, A Joint Inspection by HMI Probation and HMI Constabulary, London

CJJI (Criminal Justice Joint Inspection) (2011) *Putting the Pieces Together: An Inspection of Multi-Agency Public Protection Arrangements*, HM Inspectorate of Probation and HM Inspectorate of Constabulary, London

CJJI (Criminal Justice Joint Inspection) (2015) *A Follow Up Inspection of Multi-Agency Public Protection Arrangements*, October, Manchester

Cobley C (1997) Keeping track of sex offenders: Part I of the Sex Offenders Act 1997, *The Modern Law Review* 60 (5): 690–699

College of Policing (2020) Major investigation and public protection: notification requirements, available at: https://www.app.college.police.uk/app-content/major-investigation-and-public-protection/managing-sexual-offenders-and-violent-offenders/notification-requirements/ (accessed 15 September 2020)

College of Policing (2020a) Information management: management of police information, available at https://www.app.college.police.uk/app-content/information-management/management-of-police-information/ (accessed 22 February 2020)

CoE (Council of Europe) (1950) *European Convention on Human Rights*, Strasbourg

CoE (Council of Europe) (1959) *European Convention on Mutual Assistance in Criminal Matters (ETS 30)*, Strasbourg

CoE (Council of Europe) (1988) *Regulating the Use of Personal Data in the Police Sector* (Recommendation R(87)15), Strasbourg

Corby B, Doig A and Roberts V (2001) *Public Inquiries into Abuse of Children in Residential Care*, JKP, London

Cosgrove Report (2001) *Reducing the Risk: Improving the Response to Sex Offending*, A report to Ministers of the Scottish Executive (available at: https://lx.iriss.org.uk/sites/default/files/resources/083.%20Reducing%20the%20Risk%20-%20Improving%20the%20Response%20to%20Sex%20Offending.pdf accessed 16 August 2020)

CPS (Crown Prosecution Service) (2018) Man jailed for possessing paedophile manuals (press release), 5 November, London (available at https://www.cps.gov.uk/london-north/news/man-jailed-possessing-paedophile-manuals accessed 4 January 2020)

CPS (Crown Prosecution Service) (2019) Ten men prosecuted in first year of up-skirting legislation (press release), 31 December

CPSI (Crown Prosecution Service Inspectorate), HM Inspectorate of Constabulary, HM Magistrates Courts Service Inspectorate, HM Inspectorate of Prisons, HM Inspectorate of Probation, and Social Services Inspectorate (2000) *Casework Information Needs within the Criminal Justice System* (Vols. 1 and 2), Home Office, London

Craven S, Brown S and Gilchrist E (2006) Sexual grooming of children: review of literature and theoretical considerations, *Journal of Sexual Aggression* 12 (3): 287–299.

Craven S, Brown S and Gilchrist E (2007) Current responses to sexual grooming: implications for prevention, *Howard Journal of Criminal Justice* 46 (1): 60–71.

Curtis P and White M (2006) Kelly admits more sex offenders in school jobs, *The Guardian*, 12 January

Davies Review (2013) *Civil Prevention Orders Sexual Offences Act 2003: ACPO Commissioned Review of the Existing Statutory Scheme and Recommendations for Reform* (available at https://3rblaw.com/wp-content/uploads/civil.prevention.orders.pdf accessed 18 November 2019)

Davies H (2015) Parents against child sexual exploitation, available at: http://www.paceuk.info/changes-sexual-risk-order-system-opportunity-empower-parents-part-1/ accessed 26 October 2015)

Department for Communities and Local Government (2017) *Mayors Consultation on Updating Disqualification Criteria for Local Authority Members*, September, London

DfE (Department for Education) (2014) *First Annual Report – National Panel of Independent Experts on Serious Case Reviews*, July, London

DfE (Department for Education) (2016) *Amending the Child Care Disqualification Arrangements in Schools and No-Domestic Registered Settings: Government Consultation*, 6 May, London

DfE (Department for Education) (2018a) *Amending the Child Care Disqualification Arrangements in Schools and No-Domestic Registered Settings: Government Consultation Response*, London

DfE (Department for Education) (2018b) *Disqualification under the Childcare Act 2006*, 31 August, London

DJE (Department of Justice and Equality) (2006) *New memo of understanding signed regarding sex offenders* (press release) 27 November, Dublin

DJELR (Department of Justice, Equality and Law Reform) (2008) Ministers Ahern and Goggins welcome information-sharing on sex offenders (press release), 7 October, Dublin

DoH (Department of Health) (1997) *Guidance to Hospital Managers and Local Authority Social Services Departments on the Sex Offenders Act 1997* (circular ref. HSG (97) 37)

DoH (Department of Health) and Home Office (2000) *Reforming the Mental Health Act, Part i: The New Legal Framework, Part ii: High Risk Patients*, The Stationery Office, London

DoH (Department of Health), Home Office, Department for Communities and Local Government, Ministry of Justice and Department of Education (2015) *Our Joint Commitment to Share Information Effectively for the Protection of Children* (letter), 3 March, London

DoJ (Department of Justice) (2014a) *Guidance on Review of Sex Offender Indefinite Notifications*, 23 May, Belfast

DoJ (Department of Justice) (2014b) *Criminal Justice Act (Northern Ireland) 2013 – Explanatory Notes*, Belfast (available at http://www.legislation.gov.uk/nia/2013/7/notes/data.pdf accessed 12 March 2020)

DBS (Disclosure and Barring Service) (2020) *Disclosure and Barring Service*, available at: https://www.gov.uk/government/organisations/disclosure-and-barring-service (accessed 13 February 2020)

Dolowitz D and Marsh D (1996) Who learns what from whom: a review of the policy transfer literature, *Political Studies* 44 (2): 343–357

Dolowitz D P and Marsh D (2000) Learning from abroad: the role of policy transfer in contemporary policy-making, *Governance* 13 (1): 5–23

Doyle J (2013) Child rapists taken off sex offenders' register in secret … and police say it's to protect their human rights, *MailOnline*, 6 May (available at https://www.dailymail.co.uk/news/article-2320483/Child-rapists-taken-Sex-Offenders-Register-secret–police-say-protect-human-rights.html accessed 17 September)

DVSA (Driver and Vehicle Standards Agency) (2020) *Approved Driving Instructor (ADI) Register Guide* (available at https://www.gov.uk/government/publications/whats-involved-in-being-a-driving-instructor/approved-driving-instructor-adi-register-guide#becoming-a-driving-instructor accessed 25 May 2020)

Earle R, Newburn T and Crawford A (2002) Referral orders: some reflections on policy transfer and 'what works', *Youth Justice* 2 (3): 141–150

Eccles L (2014) A culture of sexual abuse of children, *Daily Mail*, 15 July

ECPAT UK (2006) *The End of the Line for Child Exploitation: Safeguarding the Most Vulnerable Children*, August, London

ECPAT UK (2008a) *Return to Sender – Child Sex Offenders Abroad – Why More Must Be Done*, August, London

ECPAT UK (2008b) New report shows government failure in combating child sex tourism (press release), 17 August, London

ECPAT UK (2011) *Off the Radar: Protecting Children from British Sex Offenders who Travel*, February, London

ECPAT UK (2012) ECPAT UK campaign success – UK Government to close the '3-day loophole' on overseas travel by British sex offenders (press release), 8 March

ECPAT UK (2019) Landmark Inquiry evidence shows systemic and procedural failures allowed British nationals to sexually exploit children abroad with impunity (press release), 25 February, London

Edwards D (2003) ViSOR – Violent and Sex Offender Register, *Criminal Justice Matters*, 51 (1): 28

Edwards R (2008) Gary Glitter refuses to board plane back to London, *Daily Telegraph*, 20 August.

Elliott C (1997) Boy aged 13 is placed on register of sex offenders, *The Guardian*, 19 November

Evans M (2016) Judge refuses to lift sex ban order completely but admits giving 24-hours' notice is 'unpoliceable', *Daily Telegraph*, 19 August

Facebook (2020) *Terms of Service*, available at https://www.facebook.com/legal/terms (accessed 5 July 2020)
Featherstone L (2012) Letter to Dr Hywel Francis MP, available at http://data.parliament.uk/DepositedPapers/Files/DEP2012-1041/LFtoHywelFrancisMPSexualOffencesRemedialOrder.pdf (accessed 17 September 2019)
Fickling D (2004) Six found guilty in Pitcairn sex offences trial, *The Guardian*, 26 October.
Fitch K (2006) *Megan's Law: Does it Protect Children? (2) An Updated Review of Evidence on the Impact of Community Notification as Legislated for by Megan's Law in the United States*, NSPCC, London
Fletcher D, Taylor A, Hughes S and Breeze J (2001) *Recruiting and Employing Offenders*JRF/York Publishing Series
Ford R (1997) Police chiefs oppose plan to advertise paedophiles, *The Times*, 15 February
Gallagher P (2018) 1 in 6 doctors convicted of sex offences still able to practice medicine, *i Newspaper*, 22 March, London
Gannon T, Wood J, Pina A, Vasquez E and Fraser I (2012) *The Evaluation of the Mandatory Polygraph Pilot*, Ministry of Justice Research Series 14/12, July, London
Garland D (2001) *The Culture of Control: Crime and Social Order in Contemporary Society*Oxford University Press, Oxford.
GBC (Gibraltar Broadcasting Corporation) (2019a) RGP says thirty-three registered sex offenders in Gibraltar, 18 March (available at https://www.gbc.gi/news/rgp-say-thirty-three-registered-sex-offenders-gibraltar accessed 25 November 2019)
GBC (Gibraltar Broadcasting Corporation) (2019b) No confirmation from Government on whether it plans to make sex offender list accessible to public, 25 July (available at https://www.gbc.gi/news/no-confirmation-government-whether-t-it-plans-make-sex-offender-list-accessible-public accessed 6 November 2019)
Gillespie A (2002) Discharging sex offenders, *Criminal Law Review*, January: 53–55
Gillespie A (2004) Discharging Sex Offenders R v Longworth EWCA Crim 2125 , *The Journal of Criminal Law* 68 (6): 466–480
Gillespie A (2005) Reprimanding juveniles and the right to due process, *Modern Law Review* 68 (6): 1006–1015
Giordano C (2019) Convicted paedophile who dressed as Santa and offered to pose for pictures with children is sent back to jail, *Independent*, 3 December (available at https://www.independent.co.uk/news/uk/crime/paedophile-sex-offender-santa-claus-fenwick-jail-newcastle-a9231456.html accessed 3 December 2020)
Goode S (2010) *Understanding and Addressing Adult Sexual Attraction to Children: A Study of Paedophiles in Contemporary Society*, Routledge, Abingdon
Hackett S (2014) *Children and Young People with Harmful Sexual Behaviours*, Research in Practice, Dartington
Hamilton F (2017) Police to relax rules for 'low-risk' sex offenders, *The Times*, June 30.
Hansard (2010) *Hansard House of Commons Debates 1st July 2010 col.620WA* (available at: http://www.government.pn/Laws/Sexual%20Offences%20(Notification%20and%20Prevention)%20Ordinance.pdf accessed 8 April 2020)
Hanvey S, Philpot T and Wilson C (2011) *Community Based Approach to the Reduction of Sexual Re-offending: Circles of Support and Accountability*, Jessica Kingsley Publishing, London
Harnden T (2006) Minister signals climb-down over UK version of Megan's Law, *Daily Telegraph*, 23 July, London

Harrison K, McCartan K and Manning R (2010) Paedophilia: definitions and aetiology, in K Harrison (ed.), *Managing High Risk Sex Offenders in the Community: Risk Management, Treatment and Social Responsibility*, Willan Publishing, Cullompton

Hayes M (1992) R v Devon County Council ex. p L: bad practice, bad law and a breach of human rights? *Family Law*, 22 June: 245–257

Hebenton B and Seddon T (2009) From dangerousness to precaution: Managing sexual and violent offenders in an insecure and uncertain age, *British Journal of Criminology* 49 (3): 343–362

Hebenton B and Thomas N (2004) *Introducing Lay People into Multi-Agency Public Protection Arrangements: Pilot Study of Eight Areas – Executive Summary*, Home Office, London

Hebenton B and Thomas T (1997) *Keeping Track? Observations on Sex Offender Registers in the US*, Crime Detection and Prevention Series Paper 83, Police Research Group, Home Office, London

HMG (HM Government) (2008) *Saving Lives. Reducing Harm. Protecting the Public. An Action Plan for Tackling Violence 2008–11*, London

HMG (HM Government) (2009) *Saving Lives. Reducing Harm. Protecting the Public. An Action Plan for Tackling Violence 2008–11 One Year On*, London

HMG (HM Government) (2015) *Information Sharing: Guidance for Practitioners and managers*, March, London

HMG (HM Government) (2018a) *Information Sharing – Advice for Practitioners Providing Safeguarding Services to Children, Young People, Parents and Carers* July, London

HMG (HM Government) (2018b) *Working Together to Safeguard Children: A Guide to Inter-agency Working to Safeguard and Promote the Welfare of Children* July, London

HMIC (HM Inspectorate of Constabulary) (2015) *National Child Protection Inspections – Nottinghamshire Police 1–11 September 2014*, February, London

HMIC (HM Inspectorate of Constabulary) (2016) *National Child Protection Inspections The Metropolitan Police Service 1 February – 27 May 2016*, London

HMICFRS (HM Inspectorate of Constabulary, Fire and Rescue Services) (2017) *National Child Protection Inspections Cleveland Police 8–19 May 2017*, September, London

HMICFRS (HM Inspectorate of Constabulary, Fire and Rescue Services) (2018a) Merseyside Police committed to child protection, but backlog has 'serious impact' on sex offender management (press release), 30 August

HMICFRS (HM Inspectorate of Constabulary, Fire and Rescue Services) (2018b) *National Child Protection Inspections: Merseyside Police 23 April-4 May 2018*, August, London

HMICFRS (2020) *National Child Protection Inspections*, London (available at: https://www.justiceinspectorates.gov.uk/hmicfrs/our-work/article/child-abuse-and-child-protection-issues/national-child-protection-inspection/ accessed 23 February 2020)

HMICS (Inspectorate of Constabulary in Scotland) and the Care Inspectorate (2015) *Joint Thematic Review of MAPPA in Scotland November*, Edinburgh

HMICS (Inspectorate of Constabulary in Scotland) and the Care Inspectorate (2017) *Joint Thematic Review of MAPPA in Scotland – Progress Review*, June, Edinburgh

HMIP (HM Inspectorate of Probation) (2003) *National Probation Service IT: Interim review by HM Inspectorate of Probation*, September, London

HMIP (HM Inspectorate of Probation) and HMIC (HM Inspectorate of Constabulary) (2005) *Managing Sex Offenders in the Community: A Joint Inspection*, London
HM Prison Service (2000) *Home Detention Curfew*, Prison Service Order 6700, January
Holt A (2010) Managing 'spoiled identities': parents experiences of compulsory parenting support programmes, *Children and Society* 24 (5): 413–423.
Home Office (1976) *Non-accidental Injury to Children: The Police And Case Conferences* (circular no. 179/1976)
Home Office (1986) *Coordination of Computerisation in the Criminal Justice System* (Goldman Report), London
Home Office (1996a) *Protecting the Public: the Government's Strategy on Crime in England and Wales*, Cm 3190, March, HMSO, London
Home Office (1996b) *Sentencing and Supervision of Sex Offenders: a Consultation Document*, Cm.3304, June, London
Home Office (1997a) Home Office welcomes judicial review judgement on disclosure of information (press release), 10 July, London
Home Office (1997b) Sex offenders to face tougher penalties – Maclean (press release), 27 January, London
Home Office (1997c) Guidelines for operating sex offenders register published (press release), 11 August.
Home Office (1997d) *Sex Offenders Act 1997* (circular 39/1997), 11 August, London
Home Office (1997e) Sex offender register comes into effect (press release), 31 August, London
Home Office (1997f) *Community Protection Order*, November, HMSO, London
Home Office (1998a) *Crime and Disorder Act 1998: Sex Offender Orders – Guidance*, London
Home Office (1998b) *Home Detention Curfew: Police guidance* (circular 31/1998), 27 July
Home Office (1998c) *Home Detention Curfew: Police guidance* (circular 51/1998), 21 December
Home Office (1999a) *Early Warning Mechanism for the Release or Discharge of Potentially Dangerous Offenders*, Probation Circular 15/1999, February, London
Home Office (1999b) *Draft Guidance on the Disclosure of Information about Sex Offenders who May Present a Risk to Children and Vulnerable Adults*, Police Science and Technology Unit, 31 August, London
Home Office (1999c) Sex offences review: terms of reference announced (press release), 25 January, London
Home Office (2000a) Government proposals better to protect children from sex and violent offenders (press release), 15 September.
Home Office (2000b) Sex Offender's register to be reviewed (press release) 26 June.
Home Office (2000c) *Setting the Boundaries: Reforming the Law on Sex Offences*, Volume 1, July, London
Home Office (2001a) *Statement from the Home Secretary* (press release), 18 December, London
Home Office (2001b) Strengthening the Sex Offenders Act: public consultation published today (press release), 30 July.
Home Office (2001c) *Criminal Justice and Court Services Act 2000: Amendments to the Sex Offender Act 1997* (circular no. 20/2001), 1 June, London
Home Office (2001d) *Initial Guidance to the Police and Probation Services on sections 67&68 of the Criminal Justice and Court Services Act 2000*, London

Home Office (2002a) *Protecting the Public: Strengthening Protection against Sex Offenders and Reforming the Law on Sexual Offences* (Cm 5668), London

Home Office (2002b) *Sex Offender Orders: Amendments in the Police Reform Act 2002* (circular no. 66/2002), December, London

Home Office (2002c) *Responses to the Consultation Paper on the Review of Part One of the Sex Offenders Act 1997*, London

Home Office (2002d) New moves to tighten sex offenders' 'register' (press release) 2 October, London

Home Office (2003a) *Further Guidance (1) to the Police and Probation Services on the Criminal Justice and Court Services Act 2000*, sections 67&68, London

Home Office (2003b) *Further Guidance (2) to the Police and Probation Services on the Criminal Justice and Court Services Act 2000*, sections 67&68, London

Home Office (2003c) Sexual Offences Bill to further tighten sex offender monitoring (press release), 6 October

Home Office (2003d) Government action on sex tourism (press release), 5 March, London

Home Office (2003e) *Safety and Justice: The Government's Proposals on Domestic Violence* Cm 5847, London

Home Office (2004a) Public to play vital role in managing sex and violent offenders in community (press release), 14 April, London

Home Office (2004b) *The Removal of Offenders Convicted of Buggery and Indecency between men from the 'Sex Offender Register'* (Schedule 4 Sexual Offences Act 2003) (circular no. 019/2004), 24 March, London

Home Office (2005a) *Guidance on offences against children* (circular ref 16/2005), 24 March, London

Home Office (2005b) Letter from the Home Office to police forces about 'extended sentences', 12 April, London (copy available from website of the campaign group Unlock http://hub.unlock.org.uk/wp-content/uploads/SORExtendedSentence.pdf accessed 11 November 2019)

Home Office (2005c) *Code of Practice on the Management of Police Information*, July, London

Home Office (2005d) *ViSOR: protecting the public from dangerous offenders* (press release), 19 August, London

Home Office (2006a) *Memorandum of Understanding between the Government of the United Kingdom of Great Britain and Northern Ireland and the Government of Ireland on Information Sharing Arrangements Relating to Sex Offenders* (circular 043/2006) 27 November, London

Home Office (2006b) *Information Sharing Arrangements Relating to SEX OFFENDERS* (circular no. 036/2006), 28 November

Home Office (2007a) *Review of the Protection of Children from Sex Offenders*, London

Home Office (2007b) *Power of Search and Entry to Risk Assess Sex Offenders Subject to the Notification Requirements* (circular no. 017/2007), London

Home Office (2008a) Violent Crime Action Plan published (press release), 18 February

Home Office (2008b) Tightening rules for sex offenders (press release), 20 August

Home Office (2009a) Protecting children from sexual abuse (press release), 16 March

Home Office (2009b) Child sex offender warning scheme expanded (press release), 16 March

Home Office (2010a) *The Child Sexual Offender (CSO) Disclosure Scheme – The Child Sexual Offender (CSO) Disclosure Scheme Guidance Document 1 (circular reference no.* 007/2010), London

Home Office (2010b) Protecting children: child sex offender disclosure scheme – start of nationwide roll-out (press release) 3 March, London

Home Office (2010c) Child protection scheme roll out (press release), 2 August, London

Home Office (2010d) *Sections 22–25 of the Policing and Crime Act 2009 (circular no.* 005/2010), 29 March, London

Home Office (2010e) *Guidance Part 2 of the Sexual Offences Act 2003*, October

Home Office (2010f) *Child Exploitation and Online Protection Centre (CEOP): The Way Forward*, Cm 7785, London

Home Office (2011a) *Reforming the Notification Requirements of Registered Sex Offenders (Part 2 of the Sexual Offences Act 2003): A Targeted Consultation*, June, London

Home Office (2011b) *Reforming the Notification Requirements of Registered Sex Offenders (Part 2 of the Sexual Offences Act 2003): Summary of Consultation Reponses and Conclusions*, London

Home Office (2012a) *Calculation of notification periods for Registered Sex Offenders who have an extended sentence* (FOI request), 14 September, London (available https://www.gov.uk/government/publications/calculation-of-notification-periods-for-registered-sex-offenders-who-have-an-extended-sentenceaccessed 13 February 2020)

Home Office (2012b) *Memorandum to the Home Affairs Committee Post-Legislative Assessment of the Violent Crime Reduction Act 2006*, Cm 8327, London

Home Office (2012c) 'Sarah's Law' protects more than 200 children in first year (press release) 4 April, London

Home Office (2012d) *Proposal for the Sexual Offences Act 2003 (Remedial) Order 2011 – the Government Response to the Nineteenth Report of the Joint Committee on Human Rights Session 2010–2012*, HC1549

Home Office (2012e) *Guidance on Review of Indefinite Notification Requirements issued under section 91F of the Sexual Offences Act 2003*, 12 July, London

Home Office (2013a) New powers for tighter restrictions on sex offenders (press release), 9 October, London

Home Office (2013b) *Anti-social Behaviour, Crime and Policing Bill – European Convention on Human Rights – Supplemental Memorandum by the Home Office*, 8 October (available at https://assets.publishing.service.gov.uk/government/uploads/system/uploads/attachment_data/file/249618/Supplementary_ECHR_memo_-_amendments_to_Sexual_Offences_Act.pdf accessed 14 April 2020)

Home Office (2014) *Multi Agency Working and Information Sharing Project Final Report*July, London

Home Office (2016) Police Workforce, England and Wales, 31 March 2016 Statistical Bulletin 05/16 July, London

Home Office (2018) *Guidance on Part Two of the Sexual Offences Act 2003*, September, London

Home Office (2019a) *The Government Response to the Tenth Report from the Home Affairs Select Committee Session 2017–19 HC 515: Policing for the Future*, March CP 62

Home Office /DoH (Department of Health) (1999) *Managing Dangerous People with Severe Personality Disorder: Proposals for Policy Development*, July, London

Home Office, Department of Health, Department of Education and Science, Welsh Office (1991) *Working Together: Under the Children Act 1989: A Guide to Arrangements for Inter-agency Co-operation for the Protection of Children from Abuse*HMSO: London.

Home Office/NPCC (National Police Chief's Council) (2017) *Sex Offender Notification Requirements: Review Mechanism What Are My Rights as a Victim?* July, London

Home Office/NPS (National Probation Service) (2003) *Extension of MAPPA Guidance*, March, London (available at http://nomsintranet.org.uk/roh/official-documents/PC54_2004_MAPPAGuidanceUpdate.pdf accessed 27 January 2020)

Home Office/Scottish Executive (2001) *Consultation Paper on the Review of Part 1 of the Sex Offenders Act 1997*, July, London.

House of Commons (2003) *Sexual Offences Bill Fifth Home Affairs Committee*, Report of Session 2003–2003, HC639, 24 June, London

House of Commons (2005) *The Sexual Offences Act 2003 (Amendment) Bill (Bill 26 of 2004–05)* Research Paper 05/19, 2 March, London

House of Commons (2015) *The Wass Inquiry Report into Allegations Surrounding Child Safeguarding Issues on St Helena and Ascension Island (Redacted Version)* December HC 662

House of Commons (2016) *The Wass Inquiry Report into Allegations Surrounding Child Safeguarding Issues on St Helena and Ascension Island: Progress Report on Implementation of Recommendations* (available at https://assets.publishing.service.gov.uk/government/uploads/system/uploads/attachment_data/file/536027/Wass_Inquiry_Report_-_progress_report_on_implementation_of_recommendations.pdf accessed 18 March 2020)

House of Commons (2018a) *Policing for the Future*, Tenth Report of Home Affairs Committee Session 2017–2019, HC 515, 25 October, London

House of Commons (2018b) *Domestic Abuse*, Ninth Report of the Home Affairs Committee Session 2017–2019 HC 1015, London

House of Lords/House of Commons (2003) *Scrutiny of Bills: Further Progress Report*, Seventh Report of the Joint Committee on Human Rights Session 2002–2003, HL Paper 74/HC 547, London

House of Lords/House of Commons (2011) *Proposal for the Sexual Offences Act 2003 (Remedial) Order 2011*, Nineteenth Report of the Joint Committee on Human Rights Session 2010–2012 HL Paper 200/HC 1549, October, London

House of Lords/House of Commons (2012) *Draft Sexual Offences Act 2003 (Remedial) Order 2012*, First Report of the Joint Committee on Human Rights Session 2012–2013 HL Paper 8/HC 166, May, London

House of Lords/House of Commons (2013) *Legislative Scrutiny: Anti-social Behaviour, Crime and Policing Bill*, Fourth Report of the Joint Committee on Human Rights Session 2013–2014 HL Paper 56/HC 713, October, TSO, London

House of Oireachtas (1997) *Official Report*, 9 December

Howard League (1996) *Information*, 1 August, London

HRW (Human Rights Watch) (2013) *Raised on the Registry – The Irreparable Harm of Placing Children on Sex Offender Registries in the US*, 1 May (available at https://www.hrw.org/report/2013/05/01/raised-registry/irreparable-harm-placing-children-sex-offender-registries-us accessed 13 March 2020)

Hudson K (2005) *Offending Identities: Sex Offenders' Perspectives on Their Treatment and Management*, Willan Publishing, Cullompton

Hudson K J and Henley A J (2015) Disparities in public protection measures against sexual offending in England and Wales: an example of preventative injustice? *Criminology and Criminal Justice* 15(5): 561–577

Hudson, K J, Taylor, C and Henley, A J (2015) Trends in the management of registered sexual offenders across England and Wales: a geographical approach to the study of sexual offending, *Journal of Sexual Aggression* 21 (1): 56–70
Hughes B, Parker H and Gallagher B (1996) *Policing Child Sexual Abuse: The View From Police Practitioners*, Police Research Group, Home Office, London
Humphries J (2018) High risk paedophiles in community not visited enough by 'seriously overstretched' police, *Liverpool Echo*, 30 August
Independent Jersey Care Inquiry (2017) *Final Report*, July, Saint Helier, Jersey (available at http://www.jerseycareinquiry.org/final- report February 2020)
Inside Time (2016) Sex offender's passports, *Inside Time*, 29 July (available at https://insidetime.org/sex-offenders-passports/ accessed 1 October 2019)
Inside Time (2017)'Employment for people with convictions relating to sex offences, *Inside Time*1 March (available at https://insidetime.org/employment-for-people-with-convictions-relating-to-sex-offences/ accessed 5 July 2020)
IOPC (Independent Office for Police Conduct) (2018) *Handling of Reports of Sexual Assault – North Yorkshire Police*, June 2016 – IOPC 7 January
IOM Today (2017) Number on sex offenders' register revealed; four UK sex offenders living here, *IOM Today*, 4 July (available at: http://www.iomtoday.co.im/article.cfm?id=34560&headline=Number%20on%20sex%20offenders%27%20register%20revealed;%20Four%20UK%20sex%20offenders%20living%20here&sectionIs=news&searchyear=2017 accessed 22 February 2020)
Irving G (2005) *Registering the Risk: Review of Notification Requirements, Risk Assessment, and Risk Management of Sex Offenders* (the Irving Report), Scottish Executive, Edinburgh
Janus E (2000) Civil commitment as social control: managing the risk of sexual violence, in M Brown and J Pratt (eds), *Dangerous Offenders: Punishment and Social Order*, Routledge, London.
Jay Report (2014) *Independent Inquiry into Child Sexual Exploitation in Rotherham 1997–2013*, Rotherham MBC, South Yorkshire
Jenkins L (1997) Abuse couple seek privacy from police, *The Times*, 1 July
Jewkes Y and Wykes M (2012) Reconstructing the sexual abuse of children: 'cyber-paeds', panic and power, *Sexualities* 15 (8): 934–952
Johnson B (2008) Paedophiles face curbs on internet use, *The Guardian*, 4 April
Johnston P (1997) Police block on paedophile alert to neighbours, *Daily Telegraph*, 1 April
Jones G (1996) Major accused of U-turn on new legislation, *Daily Telegraph*, 24 October.
Justice (2019) *Prosecuting Sexual Offences: A Report by JUSTICE* (chaired by P Rook), London
Justice and Home Affairs Department (2019) *Jersey Multi-Agency Public Protection Arrangements Annual Report 2018 March*, States of Jersey, Saint Helier, Jersey
Kaul A (2001) Confidentiality in dual responsibility settings, in C Cordess (ed.), *Confidentiality and Mental Health*, Jessica Kingsley Publishers, London
Kemshall H (2001) *Risk Assessment and Management of Known Sexual and Violent Offenders: A Review of Current Issues*, Police Research Series, Paper 140, Home Office, London
Kemshall H and Weaver B (2012) The Sex Offender Public Disclosure Pilots in England and Scotland: lessons from 'marketing strategies' and risk communication with the public, *Criminology and Criminal Justice*, 12 (5): 549–565

Kemshall H, Dominey J and Hilder S (2012) Public disclosure: sex offender perceptions of the pilot scheme in England – compliance, legitimacy and living a 'good life', *Journal of Sexual Aggression* 18 (3): 311–324

Kemshall H and Wood J with Westwood S, Stout B, Wilkinson B, Kelly G and Mackenie G (2010) *Child Sex Offender Review (CSOR): Public Disclosure Pilots, A Process Evaluation*, Home Office, London

Kewley S (2017) Policing registered sex offenders, *Journal of Forensic Practice*, 19 (4): 296–300

King R (1996) City aims for sex fiend file, *Manchester Evening News*, 5 September, Manchester

Knock K (2002) *The Police Perspective on Sex Offender Orders: A Preliminary View of Policy and Practice*, Police Research Series Paper 155, Home Office, London

Lagan S (2018) MPs approve register for sex offenders, *The Royal Gazette*, 15 December, Bermuda (available at: http://www.royalgazette.com/news/article/20181215/mps-approve-register-for-sex-offenders accessed 18 March 2020)

Legislation (2020) *Draft Statutory Instruments, Criminal Law, England And Wales, The Sexual Offences Act 2003 (Remedial) Order 2011* (available at: https://www.legislation.gov.uk/ukdsi/2011/9780111512357 accessed 15 September 2020)

Levenson J S and Cotter K P (2005a) The effect of Megan's Law on sex offender reintegration, *Journal of Contemporary Criminal Justice* 28 (1): 49–66

Levenson J S and Cotter K P (2005b) The impact of sex offender residency restrictions: 1000 feet from danger or one-step from absurd, *International Journal of Offender Therapy and Criminology* 49 (2): 168–178

Levenson J and Tewksbury R (2009) Collateral damage: family members of registered sex offenders, *American Journal of Criminal Justice* 34: 54–68

Lewis P (2008) Britain accused of turning a blind eye to child sex tourism, *The Guardian*, 18 August

Liberty (1997) Briefing on the Sex Offenders Bill, 23 January, London

Liberty (2008) *Briefing on the Criminal Justice and Immigration Bill in the House of Lords*, January, London

Liberty (2011) *Liberty's Submission to the Joint Committee on Human Rights Report on the Draft Sexual Offences Act 2003 (Remedial) Order 2011*, August, London

Logan W (2003) Sex offender registration and notification: emerging legal and research issues, in R Prentky, E Janus and M Seto, *Sexually Coercive Behaviour: Understanding and Management*, Annals of the New York Academy of Sciences 989: 337–351

Logan W (2009) *Knowledge as Power: Criminal Registration and Community Notification Laws in America*, Stanford University Press, Stanford, CA

LSCB (Leeds Safeguarding Children's Board) (2012) *Serious Case Review – Child K6* March, Leeds

Lucy Faithful Foundation (2013) *Child Safety Review – Ascension Island/St Helena – Public Summary*, August, Bromsgrove

Lusher A, Bamber D and Hyder K (2000) UK has 250,000 paedophiles, says police study, *Daily Telegraph*, 31 December

McCartan K, Hoggett J & O'Sullivan, J. (2018) Police officer attitudes to the practicalities of the sex offenders' register, ViSOR and Child Sexual Abuse Disclosure Scheme in England and Wales, *Journal of Sexual Aggression* 24 (1), 37–50.

Maguire M, Kemshall H, Noaks L, Wincup E and Sharpe K (2001), *Risk Management of Sexual and Violent Offenders: the work of Public Protection Panels*, Police Research Series Paper 139, Home Office, London

MacLean Report (2000) *Report of the Committee on Serious Violent and Sexual Offenders*, June, Edinburgh
Mann N and Lundrigan S (2020) *A National Evaluation of the Active Risk Management System*, March
MAPPA (2015) *General Introduction to Guernsey's Multi Agency Public Protection Arrangements* (available at https://www.gov.gg/CHttpHandler.ashx?id=92868&p=0 accessed 22 February 2020)
Marshall P (1997) *The Prevalence of Convictions for Sexual Offending*, Research Finding no.55, Research and Statistics Directorate, Home Office, London
Marshall D J and Thomas T (2015) Polygraphs and sex offenders: the truth is out there, *Probation Journal* 62: 128–139
Martin D (2007) Eleven doctors with sex convictions 'still working in the NHS', *MailOnline*, 24 September (available at: https://www.dailymail.co.uk/health/article-483605/Eleven-doctors-sex-convictions-working-NHS.html accessed 4 May 2020)
Martin D (2009) Jacqui Smith: I'd never run a thing before the Home Office, *MailOnline*, 17 July (available at https://www.dailymail.co.uk/news/article-1200108/Jacqui-Smith-admits-wasnt-Home-Secretary.html accessed 31 May 2020)
Mawby R & Worrall A (2004) 'Polibation' revisited: policing, probation and prolific offender projects, *International Journal of Police Science and Management* 6 (2): 63–73
Mawby R C & Worrall A (2011) 'They were very threatening about do-gooding bastards': probation's changing relationships with the police and prison services in England and Wales, *European Journal of Probation* 3 (3): 78–94
Mawby R C, Crawley P & Wright A (2007) Beyond 'polibation' and towards 'prisipolibation'? Joint agency offender management in the context of the Street 163 Crime Initiative, *International Journal of Police Science and Management* 9 (2): 122–134.
McCartan K F, Kemshall H & Hudson K (2012) Scotland – Briefing paper. Understanding public disclosure of sex offender information in Scotland: access, impact and value-added, 21 July (available at http://www1.uwe.ac.uk/hls/research/sexoffenderpublicdisclosure/outputs.aspx)
McCartan K F, Hoggett J and O'Sullivan J (2018) Police officer attitudes to the practicalities of the sex offenders' register, ViSOR and child sexual abuse disclosure scheme in England and Wales, *Journal of Sexual Aggression* 24 (1): 37–50
McLaughlin C (2000) Passport stamp for child abusers, *Sunday Mirror*, 10 July, London
McWilliams B and Pease K (1990) Probation practice and an end to punishment, *Howard Journal of Criminal Justice* 29 (1): 14–25
Miles A (2006) Get some policies Mr Reid, and stop hiding behind an odious sex offender, *The Times*, 14 June
Milliken R and Cooper G (1997) This woman has named 600 child abusers in Australia. Now she plans a British list, *The Independent*, 19 February
Ministry of Housing, Communities and Local Government (2018) *Consultation on Updating the Disqualification Criteria for Councillors and Mayors: A Summary of Consultation Responses and the Government Response*, October, London
MoJ (Ministry of Justice) (2008) *Criminal Justice and Immigration Act 2008 (provisions commencing in July 2008)* (Circular ref. no. 2008/01), 7 July.
MoJ (Ministry of Justice) (2015) *Serious Crime Act 2015 Fact sheet: Offence of Possession of Paedophile Manuals*, March (available at https://assets.publishing.service.gov.uk/government/uploads/system/uploads/attachment_data/file/415982/Fact_sheet_-_Paedophile_manuals_-_Act.pdf accessed 2 January 2020)

MoJ (Ministry of Justice) (2017a) *Sexual Communication with a Child: Implementation of section 67 of the Serious Crime Act 2015* (circular no. 2017/01), 3 April, London

MoJ (Ministry of Justice) (2017b) *Multi-Agency Public Protection Arrangements – Annual Report 2016/17 – Ministry of Justice Statistics Bulletin*, 26 October

MoJ (Ministry of Justice) (2018) *Multi-Agency Public Protection Arrangements – Annual Report 2017/18 – Ministry of Justice Statistics Bulletin*, 25 October

MoJ (Ministry of Justice) (2019a) *Multi-Agency Public Protection Arrangements – Annual Report 2018/19 – Ministry of Justice Statistics Bulletin*, 31 October

MoJ (Ministry of Justice) (2019b) *Voyeurism (Offences) Act 2019: Implementation of the Voyeurism (Offences) Act 2019* (Circular No. 2019/01), London

MoJ (Ministry of Justice) (2020a) *Multi-Agency Public Protection Arrangements – Annual Report 2019/20*, Ministry of Justice Statistics Bulletin, 29 October

MoJ (Ministry of Justice) (2020b) Measures announced to protect NHS from coronavirus risk in prisons (press release), 4 April

MoJ (Ministry of Justice)/HM Prison and Probation Service (2019) *Home Detention Curfew (HDC) Policy Framework Reference*, 28 March (available at: https://assets.publishing.service.gov.uk/government/uploads/system/uploads/attachment_data/file/790670/home-detention-curfew-pf.pdf accessed 31 August 2019)

MoJ (Ministry of Justice) and YJB (Youth Justice Board) (2013) *Youth Cautions: Guidance for Police and Youth Offending Teams*, London

MoJ (Ministry of Justice), National Probation Service, HM Prison Service and Association of Chief Police Officers (2007) *MAPPA Guidance 2007 Version 2.0*, NOMS, London

MORI Polls (2000a) Crime and sentencing poll, 23 July, London

MORI Polls (2000b) Naming and shaming poll, 20 August, London

Moriarty G (2006) Protocol to track sex offenders agreed, *Irish Times*, 28 November, Dublin

Morris N (2007) Home Office blunder leave serious offenders off police crime records, *The Independent*, 10 January

Morris N (2010) 'Sarah's Law' may backfire, say campaigners, *Independent*, 2 August, London

Moyes J and Bennetto J (2000) Tabloid ends its naming of sex offenders, *Independent*, 5 August

Mulholland H (2006) Blair reigns in Reid over paedophile law, *The Guardian*, 19 June, London

Mulholland H and Tempest M (2006) System 'not fit for purpose', says Reid, *The Guardian*, 23 May

Myers S (2001) The registration of children and young people under the Sex Offenders Act (1997): time for a change? *Youth Justice* 1 (2): 40–48

NACRO (National Association for the Care and Resettlement of Offenders) (2004) The Sexual Offences Act 2003 – young people and the notification requirements, Youth Crime Briefing, September, London

Nash M (1999) Enter the 'Polibation Officer', *International Journal of Police Science and Management* 1 (4): 360–368

Nash M (2006) *Public Protection and the Criminal Justice Process*, Oxford University Press, Oxford

Nazia P (2018) Merseyside Police failing to monitor sex offenders, says watchdog, *The Guardian*, 30 August

NCH (National Children's Homes) (1992) *The Report of the Committee of Enquiry into Children and Young People who Sexually Abuse Other Children*, NCH, London
NE Thames and SE Thames Regional Health Authorities (1994) *The Report of the Inquiry into the Care and Treatment of Christopher Clunis*, HMSO, London
NHS Executive (1994) *Introduction of Supervision Registers for mentally ill people from 1 April 1994*, (reference HSG (94) 5) February
NHS Executive (1997) *Guidance to Hospital Managers and Local Authority Social Services Departments on the Sex Offenders Act 1997* (ref. no. HSG (97) 37), 17 August, London
NHS and SSI (Social Services Inspectorate) (1999) *Effective Care and Coordination in Mental Health Services: Modernising the Care Programme Approach*, Department of Health, London
Niven D (1996) Suffer the little children, *The Guardian*, 16 October, London
NOMS (National Offender Management Service) (2007) *MAPPA Guidance 2009 Version 2.0*National MAPPA Team, London
NOMS (National Offender Management Service) (2009) *MAPPA Guidance 2009 Version 3.0* National MAPPA Team, London
NOMS (National Offender Management Service) (2012) *MAPPA Guidance 2012 Version 4.5* [Updated July 2019] National MAPPA Team, London
NOMS (National Offender Management Service) (2014a) *Mandatory use of ViSOR* (ref. PSI 40/2014/PI 56/2014), NOMS Agency Board, London
NOMS (National Offender Management Service) (2014b) *Sex Offender Management and Dynamic Risk: Pilot evaluation of the Active Risk Management System (ARMS)*, NatCen Social Research Crime and Justice Team Ministry of Justice Analytical Series, London
NOMS (National Offender Management Service) (2016) *Public Protection Manual*, London (available at https://www.justice.gov.uk/downloads/offenders/psipso/psi-2016/psi-18-2016-pi-17-2016-public-protection-manual.pdf accessed 6 November 2019)
Norton J (2020) Sex offenders allowed to sign off danger list, *Daily Mail*, 3 January
NPCC (National Police Chiefs Council) (2011) ACPO comment on F and Thompson – ruling on sex offender notification requirements, 16 February (available at https://news.npcc.police.uk/releases/acpo-comment-on-f-and-thompson-ruling-on-sex-offender-notification-requirements accessed 18 September 2019)
NPCC (National Police Chiefs Council) (2017) New tailored approach to managing registered sex offenders introduced (press release), 29 June, London
NPS (National Probation Service) (2007) *Critical Public Protection Cases* (Probation Circular, 06/2007), London
NSPCC (National Society for the Prevention of Cruelty to Children) (1997) NSPCC concerned re inclusion of juvenile offenders on sex offenders register (press release), 24 October, London.
ODPR (Office of the Data Protection Registrar) (1998) Privacy threatened by new databases (press release), 15 July, Wilmslow
Olliers Solicitors (n.d.) The curious case of R v Wiles, its implementation and the Sex Offenders Register (available at https://www.olliers.com/news/sex-offenders-notification-requirements/ accessed 11 November 2019)
O'Neil S (2000) Straw attacks tabloid editor for identifying paedophiles, *Daily Telegraph*, 25 July, London
Osley R and Philippidou P (2008) Gary Glitter goes into hiding as police assess vigilante risk, *Independent*, 24 August

O'Sullivan J, Hoggett J, Kemshall H and McCartan K F (2016) Understandings, implications and alternative approaches to the use of the sex offenders register in the UK, *Irish Probation Journal* 13: 84–101

Outrage (2000) *Age of Consent Bill flawed* (press release), 3 March, London

PAC (Policy Advisory Committee) on Sexual Offences (1981) *Report on the Age of Consent in Relation to Sexual Offences* (Cmnd.8216), HMSO, London

Paladin (2020) *Serial Perpetrator Register and Order* (available at: https://paladinservice.co.uk/serial-perpetrator-register-and-order/ accessed 15 September 2020)

Parker H, Gallagher B and Hughes B (1996) The policing of child sexual abuse in England and Wales, *Policing and Society* 6: 1–13

Parris M (1997) All party witch hunt, *The Times*, 24 January

Parton N (2006) *Safeguarding Childhood: Early Intervention and Surveillance in a Late Modern Society*, Palgrave Macmillan, Basingstoke

Payne S (2005) *A Mother's Story*, Hodder and Stoughton, London

PBNI (Probation Board of Northern Ireland)/The Probation Service (2017) *Information Sharing Protocol – Between the Probation Board for Northern Ireland (PBNI) and the Probation Service (Ireland) In Respect of The Management of Sex Offenders and Offenders assessed as Significant Risk of Serious Harm to Others*, Belfast/Dublin (available at https://www.pbni.org.uk/wp-content/uploads/2018/08/Information-Sharing-Protocol-PBNI-and-PS-Ireland.pdf accessed 3 May 2020)

Perry K (2000) Families flee estate hate campaign, *The Guardian*, 10 August

PAG (Police Authority Gibraltar) (2015) *Annual Policing Plan 2015–2016*: 8

Peck M (2011) *Patterns of Reconviction Among Offenders Eligible for MAPPA*, Ministry of Justice, London

Pittman N (2013) *Raised on the Registry: The irreparable harm of placing children on sex offender registries in the US*, Human Rights Watch, New York, NY

Plotnikoff J and Woolfson R (2000) *Where Are They Now? An Evaluation of Sex Offender Registration in England and Wales*, Police Research Series, Paper 126, Home Office, London

PSI (Prison Service Instruction) (2014) *Mandatory Use of ViSOR* (ref. PSI 40/2014)

PI (Probation Instruction) (2014) *Mandatory Use of ViSOR* (ref. PI 56/2014)

PPANI (Public Protection Arrangements Northern Ireland) (2020) *Statistics 2020* (available at www.publicprotectionni.com/statistics/2020 accessed 20 September 2020)

Preece R (2010) Yorkshire sex offenders among 300 on the loose in Britain, *Yorkshire Post*, 27 April

Probation Circular (1999) *Early Warning Mechanism for the Release or Discharge of Potentially Dangerous Offenders.*

Rayner G and Koster O (2006) Outrage over five week sentence for paedophile, *Daily Mail*, 14 June

The Record (2019) A cautionary tale if you're looking to start a relationship with somebody who has been convicted of a sexual offence, *The Record*, 25 November (available at http://www.the-record.org.uk/unlock-people-with-convictions/a-cautionary-tale-if-youre-looking-to-start-a-relationship-with-somebody-who-has-been-convicted-of-a-sexual-offence/ accessed 23 July 2020)

Riley E (2019) Convicted paedophile, 34, travelled 500 miles to abuse schoolgirl, 14, he met in online self-harm support group after seven transport police officers failed to stop him, *Mailonline*, 25 June (available at https://www.dailymail.co.uk/news/article-7179837/Convicted-paedophile-34-travelled-500-miles-abuse-schoolgirl.html accessed 4 July 2020)

Risse, T, Ropp S and Sikkink K (eds) (1999) *The Power of Human Rights: International Norms and Domestic Change*, Cambridge University Press, Cambridge

Rose, R. (1993) *Lesson-Drawing in Public Policy*, Chatham House, Chatham NJ

Ross T (2015) Paedophiles and rapists are caught out breaking the terms of their release from prison after undergoing new polygraph tests, Ministry of Justice figures show, *Daily Telegraph*, 22 August

Schaefer S (2000) Anger as Tyson is granted visa for Glasgow fight, *The Independent*, 19 May

Schram D and Milloy C D (1995) *Community Notification: A Study of Offender Characteristics and Recidivism*, prepared for the Washington State Institute for Public Policy, Olympia WA

Scottish Executive (1997) *The Sex Offenders Act 1997: Guidance for Agencies* (available at https://content.iriss.org.uk/throughcare/files/pdf/f1_legis2.pdf accessed 6 November 2019)

Scottish Government (2016) *Multi-Agency Public Protection Arrangements (MAPPA) National Guidance*, March, Edinburgh (available at https://www2.gov.scot/Topics/Justice/policies/reducing-reoffending/sex-offender-management accessed 18 March 2020)

Self W (2013) I was reported as 'suspected paedophile' when out with my son, *The Guardian*, 18 August (available at https://www.theguardian.com/books/2013/aug/18/will-self-reported-suspected-paedophile accessed on 27 July 2020)

Selfe D and Burke V (2001) *Perspectives on Sex, Crime and Society* (2nd ed.) Cavendish Publishing Limited, London

Sex Offender Register Bill (2009) *Consultation Draft* (available at http://www.legislativeassembly.ky/portal/pls/portal/docs/1/9781699.PDF accessed 8 April 2020)

Silverman J and Wilson D (2002) *Innocence Betrayed: Paedophilia, the Media and Society*, Polity, Cambridge

Smith L (2001) British Airways says men cannot sit with lone children, *The Times*, 16 March

Smith C, Allardyce S, Hackett S, Bradbury-Jones C, Lazenbatt A & Taylor J (2014) Practice and policy in the UK with children and young people who display harmful sexual behaviours: an analysis and critical review, *Journal of Sexual Aggression* 20 (3): 267–280

Social Work Inspection Agency, HM Inspectorate of Constabulary for Scotland and HM Inspectorate of Prisons (2009) *Multi-Agency Inspection – Assessing and Managing Offenders Who Present a High Risk of Serious Harm: A Joint Report*, June, Edinburgh

Soothill K and Francis B (1998) Poisoned chalice or just desserts? (The Sex Offenders Act 1997), *The Journal of Forensic Psychiatry* 9 (2): 281–293

Soothill K, Francis B and Sanderson B (1997) A cautionary tale: the Sex Offenders Act 1997, the police and cautions, *Criminal Law Review*July: 482–493

SOR National User Group (2013) *ViSOR Standards: Version 3.1*. ViSOR Product Management Team (available at: http://library.college.police.uk/docs/college-of-policing/VISOR-standards-2013.pdf)

Spencer D (2009) Sex offender as homo sacer, *Punishment and Society*, 11 (2): 219–240

States of Guernsey (2015) *MAPPA: Multi-Agency Public Protection Arrangements Annual Report*, Home Department, Guernsey

States of Guernsey (2020) *MAPPA – Annual Report 2019*, Guernsey

States of Jersey (2011) *Sex Offenders (Jersey) Law 2010: Jersey Multi-Agency Public Protection Arrangements – Guidance 2010*, 21 July, St Helier, Jersey

States of Jersey (2019) *Jersey-Multi-Agency Public Protection Arrangements Annual Report 2018*, March, St Helier, Jersey

Steele J (1997) Heads attack guidelines on naming paedophiles, *Daily Telegraph*, 12 August

Stoddart C (2012) Get your facts right, *The Journal of the Law Society of Scotland*, 13 August (available at https://www.lawscot.org.uk/members/journal/issues/vol-57-issue-08-1/get-your-facts-right/ accessed 22 February 2020)

Straw J (2012) *Last Man Standing: Memoirs of a Political Survivor*, Macmillan, London.

Sunday Times (1997) Paedophiles go South to avoid sex offender register, 7 December.

SWSI (Social Work Services Inspectorate) for Scotland (2002) *Managing the Risk: An Inspection of the Management of Sex Offender Cases in the Community*, Edinburgh

Tempest M (2001) Sex offender loophole closed, *The Guardian*, 30 July

Tewksbury R and Lees M (2006) Perceptions of sex offender registration: collateral consequences and community experiences, *Sociological Spectrum* 26: 309–334

The Scottish Government (2007) *MAPPA Guidance Criminal Justice Directorate 3rd Version* (circular no. 15/2006), 26 September

The Scottish Government (2010a) Sex Offender Disclosure Scheme (press release), 25 October

The Scottish Government (2010b) *Evaluation of the sex offender community disclosure pilot* Research Findings no.26/2010, October, Edinburgh

Thomas T (2003) Sex offender community notification: the American experience, *Howard Journal of Criminal Justice* 42(3): 217–228.

Thomas T (2007) *Criminal Records: A Database for the Criminal Justice System and Beyond*, Palgrave, London

Thomas T (2008a) The sex offender register: a case study in function creep, *Howard Journal of Criminal Justice* 47 (3): 227–237

Thomas T (2008b) The sex offender register – a measure of public protection or a punishment in its own right? *Papers from the British Criminology Conference* 8: 85–96, Panel Paper (available at http://www.britsoccrim.org/volume8/BCCvol82008.pdf accessed 24 May 2020)

Thomas T (2009) Children and young people on the UK sex offender register, *International Journal of Children's Rights* 17 (3): 491–500

Thomas T (2016) *Sex Crime: Sex Offending and Society* (3rd edn), Routledge, Oxon

Thompson D and Thomas T (2017) *The Resettlement of Sex Offenders after Custody: Circles of Support and Accountability*, Routledge, London

Tonry M (2004) *Punishment and Politics: Evidence and Emulation in the Making of English Crime Control Policy*, Willan Publishing, Cullompton

Travis A (1997) Howard set to name sex offenders, *The Guardian*, 12 February

Travis A (2000) Figure it out, *The Guardian*, 23 August

Travis A (2003) Gay sex 'offenders' to be taken off register, *The Guardian*, 7 October

Travis A (2005) Criminals danger list goes online, *The Guardian*, 19 August

Travis A (2011) David Cameron condemns supreme court ruling on sex offenders, *The Guardian*, 6 February

UNLOCK (2015) Charity for people with convictions calls for 'ridiculous' 'disqualification' regulations for primary schools to be urgently reviewed (press release), 20 January (available at http://www.unlock.org.uk/press-release-charity-for-people-with-convictions-calls-for-ridiculous-disqualification-regulations-for-primary-schools-to-be-urgently-reviewed/ accessed 1 December 2020)

UK and Ireland Database (2020) *UK and Ireland Database* (available at https://uk-database.net/ accessed 15 September 2020)

Valios N (1998) Social workers warn register is flawed, *Community Care*27 August – 2 September, London

Walawalkar A (2020) Priti Patel: how the bullying allegations have mounted up, *The Guardian*, 29 February, London

Ward T and Gannon T (2006) Rehabilitation, etiology and self-regulation: the Good Lives Model of sexual offender treatment, *Aggression and Violent Behaviour* 11 (1): 77–94.

Ward, T, Mann R and Gannon T (2007) The good lives model of offender rehabilitation: clinical implications, *Aggression and Violent Behaviour* 12: 87–107.

Waugh P (1991) The use of computers in the administration of justice in the United Kingdom, *Yearbook of Law, Computers and Technology*, Volume 5, Butterworths, London

Weaver B (2009) *Sex Offender Community Notification in Scotland Briefing no. 03/2009*, The Scottish Centre for Crime and Justice Research, December, Glasgow

West Yorkshire Police (2000) *The Sex Offender Register (The Sex Offenders Act 1997) Annual Report and Statistics 1999–2000*, West Yorkshire Public Protection Group, 18 September, Wakefield

Whitehead T (2009) Home visits for high risk sex offenders cut, *Daily Telegraph*, 27 May

Whitehead T (2010) Sex offenders face less supervision to cut costs, *Daily Telegraph*, 26 October

WHO (World Health Organisation) (2019) 6D32 Pedophilic disorder, in *ICD-11 for Mortality and Morbidity Statistics* (available at: https://icd.who.int/browse11/l-m/en#/http%3a%2f%2fid.who.int%2ficd%2fentity%2f517058174 accessed 13 January 2020)

Wilson J (2003) Pete Townshend put on sex offenders register, *The Guardian*, 8 May, London

Wood Report (2016) *Review of the Role and Functions of Local Safeguarding Children Boards*, March

Wood J, Kemshall H, Westwood S, Fenton A and Logue C (2010) Investigating disclosures made by sexual offenders: preliminary study for the evaluation of mandatory polygraph testing, Ministry of Justice, Research Summary 6/10, September

Wooding D (2013) Win on rights is pervs' delight, *The Sun on Sunday*, 22 December

YJB (Youth Justice Board) (2008) *Young People Who Sexually Abuse: Source Document* (Author: R Grimshaw), London (available at https://www.crimeandjustice.org.uk/sites/crimeandjustice.org.uk/files/Young_People_who_Sexually_Abuse.pdf accessed 13 March 2020)

Index

For Product Safety Concerns and Information please contact our EU
representative GPSR@taylorandfrancis.com
Taylor & Francis Verlag GmbH, Kaufingerstraße 24, 80331 München, Germany

www.ingramcontent.com/pod-product-compliance
Ingram Content Group UK Ltd.
Pitfield, Milton Keynes, MK11 3LW, UK
UKHW020147200926
475702UK00016B/2591
9780367542849